Hemlock Books
England

PICTURE CREDITS: *American International Pictures (AIP), Anglo-Amalgamated Film Distributors, Associated Artists Productions, Astor Pictures Corporation, Blue Chip Productions, Britannia Films, British Lion Film Corporation, Cannon Film Distributors, Chevron Pictures, Columbia Pictures, Compton-Cameo Films, DCA, Denis Meikle, Eros Film, Grand National Pictures, John Hamilton, London Independent Producers, Maron Films, M-G-M, Paramount Pictures, Planet Film Distributors, Regal Films International, Renown Pictures Corporation, RKO Radio Pictures, Saxton Films, Schoenfeld Films, Titan Film Distribution Ltd, Tom Weaver, Trans Lux, Universal Pictures, Valiant Films, Warner Bros-Seven Arts, Warner Pathe. Any omissions will be corrected in future editions.*

Visit our website:
www.hemlockbooks.co.uk

First published in 2012 by
Hemlock Books Limited,
The Bristol Office,
2nd Floor,
5 High Street,
Westbury-on-Trym,
Bristol
BS9 3BY

©John Hamilton, 2012. John Hamilton has asserted his right to be identified as the Author of this work, in accordance with the Copyright, Designs and Patents Act, 1988.

All rights reserved. No part of this publication may be reproduced, stored in a retrieval system, or transmitted, in any form, or by any means, without the prior written permission of the Publishers, nor be otherwise circulated in any form of binding or cover other than that in which it is published and without a similar condition being imposed on the subsequent purchaser.

A CIP catalogue record for this book is available from the British Library.

ISBN 978-0-9557774-5-5

Editor: Jim O'Brien. Design by Hemlock Books Limited.

Printed and bound by CPI Group (UK) Ltd, Croydon, CR0 4YY.

John Hamilton

Acknowledgements

Unless otherwise credited, all quotes come from interviews and correspondence with the author and I owe an enormous debt of gratitude to a number of individuals who have shared both their time and their memories with me over the last few years—some for this specific project and others simply because I asked them. Among those I need to single out are: Robert S Baker, John Cairney, Didier Chatelain, Gail Cohen, Frixos Constantine, Hazel Court, Vera Day, Janine Faye, Freddie Francis, Renee Glynn, Richard Gordon, Pamela Green, Bernard Kay, Anna Massey, Warren Mitchell, Stanley Morgan, John Llewellyn Moxey, Derren Nesbitt, Jimmy Sangster, John Scott, Vernon Sewell, Jeffrey Stone, Fiona Subotsky, Tony Tenser, Christopher Toyne and David Warbeck.

Also deserving of thanks are my friend, editor and publisher (in that order) Denis and his 'girl Friday' Jane, as well as my beautiful wife Alison, without whose unflinching support there would be no book—and no point.

CONTENTS

Introduction   9

Chapter 1: *Rocks of Obscurity*   13
Chapter 2: *Practising Sadism*   29
Chapter 3: *Horror and a Dash of Sex*   91
Chapter 4: *Excruciating Bad Taste*   149

Afterword:
Remembering Richard Gordon   209

Filmography   213

Bibliography   243

This book is respectfully dedicated to my friend Dick Gordon.

The Board's Examiners choose what they think the right category for the film, but this may not suit the company commercially and they will then ask for cuts to make the film suitable for the category they want, or occasionally ask for an 'X' certificate for a film which was considered suitable with a few cuts as an 'A' film. The Board cannot reasonably refuse to make cuts for this purpose, since even if they think this will spoil a good film it is the right of the company to cut its own film if it wants to. Equally if a company refuses to make even one cut for the 'A' category the Board cannot refuse an 'X' certificate even though by putting the film in the 'X' category the Board may later be criticised. I used to do my best to persuade film companies to accept what seemed to us to be the right category for a film, but I was not always successful.

—John Trevelyan, *What the Censor Saw* (1973)

—An example of the commercialisation of the 'X' certificate: *Certificate X! magazine* (1965)

X-Cert

Introduction

'D' for Disgusting

Let me begin this introduction by tackling the thorny question of what constitutes an 'independent British horror' picture—at least to my mind.

The most common representation of 'independent' comes from Hollywood at a time when the major studios had huge payrolls of contracted staff spread across production and post-production facilities, sales and distribution networks, all the way through to the cinemas in the high street. Anyone who did not fit under these massive permanent umbrellas, and was therefore free to offer their services to the highest bidder, was classed as an 'independent'—a term which was applied equally to producers or production companies, irrespective of size or influence. In terms of companies, one of the most obvious examples was American International Pictures (AIP) which started as two men and a desk in an unfashionable part of Los Angeles and remained an independent in the eyes of the majors despite eventually growing to employ hundreds of people in an office block in Beverly Hills and having a worldwide sales and production network.

The film business in Britain is structured very differently to its US counterpart and apart from a handful of exceptions, huge chunks of the industry could reasonably be defined as independent. To solve the conundrum, I used AIP's 'two men and a desk' analogy as a starting point to reach a definition of independent appropriate for this side of the Atlantic. By ruling out companies with a recognised and enduring corporate structure, I removed the likes of British Lion and Rank from the list, along with the more famous horror film makers, Hammer, Amicus, Tigon, and even AIP's London office. I then discounted the major American studios, which frequently used Britain as a location for their films, and thus I ruled out films like *The Innocents* (1961) and *The Haunting* (1963). The companies that remained on the list included Caralan, Tempean and Proteclo, and producers like Sidney J Furie, Robert S Baker, Monty Berman and Richard Gordon.

Having arrived at a satisfactory definition of independent, I found that 'British' was equally ambiguous. In 1967, the National Film Finance Company estimated that 80% of the films made in the UK had American financial support that ranged from distribution deals to co-production or even full production costs—effectively, a truly British film was a rare beast indeed. To add to the confusion, tax advantages and access to foreign investment was enough of an attraction for a number of British-based producers to mount their films abroad—Harry Allan Towers, for example, who shot his films almost everywhere except in Britain. The opposite side of that argument involves overseas filmmakers and production companies who came to the UK to make their films, a trend which became increasingly common in the 1970s. To remove much of the complexity, I limited my scope to those films made in the UK by a *British-registered* company.

Of the three words in contention, the most difficult to define is 'horror', and with so many films that traditionally roosted in the horror genre being equally at home as science fiction, thrillers or even comedy, the final choice was always going to be arguable. Nevertheless, I based my selection on those films which were constructed with the clear and deliberate intent of scaring or unsettling audiences by utilising themes or situations that could be considered unreal or supernatural. This definition captures Terence Fisher's 'science fiction' films, *Island of Terror* (1966) and *Night of the Big Heat* (1967), both of which featured monsters terrorising innocent citizens, but excludes *The Day of the Triffids* (1962), which employs science fiction motifs to deal with much broader themes—although I concede that there were inserts shot after principle photography which were designed solely to increase the chills.

Even with such clearly-defined criteria, subjectivity can (and no doubt has) crept into the selections or exceptions—such as Compton's 1964 Gothic melodrama *The Black Torment*—and all such instances should be marked down to the author's creative license and passed over quickly.

Having established the type of films that qualify for inclusion, the decision to time-box this volume to the period 1951-1970 was far more straightforward. The British had been making horror films at least as long as Hollywood, but the stately pace of *The Ghoul* (1933) and the histrionics of the portly Tod Slaughter never fired the public imagination in the same way as did American monster movies. The horror genre prior to 1951 was critically reviled and artistically mocked and had little to attract British filmmakers, either among the mainstream or the independents. This situation began to change when the British Board of Film Censors (BBFC) decided that the time was right to overhaul the system of film classification in the UK.

The BBFC had ruled over film censorship in Britain since before the First World War, when a collection of industry worthies decided that they needed safeguarding from government legislation as much as the great British public needed protection from the morally corrosive influence of moving pictures. Clothing its new venture in appropriately altruistic motives, the BBFC listed the areas considered unsuitable for public display, including: cruelty to animals, gruesome murders, indelicate sexual situations and 'native customs in foreign lands abhorrent to British ideas.'

To ensure that public sensibilities were suitably protected, the Board established two quite distinct levels of film classification: 'U' for universal, which signified a film's availability to the widest possible market, and 'A' for adult, for films which were only to be viewed by children under the age of 14 if accompanied by a parent or guardian. It was not until the 1930s, when the macabre screen antics of *Dracula* and *Frankenstein* (both 1931) reached these shores, that the Board introduced a third category—'H' for horror—which further restricted the cinema audience to those over the age of 16.

UK filmmakers were largely indifferent to the new category and only a handful of domestically-made films ever acquired the H classification, *The Dark Eyes of London* (1939) and *The Fall of the House of Usher* (1948) among them. None of the British-made efforts were ever successful enough either in this country or abroad to break the perception that cinematic horror was an American preoccupation. By 1950, public tastes had moved elsewhere and the import of horror films had dwindled to a trickle but the BBFC was struggling to protect Britain from the new vogue for adult content coming in mainly from Europe. A parliamentary committee recommended a major overhaul of the ratings system and the following year, the

Introduction

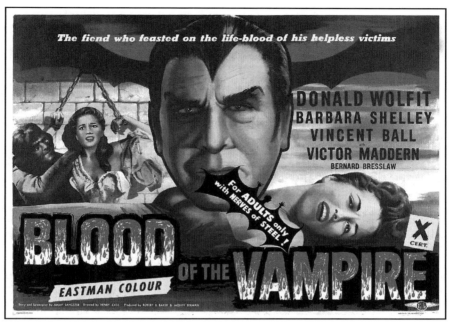

BBFC, under the direction of its then-president Sir Sidney Harris and Secretary Arthur Watkins, scrapped the H and brought in the 'X' certificate, which also only permitted a film to be exhibited to persons over the age of 16. (In the London area, the H lingered on before finally being subsumed into the new category).

Initially the new X certificate was greeted by film producers with the same lack of interest as the old H; the accepted view was that restricting the audience in this way only made the films financially unviable. This position allowed Britain's largest film production/distribution company, John Davis's Rank Organisation, to combine basic economics with the moral high ground and refuse to make or exhibit any X certificate films—which further restricted potential audience numbers. It was those perceptive showmen at Hammer Films who transformed the classification into a brand of its own by featuring the certificate prominently in their advertising as a blatant 'come on' to audiences, and even going so far as to incorporate it into titles: *The Quatermass Xperiment* (1955) and *X The Unknown* (1956). The numbers of willing adults who then flocked to X films more than offset any decline in overall audience size, but it was not until Hammer made the move from science fiction into horror that it discovered a massive worldwide audience for its product.

In many ways *The Curse of Frankenstein* (1957), the precursor to a whole gamut of horror films from Hammer, was a natural extension of the films which the studio was already making that offered a hint of sex, a whiff of violence and the implicit (but largely unfulfilled) promise of a lot more of both. The Hammer Frankenstein added one crucial new ingredient—colour—and on the screen, the blood flowed very red indeed. The effect on box-office receipts was exhilarating, and Baron Frankenstein was soon followed a year later by the even more successful *Dracula*, again in colour and offering the same calculated disregard for taste and subtlety. The critics were stupefied; the *Daily Telegraph* proclaimed, 'This British film has an X certificate. This is too good for it. There should be a new certificate - "S" for sadistic or just "D" for disgusting.' The assumption that X certificates had limited box-office potential

X-Cert

or that British films did not have international appeal was shattered once and for all, particularly in the American heartlands, where the Queen's English was regarded as something akin to a foreign language. Suddenly the incongruity of cockney landlords in Eastern European taverns, and Roedean-accented starlets succumbing to Rank-trained Transylvanian vampires was as acceptable as anything Hollywood crafted. The Hammer formula—blood, sex, stout-hearted heroes and villains vanquished in the final reel—provided the template for dozens of films that followed and made the name of Hammer synonymous with horror.

The impact on the world of independent film production was equally seismic. Filmmakers who had previously been gainfully employed churning out B-movie thrillers designed to mimic Hollywood gangster films suddenly found that there was a ready-made audience craving more full-blooded diversions. *Grip of the Strangler* (1958), *Blood of the Vampire* (1958), *Doctor Blood's Coffin* (1961) and dozens more poured from British studios in the immediate aftermath of Hammer's success as screens were filled with psychotic criminals, crazed vampires and demonic doctors. Later they would be joined by walking stone statues, voodoo curses and even a half-man/half bird enacting an ancient curse, as independent producers scrambled to cash in on the seemingly limitless appetite for British horror movies.

It is probably fair to say that these films and the people who made them have been unjustly neglected over the years as attention has been heaped instead on the likes of Hammer, Amicus and Tigon. In some cases that neglect is more than justified by the quality of the films themselves; few film lovers would list *The Frozen Dead* (1967) or *Trog* (1969), for example, in their personal top ten. But there *are* gems to be uncovered. My intention in writing this book is to shine a light into the dark corners where these films have remained hidden over the years and once again allow titles like *Night of the Eagle* (1962), *Devil Doll* (1964) and *The Corpse* (1969) a fleeting return to daylight.

Chapter 1

Rocks of Obscurity

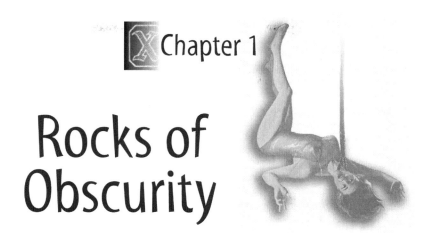

If British filmmakers in 1951 were slow to realise the commercial potential of the BBFC's new 'X' certificate, it may have been because the vast majority of them had something a little more pressing on their minds—survival. Box-office takings had gradually declined since the end of the Second World War and while the numbers of films produced remained consistent, these had been artificially boosted by the Rank organisation's ambitious and totally unsustainable expansion programme. J Arthur Rank's cinematic empire, at its height, consisted of a plethora of major production companies including Gainsborough, Ealing and Independent Producers, as well as studios at Pinewood and Ealing, a world-wide distribution network, and over 600 cinemas spread throughout Britain. Rank also boasted a multitude of peripheral activities ranging from the 'Rank Charm School' to the Gaumont British Animation unit, a £2.5 million attempt to challenge Disney for the children's cartoon market. There was no corner of the UK industry that was not touched in some way by the Organisation and huge swathes of it were dependent on Rank's continued prosperity. To coin a phrase: if Rank sneezed, the British film industry caught a cold. By the end of the 1940s, the economic decline of the country, a run of poor investment decisions by the current Rank board and some unmitigated bad luck rendered the bedrock of filmmaking in Britain a hospital case.

Harold Wilson, then President of the Board of Trade and a future Labour prime minister, articulated the government's concern when he said there was a real risk that without the Rank Organisation, all British film production would cease. Sir John Davis, Rank's managing director, was ruthless in his mission to save the company and he enacted wholesale redundancies, initiated the sale of studios and offices, and severely restricted the company's filmmaking activities. The movers and shakers in British film huddled in their Wardour Street offices and prepared for a very bleak future.

For once, the politicians did more than just talk and the new post-war Labour administration introduced a series of measures designed to safeguard and nurture the ailing industry. Fundamentally protectionist in design, these did little to address the inherent problems in film distribution and exhibition in the UK but they did provide some respite for hard-pressed producers and, significantly, they became the building blocks that would later underpin independent film production in Britain.

The first of these measures, the Cinematograph Films Act, came in as early as 1948 and set a new requirement for exhibitors to show a minimum 'quota' of domestic as opposed to imported films. Quota thresholds had been in place in one form or another since 1927 but this Bill set a higher baseline at 45% (it was reduced to 30% in 1950, where it remained until it was abolished by Margaret Thatcher's government in 1983). The films produced to meet the quota are often derided for their quality and it is true that many cinema managers resorted to showing British films early in the morning or late at night to avoid interrupting the more popular Hollywood pictures. But the value of the legislation was not in the pictures produced but in the talent that was cultivated and many of those involved would go on to work in more prominent features, including the likes of directors John Gilling, Vernon Sewell and Terence Fisher, as well as screenwriters, technicians and actors of the calibre of Christopher Lee, Hazel Court and Donald Houston.

A more tangible development was the establishment of the National Film Finance Corporation, with a five-year tenure and publicly-funded purse of £5 million for investment in new films. Targeting low to medium-budget films, the NFFC would typically put up around 15 to 20% of a film's finance, subject to various guarantees from the producers and distributors. The fact that the NFFC accepted the residual value of films already completed against a guarantee of future earnings was a huge incentive for B-movie filmmakers to start work on their next film while the previous picture was still on release. The NFFC was to become the cornerstone of the British horror genre, providing support to companies such as Hammer in the early 1950s as well as funding the British horror film revival in the 1960s. Far outliving its original term, the Corporation finally fell foul of Thatcher's anti-protectionist policies.

Another of Wilson's measures, intended as a short-term gesture, was the Eady Levy (named after Treasury official Sir Wilfred Eady), which imposed a toll of 12% on cinema tickets. This tax was collected by Her Majesty's Customs and Excise and subsequently distributed to British-based film producers in proportion to the revenues their films generated in UK theatres. The more successful a film was at the

Dead of Night (Ralph Michael, Googie Withers)

Latin Quarter (Beresford Egan)

1: Rocks of Obscurity

UK box-office, the larger the producers' share of the Eady pot and, unlike similar schemes in Europe, there was no obligation for the money to be reinvested in future production—a significant enticement for overseas filmmakers to come to Britain. The Eady Levy remained in place until 1985.

The combined impact of the Labour government's various legislative measures cannot be underestimated; filmmaking in the UK was now vigorously encouraged, and to a large extent subsidised, while at the same time inward investment from overseas, predominantly the USA, was being actively rewarded. All that was needed to kick-start growth was film producers with the courage to put their own money where the box-office rewards were but unfortunately, and despite the change in the classification, this was not in the horror genre.

In the years leading up to the introduction of the X certificate, British-made horror films remained noticeable by their absence. A whole gamut of monsters (most of them inspired by English literature's Gothic heritage) had already stomped through the Californian backlots and inflicted all manner of 'sons', 'returns', 'ghosts' and 'houses' on audiences. British film producers, for the most part, ran shy of the genre, with the exception of a handful of efforts which were generally considered to be poor cousins to the Americans. There were some exceptions to this rule; *Dead of Night* (1945), for example, was a well-regarded anthology of ghost stories from Ealing Studios, a company more commonly associated with genteel comedies. The format would later inspire the Amicus horror films but in post-war Britain, even this critical and commercial success did little to encourage would-be horror filmmakers. *Latin Quarter* (aka *Frenzy*), released the same year, marked a rare outing into the world of A features for Vernon Sewell, a director who was to remain happily mired in supporting features for most of his career but who would also contribute some memorable additions to the horror genre. Sewell's successful melding of murder mystery and the supernatural nevertheless failed to incite others to the cause.

By the early 1950s, even Hollywood had abandoned horror films in favour of extraterrestrial terrors (another market the British were slow to exploit) and when the first X certificate was issued on January 8, 1951, it was awarded not to a horror film but a documentary, *La Vie Commence Demain* (1950), which committed the cardinal sin of depicting artificial insemination. That is not to say the British were not making interesting films; the Gainsborough production, *So Long at the Fair* (1950), concerning a disappearance at the Paris Expo of 1889, skirted around the horror genre to deliver a superior but curiously-unsatisfying thriller. Don Sharp later reworked the same premise into the much more entertaining *The Kiss of the Vampire* in 1963. At the same time down on the banks of the Thames, Hammer Films varied their customary output of comedies and light dramas with the likes of *Room to Let* (1950), a recasting of Jack the Ripper myth not dissimilar to Hitchcock's *The Lodger* (1927). The studio came even closer to horror when Terence Fisher helmed *Stolen Face* (1952), the tale of a plastic surgeon re-engineering the face of a woman in compensation for the loss of a previous lover. The low-key approach and happy ending ensured it did not stray a jot from the path of an A certificate—despite having many of the ingredients that would later feature in *Circus of Horrors*, *Corruption* and Fisher's own *Frankenstein Created Woman* (1967).

Not all British filmmakers were quite so bashful about horror films, however—although they were still some way from recognisable X-certificate territory. George Minter, managing director and founder of the Renown Picture Corporation, merits more than a footnote for not only creating the first British screen vampire but for recalling to Britain's shores the actor who for generations of cinemagoers was the definitive representation of Stoker's Count Dracula: Bela Lugosi.

15

X-cert

Mother Riley Meets the Vampire
'It's enough to make a bat laugh!'

> The infamous Baron Von Housen schemes to take over the world using unstoppable robots. To gain access to limitless supplies of the uranium he needs to power his army, he kidnaps the daughter of an Italian scientist who has the map of a recently-discovered mine. Unfortunately Von Housen's first robot is delivered to Mother Riley by mistake while Von Housen receives her collections of bedpans and bottles. The mad scientist uses his telepathic powers to summon the unsuspecting Mother Riley to his mansion where he develops a liking for her blood group and puts her on a meat-intensive diet to enrich the iron in her blood count. Mother Riley discovers the kidnapped Italian girl and with the help of a maid manages to alert the authorities, but not before Von Housen has successfully reactivated his robot.

Lugosi's career had been on the slide for nearly two decades, almost from the moment that he declined a starring role in Universal's companion-piece to *Dracula* (1931) and cleared the path for an unknown Englishman called Boris Karloff to play Frankenstein's monster. The two actors were frequently hailed as the joint kings of horror films in the 1930s, but Karloff's stock rocketed while Lugosi was shoehorned into one inappropriate vehicle after another. By the mid-1940s, however, both men were suffering from a lack of decent parts but Karloff, the more bankable star and widely considered the more versatile actor, transferred easily into supporting roles in mainstream vehicles and an impressive run of theatre engagements. Lugosi, on the other hand, was reduced to slumming it in poverty row comedies and touring the US in a second-rate stage revival of *Dracula*. By the early 1950s, even the Count could not entice curious Americans to the theatres and the actor was hamming it up in a vaudeville horror and magic show.

Lugosi's horror film roles were a memory by then; he had swallowed his pride and spoofed his most famous creation in *Abbott & Costello Meet Frankenstein* (1948) but despite featuring in the top-grossing films of the year, it failed to dispel the view in Hollywood that the actor was all-but unemployable. Enter one of the few men who still believed in the former star, Richard Gordon, an ex-pat Englishman who befriended Lugosi while writing for British film magazines. Gordon and his brother Alex had travelled to the US on a one-way ticket at the end of the 1940s, determined to break into the film business. Alex went to California and teamed up with two enterprising executives named Samuel Z Arkoff and James H Nicholson in what would later become American International Pictures; his films for the soon-to-be exploitation giant included *Apache Woman* (1955) and *Girls in Prison* (1956) and he would become a good source of scripts and talent for Richard, who stayed on the East Coast to set up Gordon Films Inc, a distribution agent to European and British independents—including George Minter and Renown.

Desperate for work, Lugosi asked Richard Gordon to help him secure backing for a UK stage revival of *Dracula*, a project that he had been planning for a while. Gordon made introductions through his network of contacts and in the spring of 1951, Lugosi and his wife Lillian sailed from New York for what would prove a hastily-arranged and grossly underfunded British tour. The production attracted some mixed reviews as it tramped around the provinces with the vague intention of opening in the West End at some indeterminate future date. For six months, Lugosi endured on-stage mishaps, indifferent audiences and rudimentary lodgings before the tour finally ran out of steam in Derby. The remaining dates were cancelled and the actors laid off, leaving Lugosi (who had been banking on a longer run) stranded

1: Rocks of Obscurity

Mother Riley Meets the Vampire (Arthur Lucan, Bela Lugosi)/INSET: Lucan, Kitty McShane
BELOW LEFT: Richard Gordon, Lugosi, George Minter/BELOW RIGHT: Lugosi, Richard Gordon

and without even the return fare to the US. The actor then sent a telegram to the only man he knew who might be able to help—Richard Gordon.

Knowing that George Minter was keen to break into the US market, Gordon flew to London to persuade the producer that he had the opportunity of signing a major Hollywood star at a very reasonable rate. Minter, a Londoner by birth, had moved into film production with *No Orchids for Miss Blandish* (1948), a controversial gangster film that attracted the sort of notices later associated with the most extreme horror films: 'The most sickening exhibition of brutality, perversion, sex and sadism ever to be shown on a cinema screen,' screamed the *Monthly Film Bulletin*. Minter's subsequent films were far less colourful and, operating under a number of subsidiary companies, he produced such titles as *A Christmas Carol* (1951) and *Tom Brown's Schooldays* (1951). Minter's Renown outfit had also picked up the *Old Mother Riley* franchise, which had been cast aside by British National Films in 1945.

The dim-witted Mother Riley character was the alter ego of music-hall comedian Arthur Lucan, who had perfected his act in variety theatres in Ireland and the North of England before launching himself on the general public via radio and film. Acting opposite his real-life wife, Kitty McShane, who played Mother Riley's much put-upon daughter, Lucan would caper into a series of laboured mis-timings and mishaps interspersed with the odd song and dance routine, as the doltish haridan somehow managed to best scheming villains and/or condescending establishment bureaucrats. By the end of the war, the duo seemed to have run their course professionally and personally (their marital spats had become the stuff of legend) and their film career went into an enforced hiatus. Minter resurrected the pairing for *Old Mother Riley's New Venture* in 1949, followed quickly by two equally poor and equally poorly received sequels—none of which made any impact at all outside of the UK. But the unexpected availability of Bela Lugosi presented Minter with an opportunity to change strategy and he did not have to look too far for a script.

Val Valentine, who had fashioned *Old Mother Riley's Jungle Treasure* (1951) by recycling the Abbott and Costello film *Africa Screams* (1949), was already working on a variation of *Abbott and Costello Meet the Invisible Man* (1951). When Lugosi's name came up, Valentine simply dug out the actor's own encounter with the comics and fashioned a screenplay 'inspired' by the same basic plot. As Richard Gordon later admitted, 'The intention from the outset was to cash in on the success of *Abbott and Costello Meet Frankenstein* and some of the sequences were a direct steal.'

To direct proceedings, Minter engaged John Gilling, whose best work to date had been as a writer for Hammer on the films *The Man in Black* (1949) and *Room to Let* (1950) before moving on to direct a handful features for B-movie specialists Tempean Films. Gilling had started his career as an assistant director in the 1930s, graduating to the editing suite and later branching into writing where he proved himself a source of cheap but efficient thrillers. Gilling's later directing career would include a number of minor but interesting horror films, not least of which was *The Plague of the Zombies* (1966). Unfortunately as this outing was to prove, comedy was not John Gilling's forte.

Richard Gordon secured Lugosi a fee of $5,000 plus expenses for four weeks work, less than a quarter of the figure paid to Lucan and some way short of the $10,000 he had been paid for *Abbott & Costello Meet Frankenstein*, but the actor was in no position to argue. The supporting cast at least was a notch or two above the usual Mother Riley fare and included performers who would go on to much better work, such as Hattie Jacques, Richard Wattis and John Le Mesurier, as well as character actor Laurence Naismith. The middle aged Kitty McShane, now far too old for the juvenile lead, was jettisoned, much to her annoyance, for the promising

1: Rocks of Obscurity

British comedienne Dora Bryan. Minter still considered Mother Riley to be the film's principle selling point in the UK but by the time the cast assembled at Nettleford Studios in October 1951, two days before Halloween, US trade adverts were already heralding Lugosi's return to the screen in *Vampire over London*.

It was fitting that Lugosi, who had starred in the first British film to obtain an H certificate—*Dark Eyes of London* (1939), should have the opportunity to create the country's first vampire; unfortunately the BBFC had different ideas. Minter needed the film to reach the widest possible audience and the restrictive X was a potential disaster; as the censor regarded vampirism as inappropriate for a family audience, Gilling was forced to compromise to secure a U certificate. An on-screen disclaimer was added, supposedly 'explaining' this aspect of the film's villain:

'..Baron Von Housen, whom legend immortalised as a vampire. For reasons of his own, Von Housen claims to be an earthly reproduction of his notorious ancestor, owing his continuing existence to the consumption of human blood. Needless to say there is not the faintest vestige of truth in his claim.'

The fact that the screenplay repeatedly contradicts this view suggests the addition was either made at the last minute or simply ignored by Gilling in constructing his plot-line. Certainly Von Housen leaves his cohorts in no doubt as to his undead status and solemnly declares, 'Until now I have existed in the minds of people as a legend, a vampire, created by evil. Now at last, I—Von Housen—am ready to fulfil my destiny!' References also remain to 'all these women' who come to Van Housen's mansion and are never seen again, as well as Mother Riley's description of him as 'a vampire in wolf's under-clothing.' The most obvious point is of course Van Housen's insistence that his latest 'houseguest' is fattened up to enrich her blood. 'You shall have liver and steak all day, every day,' he says leering at the crone. 'You need feeding up.' Naturally the steak is served rare.

After his gruelling *Dracula* tour, Lugosi seemed to be much more relaxed—as Gilling recalled for writer Gilbert Verschooten and *Little Shoppe of Horrors*: 'We had tremendous fun on set. There were lots of spontaneous gags and laughs which really one could only invent on the spur of the moment.' All this bonhomie did not translate to the screen, however, and the 'humour' veers from the cringingly obvious to the inherently unfunny. Such comedy as does exist comes mainly from Lugosi's deliberately po-faced delivery; 'A poor specimen,' Von Housen remarks when he sees Mother Riley, 'but the right group and an excellent vintage.' Later he draws her (him!) close and hisses sweet nothings in the form of, 'Do you like baaaatz?'

Richard Gordon was less convinced about the affability of Lugosi and thought the actor struggled to cope with his co-star's constant ad-libbing, as

Arthur Lucan/ABOVE: with Lugosi, in costume as Mother Riley

well as being genuinely unsettled by Lucan's refusal to emerge from behind his Mother Riley persona. Lucan changed into costume at home and travelled to and from the studio in full Mother Riley regalia; Gordon, who visited the set on several occasions, never caught sight of the film's nominal star out of character.

Gordon and Gilling do agree on the quality of Lugosi's acting. The director told Verschooten that Lugosi was 'a superb melodramatic actor, comparable in a way to Tod Slaughter only more controlled.' Gilling, playing to this image of the actor, piles on the horror clichés—the fog swirls in the moonlight and crypts are festooned with giant cobwebs. Lugosi rises to the histrionics in what Richard Gordon felt was 'the last time you have the opportunity to see Lugosi and some of the power and magic he had as a performer. Not in the scenes where he is fooling around with Arthur Lucan but in the other scenes where he is doing his mad scientist, you could see the magic that was there.'

Gordon, aware of the potential in Lugosi's performance, suggested to Minter that it would be in everyone's interest if Gilling shot additional footage of the actor that could be used for the American market. 'I knew watching the shooting that Arthur Lucan's humour was never going to translate to American audiences,' the Englishman recalls. The producers pressed on regardless, believing the fusion of Hollywood horror and English variety would find receptive audiences on both sides of the Atlantic and Lugosi, at least publicly, seemed to share their confidence. When he finally made it back to the US, the actor was interviewed for the television show *Ship's Reporter* as he disembarked in New York and he told Jack Mangan, 'It was a rather clever story, and I think they would laugh at it very much. It's going to sell in America especially.'

Despite the star's wishful thinking, Lucan's tired routines and limp humour buried whatever quality Lugosi could bring and the British critics were damning. The *Monthly Film Bulletin* called it 'stupid, humourless and repulsive'; *Picturegoer* at least spotted some merit in the performances of the leads but concluded, 'The script defeats them both.' The film could not even find a US distributor and sat on a shelf for three years before plans emerged to remove Mother Riley entirely and shoot additional scenes with Lugosi to create a new film called *Robot Monster*. By then, its star's physical deterioration made it impossible to match the earlier footage and the proposal came to nothing. Minter's film was finally released in the US in 1963, seven years after the death of its star, under the title of *My Son, the Vampire* and with a new introduction by American comedian Alan Sherman. Sadly, Lugosi's fan base, if such a thing existed, failed to turn out and after receiving some nostalgia bookings, the film was consigned to the vaults.

Lucan, Lugosi and Gilling (second left) on set

George Minter's failure to ignite the box office with *Mother Riley Meets the Vampire* left one of the great 'what ifs...' of British cinema. In a moment of unbridled enthusiasm shortly after production started, Minter had announced *Mother Riley's Trip to Mars* and two new horror films to be shot in England with Boris Karloff and

1: Rocks of Obscurity

Bela Lugosi headlining one apiece. The abject box-office returns sent Arthur Lucan back to the music halls to see out his dotage while Lugosi was left in the Hollywood wilderness to be 'rediscovered' by the notorious Ed Wood. Had the money rolled in and the proposed Lugosi/Karloff double bill taken off, then Renown rather than Hammer may well have become the British studio most synonymous with horror and fantasy films.

As it was, Minter returned to his regular diet of programme fillers and the horror genre had to make do with a return to the mannered ghost stories of Vernon Sewell, architect of *Latin Quarter*, who dug into his own personal vaults to pull out a modest but endearing supernatural tale called *Ghost Ship*.

Ghost Ship
'Dead men spoke to solve the secret of the sea!'

> *Newlyweds Guy Thornton and his wife Margaret buy a neglected 40-year old steam-yacht in the belief it will make the ideal floating home—despite a warning from the harbour master that the boat has a somewhat dubious reputation. The Thorntons laugh off suggestions that the ship is haunted and set about hiring a crew and restoring her to her former glory. Problems start immediately after the maiden voyage off the Sussex coast when the engineer quits, insisting he has seen a ghost; a new engineer also quits refusing to sail on a haunted ship. It is only after Guy witnesses an apparition in the engine room that they call in a paranormal investigator who in turn brings with him a medium called Mrs Manley. During an on-board séance, Mrs Manley manages to establish the truth behind the disappearances of the previous owners and reveals the horrific secret hidden below the decks of the Thornton's new home.*

Not to be confused with the similarly-titled RKO film of 1943, Vernon Sewell's *Ghost Ship* was yet another adaptation of the play *L'Angoisse* by Celia de Vilyars and Pierre Mills. Sewell had purchased the rights to the play in the 1930s and fashioned the rather sedate tale of haunting and séances into a distracting short film called *The Medium* (1934). Over subsequent decades, he took the notion of parsimony to a whole new level by remaking the project first as *Latin Quarter* (1945), and then as *Ghost Ship* (1952), before reusing the entire premise yet again for one final outing as *House of Mystery* in 1961.

Born in London in 1903, Vernon Sewell began his career as a camera assistant at Nettlefold Studios in 1929, moving swiftly through the ranks of the camera department to sound recordist, art director and then editor. *The Medium* marked his directorial debut, working from a script written for him by close friend Michael Powell, and the two men continued their association when Sewell acted as production assistant on Powell's *The Edge of the World* (1937). Branching into full-time directing, Sewell carved out a reputation for polished if unambitious B features, including *The Silver Fleet* (1943) and *The World Owes Me a Living* (1945), before *Latin Quarter* registered his first significant box-office success. Sewell followed that in 1947 with a more whimsical fantasy entitled *The Ghosts of Berkeley Place*, which remained one of his personal favourites, but he quickly returned to Bs with *Uneasy Terms* (1948) and *Jack of Diamonds* (1949). His penchant for low-budget filmmaking meant that Sewell, unlike many of his contemporaries, remained relatively unknown, although it did not stop him acquiring admirers, including the influential author and critic David Pirie, who told readers of *Heritage of Horror* that Sewell was 'one of the great heroic (yet unsung) eccentrics of the British cinema.'

X-cert

Ghost Ship (Hazel Court, Dermot Walsh, Joss Ambler)

Looking back on his long career in 1997, Sewell claimed that working in 'B' pictures '..meant I had complete control. I didn't have to answer to anybody; I was my own boss and that was reason enough not to get involved with big pictures.'

The shooting of *Ghost Ship* was set up through Vernon Sewell Productions, with partial funding from distribution company Anglo-Amalgamated (A-A), a small British distributor which would later have considerable influence on the horror genre. On some prints, Anglo's managing director Nat Cohen is listed as producer but Sewell insists that after contracts were signed, he was left entirely to his own devices and was free to recruit a number of his regular collaborators. These included Eric Spear, who composed the score, Francis Bieber as editor and George Haslam as production designer.

In front of the cameras, Sewell engaged Dermot Walsh to play the male lead, an actor who had been lured from his native Eire with the promise of a Rank contract and who was touted as a future star in such films as *Hungry Hill* (1947) and *Jassy* (1947). Released by Rank as part of their down-sizing, Walsh had no difficulty in lowering his sights and became a familiar face in British B films for the next decade. Walsh's on-screen wife was played by his real-life spouse, Hazel Court, another contract artist in the Rank empire who found refuge in B movies. Like her husband, Court's career stayed firmly planted in low-budget efforts, but a subsequent sojourn in Hammer and American International horrors accorded her a cult status which Walsh never equalled. The cast-list also included Sewell's wife Joan Carol, who

1: Rocks of Obscurity

appeared in a number of his films, including the early Hammer-Exclusive sea-borne thriller, *The Dark Light* (1951).

Enjoying the familiarity of it all, Sewell booked his picture into Merton Park studios, one of his favourite haunts. 'I was good friends with Will Williams, who produced my films there,' he recalled. 'Williams was an ideal producer for me in that he left me to get on with things, which I liked, but he was also a thoroughly nice man. When he got sacked I didn't work there again.' The tiny studio located on Kingston Road in South West London was also the base for criminologist Edgar Lustgarten's popular series of crime thrillers, supposedly drawn from Scotland Yard's actual files, and it become a home from home for many independent filmmakers until the mid-1960s, hosting some 130 films—nearly all of them B pictures.

The decision to shoot the exteriors in the English Channel on board the director's own steam-yacht *Gelert* provided Sewell with another opportunity to save money. Interviewed by Brian McFarlane for his book *An Autobiography of British Cinema*, Dermot Walsh recalled that the director 'wanted to get her (*Gelert*) scraped, which meant she would have to go into dry dock, so he wrote a story and set it on the yacht. He hired his own ship for his own story, got her scraped and repainted, which he worked into the action.' Stanley Long, whose three-decade friendship with Sewell started when he worked as his director of photography, says, 'His real passion was boats and whenever a script came along which featured a marine subject, it was a good bet that Vernon's name would be in there somewhere on the credits.'

Title aside, the film plays like a psychological thriller and Sewell seems reluctant to concede that he is making a horror film at all. The matter-of-fact style and low-key tone are reminiscent of his earlier documentary work and there is altogether too much talk—most of it about the technical aspects of sailing—and too little action. The one moment that seemed custom-made to give the audience a jolt, the ghostly manifestation, is treated with a casual disregard for the conventions of the genre, with no build up or shock reveal. There is still much to admire in the film; Stanley Grant's photography is excellent, the story remains intriguing, and the principles, as one might expect, have an easy and engaging rapport. Hazel Court in particular displays an on-screen warmth and gift for comic relief seldom seen in her later films and, while Walsh struggles to maintain his transatlantic accent, Sewell was happy enough with the pairing to cast them again in his next film, *Counterspy* (1953).

Sewell's assured handling does enough to ensure that the 72 minutes of screen-time pass relatively painlessly and he is not above adding his own gently subversive humour whenever the action starts to wane. One of the more amusing moments comes when the couple arrive to collect their ghost hunter and draw the obvious but incorrect conclusion when confronted by the dramatic appearance of a dotty vicar in a billowing black cape. The real investigator arrives moments later and could not be more hum-drum.

Planned only as a supporting feature, *Ghost Ship* set low expectations but trade paper *Kinematograph Weekly* caught the director's intent and concluded of the film that it, 'Weighs anchor with alacrity, drifts a little between flashbacks but cleverly avoids the rocks of obscurity and finally makes port in exciting circumstances.'

Sewell's unpretentious efforts were never going to provide the much-needed genre uplift and with traditional monsters still out of fashion, British filmmakers continued to display their customary aversion to risk-taking. When mainstream producer Ian Dalrymple decided to turn his attentions to the horror genre, he played safe by looking to past successes for inspiration rather than trying to anticipate future tastes. Nevertheless, with *Three Cases of Murder,* Dalrymple managed a feat all too rare in British cinema up to this point in time—he made a genuinely scary film.

X-cert

Three Cases of Murder
'All it takes is a little imagination...'

> A narrator welcomes the audience to his home and promises them three stories that all have something a little 'unusual' about them. 'In the Picture' is set in an art gallery where objects inexplicably disappear and the glass frame of one particular painting is prone to shatter when no one is about. A meek tour guide, Jarvis, strikes up a conversation with a stranger and accepts his invitation to join the man literally inside the painting. In 'You Killed Elizabeth', two life-long friends are in love with the same woman, Liz. The handsome and popular Edgar is the clear favourite to win her heart but he has a drinking problem and is subject to blackouts so when Liz turns up dead, the more compliant George sees an opportunity to come out on top for once. 'Mountdrago' sees a pompous politician cross swords with a rising star of the back benches only to later realise his parliamentary rival is using supernatural forces to exact his revenge.

South African Ian Dalrymple is not a name normally associated with the horror genre, and certainly the Rugby and Cambridge-educated editor/director/writer and producer had much higher profile successes during his thirty-plus years in British films. An apprentice at Gainsborough in the 1920s, Dalrymple edited films like *The Hound of the Baskervilles* (1932) and *The Ghoul* (1933) before turning to writing and subsequently sharing an Oscar for his contribution to the script of *Pygmalion* (1938). After an association with legendary film mogul Sir Alexander Korda and a wartime role as a producer for the Crown Film Unit making morale-boosting documentaries, Dalrymple set up Wessex Film Productions Ltd under the umbrella of Rank's Independent Producers initiative. Wessex survived the upheaval at Rank and though it dipped into documentary filming every now and again, Dalrymple was more usually involved with mainstream hits like *The Wooden Horse* (1950) and the later *Hell in Korea* (1956).

One of the key influences behind *Three Cases of Murder* was another close friend of Korda's, Alexander Paal. A fellow Hungarian émigré, Paal had worked for Hammer as a writer on *Stolen Face* (1952) and then producer on *Four Sided Triangle* (1953) and would later be responsible for one of the company's more distinctive pictures, *Countess Dracula* (1971). In exchange for upfront finance, Korda's British Lion took the domestic distribution rights, and its regular producer, Hugh Perceval, came on board to oversee the production. The Korda connection was reinforced when Georges Périnal was appointed director of photography; the Frenchmen had won an Oscar for Korda's production of *The Thief of Bagdad* (1940) and had earlier shot *Things to Come* (1936) and *The Four Feathers* (1939).

Adopting the anthology format for *Three Cases of Murder*, Dalrymple and Paal looked directly to *Dead of Night*, but they also had an eye on two popular non-horror films—*Quartet* (1948) and *Trio* (1950), both originating from Gainsborough and featuring short stories by W Somerset Maugham. Dalrymple acquired one of Maugham's stories for his picture and was astute enough to ensure that the author's name was featured prominently in the film's advertising. *Lord Mountdrago*, which Maugham had written in 1939 as a treatise on psychiatry and the analysis of dreams as much as paranormal phenomena, was adapted by Dalrymple, with the other two stories, *In the Picture* and *You Killed Elizabeth*, coming from stories by Roderick Wilkinson and Brett Halliday; the latter was a pen name for American mystery writer Davis Dresser.

Like *Dead of Night*, Dalrymple engaged separate directors to helm each segment:

1: Rocks of Obscurity

Three Cases of Murder (Eddie Byrne, Hugh Pryse, Ann Hanslip, Alan Badel)

Three Cases of Murder (Andre Morell, Orson Welles)

X-cert

Wendy Toye directed *In the Picture*, David Eady made his feature film debut on *You Killed Elizabeth* and George More O'Ferrall, who had helmed Dalrymple's earlier *The Heart of the Matter* (1953), took charge of the final tale, *Lord Mountdrago*.

The film was introduced by smirking television personality Eamonn Andrews, who tells the audience that he likes his murders, 'short, sharp and efficient', before inviting them to join him in three tales of slaughter. This style of introduction, which was particularly popular on television at the time, sets a tone reminiscent of Agatha Christie's drawing-room mysteries, but there is only one story that realistically could be described as a 'whodunnit' and it was the second screened, *You Killed Elizabeth*. Easily the most frivolous and contrived of the trilogy, the segment starred John Gregson as the womanising Edgar who steals Elizabeth (Elizabeth Sellars) away from his best friend. The barman plying Gregson's alcoholic with liquor is Alan Badel, the only member of the cast to appear in all three stories.

Alan Badel, a veteran of the Royal Shakespeare Company and the Old Vic, had appeared in an award-winning short film for Wendy Toye called *The Stranger Left No Card* (1952), and it is their collaboration on the first story screened that really sets the film apart as something subversive and disturbing. Toye, a former ballet dancer and choreographer who was under contract to Korda at the time, was that rarity in the pantheon of British cinema, a successful woman director, and her only contemporary of note was Muriel Box. Eamonn Andrews pops up to set the scene by warning the audience not to be 'surprised if things take a fantastic turn, the painter was a fantastic man' before we are introduced to the unctuous Badel as 'Mr X' who persuades the lugubrious guide Jarvis (Hugh Pryse) to join him in a deeper exploration of a favoured painting. 'Come closer to the painting,' Badel says. 'Have you ever taken a really close look? I mean close enough to get to the very heart of the pigment?' Taking Jarvis literally *into* the painting, the two men find themselves in a nightmare world of weird angles and dark corners where a taxidermist (Eddie Byrne) has a predilection for human subjects and demons hover just out of sight. 'There are many brands of damnation,' says Mr X. 'Out here we

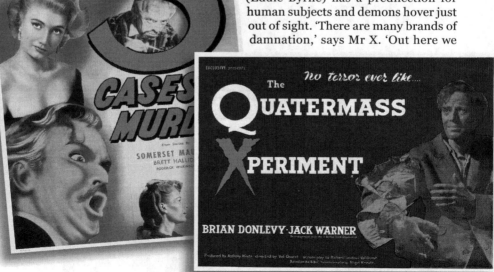

1: Rocks of Obscurity

have more varieties of it than you have pickles...' The story is unsettling enough but Badel's performance sets it apart and manages to make the acquisitive Mr X both foppish and menacing. Having captured Jarvis, he then returns to the outside world to stalk new prey.

Badel's performance in the last story is equally effective, but on this occasion he has to contend with the considerable screen presence of Orson Welles, who plays the mountainous Lord Mountdrago. Badel is a debutant Welsh MP called Owen, who is humiliated in the House of Commons by the pompous braggart and vows revenge. 'You broke my heart tonight,' Owen fumes, 'I can't break yours, because you haven't got one, but I can crush your proud spirit...and I will.' From that point on, Mountdrago is pushed closer and closer to a mental breakdown with a series of bizarre dreams: he turns up for a dinner party without his trousers on; a parliamentary debate erupts into song; and at every turn, Owen is there to enjoy the moment. 'I no sooner close my eyes than he is there!' Mountdrago wails to his doctor. 'That grinning, vulgar little cad...mocking me...' Playing the doctor who is unable to convince Mountdrago to apologise is Andre Morell, a well-known stage actor at the time who would become one of Hammer's most versatile stars, but it is Welles who dominates the segment. The Hollywood maverick was enjoying self-imposed exile in Europe, jumping from film to film to stay one step ahead of his creditors and content to lend his name (for an appropriate fee, naturally) to local producers. Welles's blustering and spluttering almost steal the show but Badel still manages to make his mark, and the suggestion that the sly Owen will pursue his revenge from beyond the grave closes the film with a delicious moment of *frisson*.

Having the name Orson Welles prominently in the credits ensured the film a US release (it opened in New York two months ahead of its British premiere), but not all American critics appreciated its finer qualities and it received mixed notices. The *New York Times* thought the stories were 'interesting in their virtuosity and cosily British in style. The only fault with them is the monotony of their terminal incidents.' The *New York Post*, on the other hand, called it 'suspense at its best'.

Three Cases of Murder opened in the UK in May 1955, only a few months ahead of the film that would finally start the horror revolution, Hammer's *The Quatermass Xperiment*, only the twelfth film to receive an X certificate—a fact that so pleased its producers that they re-worked their title to emphasise it. Directed with gusto by Val Guest and adapted from a hugely popular BBC science-fiction serial, Hammer's film was essentially a monster-on-the-loose movie told with a barefaced audacity seldom seen in British films. The public lapped it up and Hammer executives James Carreras and his partner Anthony Hinds suddenly found themselves in the horror business. *X The Unknown* (1956), with a script by Jimmy Sangster, soon remixed the same science fiction/horror ingredients as before with similar success. A second Quatermass film would trundle off the Bray production line in 1957 but by then, Hammer had turned their creative energies to something quite different: *The Curse of Frankenstein*.

The artistic qualities of Terence Fisher's film have been hotly debated for five decades but contemporary critics were in no doubt: 'For sadists only' warned the *Daily Telegraph,* while *The Observer's* reviewer despaired, 'I could not discern one moment of art or poetry.' The trade papers were more sparing but the reviews hardly mattered to the cinemagoers who queued around the block the moment the film opened—a sight that was repeated throughout the UK and across the world. The more organisations like the American National Legion of Decency stepped up to condemn the film, the louder the tills seemed to ring—much to the delight of Messrs Carreras and Hinds. The company could never claim to have invented the British horror film

X-cert

but Hammer certainly initiated X-certificate horror in all its vulgar, blood-red glory and for the first time, the ability to make money had a direct correlation to the gore, violence and sex on the screen. The British independent filmmakers who, thanks to government subsidies had survived by aping American B movies, suddenly had a home-grown role-model to follow and, while Hammer refined its excesses into a repeatable formula, the first of a new breed of independent horror film was getting ready to roll.

The Curse of Frankenstein (Christopher Lee)

Chapter 2

Practising Sadism

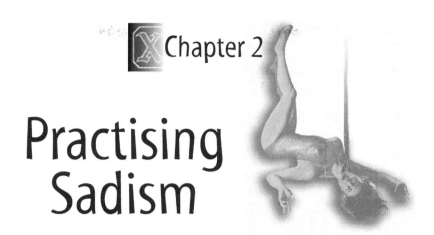

Just as Hammer was gearing up to unleash its version of the Frankenstein monster, the originator of the role, Boris Karloff, was back in Britain intent on reviving his particular brand of screen menace. The 70-year old actor was as active as ever on television and radio (with the occasional foray onto the stage) but in Hollywood, he was considered passé and his recent film appearances had consisted of unworthy cameos or encounters with low-brow comedians. Now Karloff had a leading role, a good script and a producer he trusted.

Fellow Englishman Richard Gordon identifies befriending Boris Karloff as one of the highlights of his long career and readily acknowledges the actor's generosity. 'Karloff handed me the script called *Stranglehold*,' Gordon recalled, 'which would become *Grip of the Strangler*, and it was written for him by his friend, Jan Read. Knowing that I was looking to make a film in England, he told me that if I could set it up he would appear. Although I was relatively unknown at the time, Karloff's name was such that every British distributor I approached was interested.'

GRIP OF THE STRANGLER
'Their wild beauty marked them for death!'

> Writer and philanthropist James Rankin is researching the case of the 'Haymarket Strangler', a killer sent to the gallows twenty years earlier for the brutal murder of five women—all half-strangled and stabbed. Rankin is convinced that Edward Styles, the man convicted of the crimes, was really innocent and that Dr Tennant, a surgeon attached to the case, was the true killer. Determined to prove his theory, Rankin exhumes Styles's body. In the open coffin, he finds the missing murder weapon, a surgeon's scalpel, but when he touches the blade, his features transform into a mask of cruelty. Unable to control his impulses, Rankin embarks on a murder spree to equal that of his notorious predecessor. Only then does Rankin learn the awful truth—that he and Tennant are one and the same and that in a state of total amnesia, he has been living a lie for over twenty years...

After his unfortunate encounter with Mother Riley in 1951, Richard Gordon had expanded and developed his distribution business, representing the interests of a number of British filmmakers in their attempts to break into the US market. He made his first tentative steps towards film production when he set up Amalgamated

Grip of the Strangler (Boris Karloff)

Productions in partnership with New Yorker Charles 'Chuck' Vetters, and started supplying US funding, actors and occasionally scripts for B pictures shot in Britain. *Kill Me Tomorrow* (1957), directed by Terence Fisher and Francis Searle, was just one of the pictures supported by Amalgamated Productions.

Gordon first met Karloff during one of the actor's Broadway runs and over the next few years, they often discussed working together on a film, but it was only when he was handed Jan Read's script that Gordon felt they had a project strong enough to launch Amalgamated as an independent production house. Bringing British-based producer John Croydon into the partnership, they negotiated a finance deal with the distributor Eros which guaranteed funding for 70% of the film's budget after delivery of the finished product; this guarantee was then discountable at the bank for the cash needed to meet the day-to-day production costs. The remaining 30% of the budget came from the National Film Finance Corporation (NFFC), which took the total to £80,000, with the producers themselves responsible for any over-runs. Double-bills comprising of two films usually vaguely similar in subject-matter were

2: Practising Sadism

Grip of the Strangler (Anthony Dawson, Boris Karloff)

common at the time and the terms of the Eros agreement required Amalgamated to provide a suitable supporting feature. By the time Karloff arrived in London, Gordon was already in pre-production on the second film, which would be shot more or less back-to-back but with a different cast and director. The deal with Eros, which covered the UK only, also ensured that Amalgamated had covered its costs before a single frame of either film had been shot, leaving it the luxury of selling the remaining rights at leisure. M-G-M finally picked up the two-film package shortly after completion of principle photography.

Karloff may have been crucial to selling the film but his salary was a relatively modest $6,875 a week for four weeks, with an additional $400 per week for living expenses and first-class return tickets to the US for he and his wife. To put it into perspective, the RKO picture *The Body Snatcher* (1945), which was made a decade earlier and considered a B movie, rewarded the actor with $6,000 per week without the disruption of travelling from his American base. Gordon's deal with Karloff was complicated by his agent's insistence on an option for a further feature on a 'pay or play' basis; in other words, Karloff would be paid for this second film whether it was made or not. This clause specified that the additional film had to be shot in a fixed time period after completion of the first, leaving Gordon with the challenge of overseeing the simultaneous production of two feature films while actively searching for a third.

For Karloff, the *Stranglehold* script represented the sort of acting challenge that had eluded him for more than a decade: playing a character that one moment is fainting at the sight of blood and the next is carving his way through the supporting cast. In fact Read had envisaged a far more subtle approach, with Rankin merely possessed by the killer's spirit; it was John Croydon, writing as John C Cooper, who made it a physical transformation and brought in the idea of a Jack the Ripper-style slasher. Croydon also wrote in many of the elements considered by filmmakers to be essential features with a Victorian backdrop: floggings, graveyards and chirrupy

X-Cert

Grip of the Strangler (Elizabeth Allen, Boris Karloff)

BELOW: Diane Aubrey, Tim Turner

chorus girls cavorting in French knickers. Read was reportedly unhappy with the changes but the resulting script is a rich slice of gothic melodrama that combines the grim reality of Newgate Prison with Ripper folklore, mixing in Stevenson's *Strange Case of Dr Jekyll and Mr Hyde* and a dash of Charles Dickens. The rush to get Croydon's re-write finished ahead of shooting did throw out one obvious inconsistency; given that Rankin and the killer are one and the same person, why is it that no-one recognises him? 'In the time-honoured tradition of the movies,' Gordon explains, 'We drew a veil over that; it is one of those things you just have to accept.'

With Karloff topping the bill, there was no need to pay for star names in any of the supporting roles and the best-known face was probably Jean Kent, the former Gainsborough starlet, who played the rather matronly good-time girl Cora. She is joined by pert blonde Vera Day as part of the 'entertainment' at 'The Judas Hole', a gentleman's supper club where the girls dance the can-can and leap giggling onto the laps of the male customers. Elizabeth Allen had the less physically demanding role of Rankin's long-suffering wife, who confronts him with the truth and suffers the consequences. The only other familiar face was that of Anthony Dawson, who was memorably sleazy in *Dial M for Murder* (1954) but played against type as an affable policeman; the role of the hero was taken by Tim Turner, who would go on to become a familiar *voice* on television as *The Invisible Man*.

Robert Day, an experienced cameraman, was hired to direct the film and his visual sense and attention to detail created a rich *mise-en-scène* which belied the limited budget. Two other noteworthy names behind the scenes were the highly regarded special effects wizard Les Bowie, whose work included *The Day the Earth Caught Fire* (1961) as well as a host of Hammer films, and a young assistant director named Douglas Hickox, who would go on to direct the minor Vincent Price masterpiece, *Theatre of Blood* (1973).

While the sets were being constructed at Walton Studios in Surrey, the producers wrestled with the challenge of achieving Karloff's physical transformation without expensive monster make-up. A number of designs were tried and rejected before Karloff offered a more practical alternative to greasepaint and latex. 'He turned his back,' Croydon told *Fangoria* magazine 'and seemed to be remoulding his features. When he swung back again, we were stunned. He had removed his false left upper and lower molars, and drawn his mouth awkwardly sideways, sucked in his lower lip so that the upper teeth overlapped, his cheek drawn inwards. The left eyebrow and lid were lowered, his left arm drawn up and useless, as though he had suffered a major stroke. In a thickened tone, unlike his own softly-modulated voice, he asked, "Will this do?"'

'Karloff assured us that he could maintain those facial expressions throughout the shooting,' Richard Gordon adds. 'And he was not the type of actor that made a commitment he couldn't fulfil.' The unlikely sight of Karloff gurning, as the script says 'more like a beast than a human being', turned out to be as effective off screen as it was on. Vera Day remembers, 'I jumped out my skin when I saw it. They didn't tell us what they were going to do and when Boris came out looking like that I was absolutely terrified.'

Despite the star's creativity, Robert Day was under constant pressure from his producers; he told Tom Weaver, 'When I wanted to do a reverse shot, I thought, "Well, I can't do it because I don't have the time". And then I had John Croydon up my ass all the time, talking about the budget and the schedule and so on.' The two men also clashed on content, particularly on the more graphic scenes, which Day felt were undermining his carefully-crafted atmosphere. Croydon, as he made clear to *Fangoria*, regarded himself as an 'observer and critic in the interests of the script and its integrity' and insisted that scenes such as the whipping of a half-naked wretch were filmed as scripted. Karloff, in an on-set interview with *Photoplay magazine* seemed to accept the producer's perspective: 'The public wants it,' he said. 'Every time a picture is given an X it pulls in the film-goers. And I do not object provided it doesn't offend good taste.'

Karloff, enjoying the challenge of a meaty role, was putting in a remarkably energetic shift. 'We obviously had a stand-in for Boris,' Gordon says, 'but he asked if he could do his own running and jumping which was quite out of the question. He liked the part and he had a close rapport with Robert Day so I am sure he wanted to do his very best.' Karloff's enthusiasm, his quiet dignity and humility won him plaudits from the crew and his fellow actors; Vera Day, who had the dubious pleasure of being throttled by the veteran on screen, remembered, 'An absolute gentleman, a lovely, lovely man with no sign at all of airs and graces. He was just one of us, a real trouper.'

Karloff's faith in the project was rewarded when it emerged as an effective and fast-paced horror picture, seen by many to be a bridge between the 'Golden Age' of horror films and the emerging era of Hammer. The critics on the whole agreed; the *New York Times* said, 'Karloff is indeed the villain we can unashamedly hiss and hate; his return is in a picture that measures up with his very best'; while *Time Out* thought it 'uncommonly gripping, wonderfully atmospheric, it has a real touch of the Val Lewtons.'

With *Grip of the Strangler* occupying John Croydon's attention, Richard Gordon was setting up his second feature, which originated from a story by Amelia Reynolds Long called *The Thought Monster* and eventually graced the screen under the far more evocative title of *Fiend without a Face*.

FIEND WITHOUT A FACE
'Science gone wild. Will the man of the future be...a fiend without a face?'

> When a farmer is killed close to a US air force base, the locals blame what they believe is a rogue GI hiding in the woods. Major Jeff Cummings, in charge of a top secret military project using nuclear power to boost radar signals, is not so sure and despite resistance from the community, he starts his own investigation. The pathologist examining the victim points out that there are two holes at the base of the victim's neck and the brain is missing— 'sucked out like an egg'. Major Cummings suggests they are looking for a 'mental vampire' and suspicions fall on Professor Walgate, an expert on psychic phenomena who has written books on the materialisation of thought. Jeff confronts Walgate who admits he is responsible for creating invisible creatures but it seems the discovery has come too late; the 'fiends' surround and lay siege to the house.

It was legendary editor Forrest Ackerman who found the story in a 1930 edition of *Weird Tales* magazine and alerted Alex Gordon at AIP to its potential as a low budget horror. When the Hollywood company declined an option, Richard Gordon

2: Practising Sadism

Fiend Without a Face (Stanley Maxted, Marshall Thompson)

stepped in to snap up the rights for the princely sum of $400. Television and radio writer Herbert J Leder was then engaged to update the tale for a modern audience and accommodate two of cinema's most topical obsessions: atomic radiation and invasion—usually by aliens but sometimes by the Soviet Union, depending on the genre of film concerned. Leder inventively covers all the bases by setting his story on a US base monitoring the Russians while fending off attack by mysterious creatures, the titular faceless 'fiends', which are kept invisible until the film's climax and are then revealed as brain-like, with a long coil of spine acting as a tail. This invisibility was a calculated move to save money on special effects but it proved a challenge for the filmmakers when it came to building tension along the way. The novel solution was the addition of an ominous 'heartbeat' and slurping sound effects—biological anomalies forgivable under the circumstances.

Gordon liked Leder's script but was less impressed when the writer expressed his ambitions to direct the film. 'I had no confidence in his ability,' Gordon states, 'and he never forgave me for not letting him direct this film; I accepted his screenplay and he never spoke to me again.' Leaving the screenwriter to cool his heels, Gordon opted for Arthur Crabtree, a graduate of the Gainsborough studios where his most accomplished film was probably *Madonna of the Seven Moons* (1945). The dozen or so features that followed it, including the Amalgamated-funded *The Fighting Wildcats* (1957), proved that Crabtree possessed the two qualities most admired by low budget film producers: speed and reliability.

Given its status as the lower half of the proposed double-bill, *Fiend* was allocated a shorter schedule and smaller budget, thus negating any prospect of casting a star name. Nevertheless Gordon, keen to underscore the American connection and on the recommendation of Alex Gordon, signed Marshall Thompson for the role of Major Cummings. A former contract player at M-G-M, Thompson had spent most of his career in B movies, including the horror movie *Cult of the Cobra* (1955), usually playing decent sorts and authority figures. The actor was given a rare opportunity

X-Cert

to show a darker side as a mentally disturbed killer in *Dial 1119* (1950) and did well enough to make one regret that he was not cast as villains more often. To provide the Major with a love interest, Gordon hired Kim Parker to play Barbara Griselle, sister of the first victim and the link between the investigators and the enigmatic Professor Waldgate, who was played by veteran Kynaston Reeves. Ms Parker, who had decorated *Fire Maidens of Outer Space* (1956), provided the only minor hiccup in an otherwise happy shoot when she shared a car to the studio with Boris Karloff, who was shooting *Grip of the Strangler* at the same time. It seems the veteran found his young companion's stories and language a tad inappropriate. 'He wasn't exactly complaining,' Gordon says, 'but he suggested he would rather share his car with someone closer to his own age!'

The script offered little that was new and the plot could have been lifted from any one of dozens of Hollywood films, but Crabtree is helped out by the engaging performances of Thompson and Parker, while the obviously low budget is offset by a palpable sense of paranoia and growing tension within the isolated community. It is only when the creatures finally make their onscreen appearance that the mood is broken. A small FX team working in Munich under the direction of Baron Von Nordhoff and KL Ruppel produced the stop-frame animation, but the 'fiends' never really look convincingly alive and when required to physically attack their victims, it is all too obvious they are being fired from slings or pulled on wires. Even so, the effects proved so complicated that *Fiend Without a Face* ended up costing slightly more than the main feature.

As a sop to the needs of the ad-men, Crabtree also shot a brief (and very tame) shower sequence—predictably nothing to do with the narrative—and the subsequent stills of Kim Parker were extensively used in the publicity. As it happens, there was

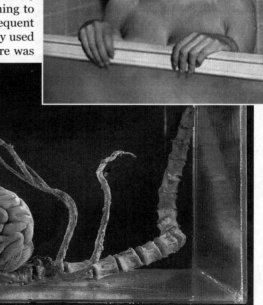

Fiend Without a Face / INSET: Kim Parker

X-Cert

no need to rely on sex to sell the film; when it opened at the Ritz in Leicester Square in June 1958, there was an immediate reaction from the press. 'The picture was passed as an X,' Gordon says, 'but when the reviews focused on what they saw as the excessiveness in the some of the scenes, they considered it a disgrace to the British film industry. I believe there was even a question asked in Parliament—that's the sort of publicity that money can't buy!'

The New York opening on Times Square

Given its chosen market, Eros was a natural home for the double-bill in the UK, but it is less clear why the films attracted the attention of M-G-M, widely seen as the most mainstream of the US majors. 'Hollywood was changing,' Gordon explains. 'This was at the time when big studios were acquiring independently produced pictures, so I imagine this was something of a new territory for them and I had differences with the marketing department on how to handle the pictures.' M-G-M's marketing strategy wasn't geared for horror/exploitation pictures and they booked the films into up-scale cinemas rather than the usual flea-pits. 'These theatres normally played films like *Gigi*,' Gordon discovered, 'and the managers were horrified to have to show their patrons pictures like this.' M-G-M's miscalculation meant a slow start at the US box-office and it was only after word of mouth spread that the audience numbers swelled. At a time when many of its higher profile contemporaries have faded away, *Fiend without a Face* has proved particularly enduring and become

2: Practising Sadism

something of a cult favourite on television and late night cinema shows. 'Even forty years after it was made,' Gordon reflects, 'a lot of people tell me that it was a film that frightened them as a child or gave them nightmares; people who have gone on to become directors or writers themselves say the same thing.' Sadly, despite persistent rumours of remakes which have circulated for some years, there has been no updating of the fiends using modern techniques and special effects.

M-G-M turned enough profit on its Amalgamated pictures to request more of the same and it proposed the mounting of a Technicolor and Cinemascope version of *Dracula*, with Karloff in the title role. The actor was apparently receptive but almost immediately the project hit problems: 'We had been led to believe that the rights were in the public domain,' Gordon says, 'but we were wrong. They were in Europe but in the US they were owned by Universal.' The project was shelved and a short time later, Gordon learned that Hammer had signed a deal with Universal-International for its own version.

While the search continued for a Karloff vehicle to headline Amalgamated's next double bill, Gordon sold M-G-M on the co-feature, another science fiction/horror based on a story called *Satellite of Blood*, which tapped into the wave of public interest following the launch of Russia's Sputnik 1. Keen to get ahead of the competition, M-G-M decided not to wait for the development of a main feature and requested that *First Man in Space* be rushed into production.

FIRST MAN INTO SPACE
'Did the deadly gamma rays turn him into a monster?'

> Test pilot Dan Prescott disobeys instructions from Mission Control and flies his experimental plane further into space than any man has gone before. The control centre loses track of the craft completely as it collides with a meteor storm and Prescott plummets back to earth, crashing close to Albuquerque, New Mexico. Dan survives the crash but he has been transformed; his face reduced to an amorphous sludge, he has developed unnatural strength and an inhuman thirst for blood. When cattle turn up mutilated, Dan's brother, Chuck Prescott, who is in charge of the test programme, suspects the truth and a manhunt is launched. Dan, maddened by thirst, raids a blood bank and kills a nurse; other deaths follow as he steals a truck to elude his pursuers. Chuck, torn between destroying and saving his brother, concocts a plan he hopes can trap him.

Satellite of Blood was another script plucked from the 'reject' drawer at AIP by the ever-vigilant Alex Gordon who correctly guessed it would be of interest to his brother. The story had been written some years earlier by Wyatt Ordan, originator of such gems as *Monster from the Ocean Floor* (1954), and it was left to John Croydon and Chuck Vetters (writing as Lance Z Hargreaves) to update the screenplay for the Sputnik generation. Their inspiration came directly from Nigel Kneale, care of Hammer. '*The Quatermass Xperiment,* which had been very successful, was a definite influence,' Gordon concedes, 'Chuck Vetters was hoping to emulate Kneale's screenplay and the success of that film.'

Once again Amalgamated turned to Marshall Thompson to bring his customary calming influence to the character of Chuck Prescott, the air force officer determinedly tracking down his brother. This was Thompson's third and final outing for Gordon, having stayed on in London following *Fiend without a Face* to appear in the thriller *The Secret Man* (1958). To play the hot-headed Dan, Gordon hired Bill Edwards, a Canadian living in England who had a number of small roles on television and in

features to his credit. Edwards had to endure hours in make-up but had the compensation of uttering the film's defining line: 'I just had to be the first man into space.'

Marla Landi was cast as Dan's fiancée on the recommendation of Hammer managing director James Carreras, who had recently featured the Italian starlet in *The Hound of the Baskervilles,* and Roger Delgado, who was to become something of a cult figure as 'The Master' in the *Dr Who* television series of the 1960s, added a bit of comic relief as the Mexican consul seeking compensation for a disrupted bull fight.

Robert Day was back in the director's chair, this time facing up to the obvious difficulties of depicting the New Mexico landscape during a rainy British January. To disguise shots of the distinctly English foliage, Alex Gordon supervised some second unit shooting in California, mainly of cars coming and going, which was then integrated into Day's shots along with stock footage of US air force planes both on the ground and in the air. Using residential houses rather than a studio helped to keep costs down, but creating the illusion of a space-age command centre was more difficult and Day had to keep the impoverished set in shadows to disguise the paucity of the dressings.

The laughably-small effects budget proved more difficult to camouflage; the script's spectacular meteor storm was created using a model aircraft bombarded by sequins, for example. Gordon was too shrewd to scrimp on the monster, though, and the make-up is by far the best thing in the film, successfully suggesting that Dan's

First Man into Space

features had been reduced to a single eye and some teeth poking out of sludge. Once again Day uses shadows to underpin the impact, and scenes such as the vampiric creature stalking the night are particularly effective. On the whole, however, the film lacks the sense of claustrophobia and threat that had pervaded *Fiend without a Face*. Also, over-wordy early sequences designed specifically to slake the public's appetite for science come across as flat and tedious, and the acting also tends towards blandness. Even the usually-reliable Marshall Thompson struggles to add credibility to lines such as 'The conquest of new worlds always makes demands on human life and there will always be men who will accept the risks.'

M-G-M neither noticed nor cared about the film's shortcomings; the unmanned Sputnik 2 had just launched and it wanted *First Man Into Space* out on the circuits before fact caught up with fiction (in fact, it was 1961 before Yuri Gagarin managed to emulate his on-screen rival). Without waiting for Amalgamated to produce a co-feature, it rushed a world premiere in Albuquerque, presumably believing it would be perceived as a local product. It is doubtful if any of the New Mexicans who gathered on the March 5, 1959, were fooled into thinking this had been filmed anywhere in their state but the critics on the whole were surprisingly kind. *Variety* spoke for the majority saying, 'A good entry in the exploitation class, it has excitement and genuine horror', and the returns from both sides of the Atlantic were good enough for Gordon and his partners to think of Amalgamated Productions as a new force in the horror/science fiction market.

With renewed confidence, Amalgamated turned its attention back to the ticklish problem of the Karloff film and briefly considered an adaptation of Poe's story *The Facts in the Case of M Valdemar*. The sudden resurgence of the horror genre meant that Karloff was once more in demand and the actor had recently signed a three-film

41

deal with B-picture producer Aubrey Shenck—which further reduced the window that Richard Gordon had to make his own film. Getting a Poe script together from scratch would take too long, so John Croydon volunteered a screenplay written by Jean Rogers called *The Doctor of Seven Dials*. Rogers's script had the right balance of history and horror to be acceptable to Karloff and more significantly M-G-M, which approved the film to be made at its Borehamwood Studios at Elstree.

CORRIDORS OF BLOOD
'His newest and most frightening role!'

> *Thomas Bolton, a surgeon in 1840s London, is horrified by the barbarity of medical practices; 'I came face to face with one of my so-called successful operations,' he says, 'his mind destroyed with shock and pain—a fine tribute to my skill!' His colleagues insist that 'pain and the knife are inseparable,' but Bolton resolves to rid surgery of such horrors and submits himself to a series of experiments using highly-addictive drugs. Despite his good intentions, a public demonstration of his anaesthesia ends in farce and Bolton is suspended and deprived of access to his drugs. With nowhere else to turn, he falls in with a gang of murderous body-snatchers operating in the notorious Seven Dials district. In return for the drugs, these villains force Bolton to sign fraudulent death certificates which eventually alert the authorities. As the Peelers close in, Bolton makes a belated attempt to stand up to his blackmailers.*

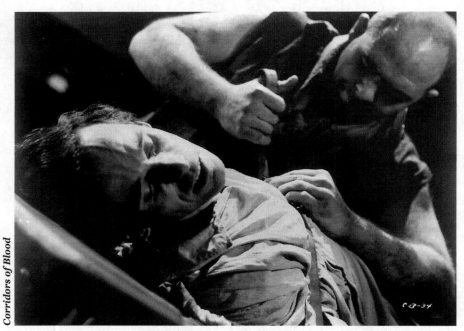

Corridors of Blood

Rogers, a writer on the ATV soap opera *Emergency Ward Ten*, based the story loosely on the real-life New England dentist, Horace Wells, who pioneered the use of anaesthesia and who had already featured in the 1944 biopic *The Great Moment*, starring Joel McCrea. Mixing fact with fiction, Rogers used a similar biographical structure to weave in social comment and melodrama, adding some anachronistic body-snatching for good measure. The approach appealed to the film's star; 'Boris

2: Practising Sadism

Corridors of Blood (Francis Matthews, Boris Karloff) INSET: Christopher Lee

liked the script very much,' Gordon confirms, 'and in particular the seriousness of the subject matter and the picture's historic background which he thought was a welcome departure from Hammer-style horror movies.'

Hammer's growing influence in the field was not completely ignored, however, thanks once again to the intervention of the company's colourful MD. 'Jimmy Carreras was always very helpful to me,' Gordon recalls. 'He knew that I was about to make a film with Boris Karloff and thought it would be to my advantage to feature Christopher Lee, who had just appeared as the Frankenstein monster. He also recommended Francis Matthews who had been in another Frankenstein film.' Matthews had played a conventional leading man for Hammer in *The Revenge of Frankenstein* and he slotted neatly into the same type for Gordon, but providing space for Lee proved more challenging. The only role available was the small part of a body snatcher named Resurrection Joe, a

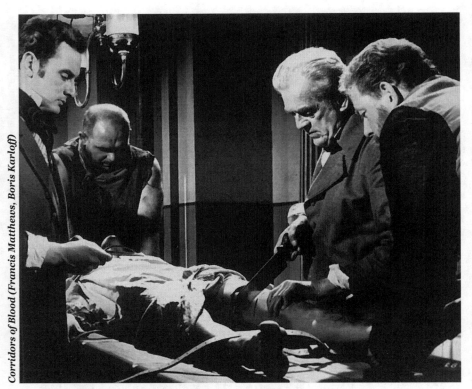

Corridors of Blood (Francis Matthews, Boris Karloff)

thuggish sidekick to the main heavy, Black Ben. To accommodate Lee, Gordon had the role expanded to include several scenes opposite Karloff himself. The move undoubtedly increased the film's saleability but Gordon found it difficult to warm to the actor. 'I found Christopher Lee somewhat pompous as a person,' he confessed, 'and working with him was not a happy experience. He said that his performance as the Frankenstein creature would eclipse that of Karloff in the original, a suggestion which he clearly believed but which had no credibility as far as I was concerned.' Whatever his comments to Gordon, Lee told his biographers Tom Johnson and Mark A Miller, 'I was very much in awe of Boris Karloff...quite simply, one of the most talented and personable people with whom I've ever been associated.'

Karloff's basically decent Dr Bolton remained the central character but Lee's Resurrection Joe lent the picture a morose and menacing presence, skulking in the background or leaping from the shadows with murderous intent. It's an interesting cameo which does not intrude on or distract from the larger-than-life wickedness of Frances de Wolfe as Black Ben or Karloff's doleful slide into drug addiction. Shortly after shooting started in May 1958, Hammer's *Dracula* opened in London, followed a week or so later by its US premiere, and Gordon happily adjusted the schedule to allow Lee to fly to New York for a personal appearance. By the time he returned to the set, the actor had taken a significant step towards becoming the most important of the post-War horror stars.

Robert Day was engaged for his third and final Richard Gordon film and, with M-G-M on board from the outset, he was afforded not only more expansive studio facilities but a larger budget of around £90,000. The increase still meant shooting in black and white, as with all the Amalgamated films, but it allowed Day

2: Practising Sadism

Corridors of Blood (Boris Karloff, Christopher Lee, Adrienne Corri, Francis de Wolfe)

to recruit a much more experienced cast. This included Finlay Currie as Charles Matheson, one of Bolton's stalwart supporters, and Adrienne Corri as Black Ben's coquettish paramour. Hollywood actress Betta St John played Bolton's niece, while upcoming starlet Yvonne Romain provided glamour as the bawdy house tart Rosa who inadvertently attracts the lustful designs of Resurrection Joe.

For Day, the improved shooting circumstances were tempered by the presence of John Croydon on his set and in particular the producer's continued insistence on ramping up the explicit violence. Resurrection Joe's demise was a particularly unpleasant example of exploitation triumphing over art. The character, up to his usual nefarious activities, gets doused in vitriol which burns the flesh of his face; Croydon insisted that Lee's agonised death throes were shown in slow motion. An earlier scene, the amputation of a child's leg, is almost too gruesome to watch but Croydon asserted, with some veracity, that surgical operations of the period were conducted on butcher's tables with doctors wearing leather aprons as protection from the spurting blood. With no anaesthetics, the conscious patients more often than not had to be dragged screaming into the operating theatre knowing there was a good chance that the shock would kill them if the operation did not. These scenes were easily as graphic as anything in Hammer's films at the time, but the decision not to shoot in colour seemed to appease the BBFC and the censor asked for only minor cuts to shots that showed scalpels ostensibly penetrating flesh. Boris Karloff was less comfortable and took the occasion of an on-set interview with *Films and Filming* to insist, 'Good taste plays a very important part in the telling of a horror story on film. Some have taste, others regrettably have not.'

Karloff's comments may well have been a subtle jab at John Croydon, who was voicing concerns about the actor's performance. He later described what he saw to *Fangoria* as 'melodrama rampant', and compared the crucial scenes set in the Seven Dials to 'Victorian melodramas like *Sweeney Todd* or *Maria Marten*.' Richard Gordon was only too aware that tension was building on the set and asserts that 'John Croydon was responsible; although I have to say he was a wonderful man who I liked very much. Robert Day knew exactly what he wanted to do; he was well prepared and he got on very well with Karloff. John Croydon did not always approve of the director's decisions and would voice his criticisms. Day and Karloff sided with each other, as you might expect, against Croydon, and it caused some minor problems...I believe there were moments when John would not address Karloff directly and would only talk to him through a third party.'

If Karloff felt any strain he did not let it show. Yvonne Romain told Tom Weaver that the unassuming Englishman was 'the gentlest, sweetest man in the whole world. The opposite from what you imagined he would be.' The crew also warmed to the star's unpretentious nature and picked up on his oft-repeated offer to help sweep up the set at the end of each day's shooting by presenting him with an inscribed broom as a memento of the film.

Richard Gordon had more on his mind than his star when after a few weeks of shooting, the production fell foul of a corporate reshuffle at M-G-M. 'The studio changed their management team,' he recalled, 'and as usually happens, the new guys were not interested in the pictures made by the previous regime. They saw this as a little picture and not in keeping with the direction they wanted to take the company.' M-G-M put Amalgamated on notice that they would not continue financing the film, though they agreed to defer repayment of monies already advanced until after the picture's release—provided that the film was completed with funds from elsewhere. Warner Brothers expressed interest but could not reach agreement with M-G-M, which left Gordon and his partners to finish the film using their own resources, without the comfort of a distribution deal, and with M-G-M retaining ownership of a film it now did not want.

Corridors of Blood

2: Practising Sadism

With no inclination to release the film, M-G-M allowed the retitled *Corridors of Blood* to languish in the vault until September 1962 before slipping it out for a UK circuit release, followed nine months later by its American opening. 'By then there had been another change of management at M-G-M,' Gordon says, 'and suddenly small pictures were seen as a good revenue stream again!' But the moment had gone; in a crowded market, *Corridors of Blood* looked staid and old-fashioned, and despite some black-hearted villainy from Lee and de Wolfe, the public's taste was now for Technicolor horrors. The *New York Times* was not alone in thinking it a 'plodding, shuddersome exercise in blood and pain.' Richard Gordon also had mixed feelings; 'as a combination of history and horror, we managed to be neither one nor the other and it didn't really work.'

The film's long-delayed release and subsequent poor box-office performance effectively put an end to Amalgamated Productions as a viable filmmaking unit and highlighted the vagaries of dealing with Hollywood majors. The company was closed down and while Richard Gordon continued making low budget British horror films, he never again looked for major studio backing.

The mixed success of Amalgamated can be contrasted with another independent film unit, Tempean Films, which had been productively making B pictures for over a decade and whose engaging owners, Robert S Baker and Monty Berman, were about to bring their considerable experience to bear on the science fiction/horror market.

Londoners both, Baker and Berman had served together in the Army Film and Photographic Unit during the Second World War and somewhere between the North African campaign and the fall of Berlin, they decided they would join forces in the safer but probably equally unpredictable pursuit of making films in post-war Britain. Founding Tempean in 1947, they supplied a steady diet of supporting features to the smaller British film distributors, predominately Eros. 'We made some comedies and musicals,' Robert Baker says, 'but realised quickly that the biggest audience was for thrillers; we stayed close to familiar themes and familiar stories and provided we spent around £20-£25,000 per film, we could make a reasonable living.'

As the market for B thrillers started to dry up, Tempean snapped up the rights to *The Trollenberg Terror*, a popular television series billed as commercial television's answer to *Quatermass*, and then they hired Hammer screenwriter Jimmy Sangster to pen what would be the first in a series of successful genre features.

THE TROLLENBERG TERROR
'A man dissolves...and out of the oozing mist comes the hungry eye, slave to the demon brain!'

> Something strange is happening on the Trollenberg peak: climbers have mysterious accidents, bodies are found decapitated and the locals are convinced that malignant spirits inhabit the region. Two sisters, Anne and Sarah, en route to Geneva, are drawn to the mountain; Anne, a stage psychic, senses something evil is lurking in the area around a government-funded observatory located near the mountain-top. They are joined by Alan Brook who has experienced similar events in the Andes, and has been summoned to provide his insights into the discovery of a mysterious radioactive cloud. Brook's investigations have arrived at one conclusion: aliens are using the Trollenberg as a base for a future invasion, killing climbers and using their reanimated bodies to attack the locals! As the invasion gathers momentum, Brooks fortifies the observatory and prepares the survivors for a last stand against the aliens.

X-Cert

In condensing Peter Key's teleplay for six 30-minute episodes into an 80-minute script, Sangster had to truncate scenes and merge characters but as Baker reflects, 'Jimmy had done this sort of thing before and we knew he could do a good job. Don't forget the *Quatermass* films started out on television too and lost very little in the translation to the big screen.' The abbreviated running time does create some unlikely leaps in logic; for example, no sooner has the possibility of alien involvement been established, than Professor Crevett at the observatory is helpfully suggesting, 'There are many galaxies besides ours. Who knows what is happening millions of miles out in space,? Perhaps the world that these creatures inhabit is coming to an end; perhaps they need to find somewhere else to live.' Other loose ends left to flap in the Alpine winds include any explanation as to why the aliens need to go to such lengths to kill the psychic after their diabolical plot has been discovered, or how a mountaineer has been killed and decapitated inside a locked cabin with no sign of forced entry..? On a more positive note, Sangster's narrative bristles with energy: the opening charts a beheading, the discovery of the body and the introduction of the lead characters all within the space of only a few minutes.

Despite the gruesome nature of the slayings, director Quentin Lawrence is surprisingly restrained and stages most of the violence off-screen, using the inherent isolation of the mountains to underpin the tension. Mountaineers are attacked on a precipice, scientists are trapped in a remote cabin, and the climactic battle is staged with the villagers shut inside the reinforced observatory with no obvious avenue of escape. Lawrence, a qualified physicist by trade, was making his debut as a feature film director but he had a commendable track record on the small screen, including the original tele-serial of *The Trollenberg Terror*.

Also retained from the small screen version was former Old Vic actor Laurence Payne who repeated the role of Truscott, an investigative reporter with a nice line

The Trollenberg Terror

The Trollenberg Terror (Janet Munro, Andrew Faulds)

in cynicism. 'If they can only exist on the tops of mountains,' he observes wryly, 'they are hardly likely to inherit the Earth'. Meeting the requirements of the obligatory American lead was Forrest Tucker, most recently of Hammer's *The Abominable Snowman* (1957). The actor's rugged demeanour made for an unlikely scientist but he was more than up for the physical demands of battling aliens and wooing leading ladies. Providing the glamour were Jennifer Jayne and Janet Munro as Sarah and Anne Pilgrim; the latter was particular good as the psychic thrown into a milieu she cannot understand, and it is a shame that the script gives her little to do after the initial premise has been established. Similar disregard is shown for the supporting roles, including Warren Mitchell as Crevett, complete with a comic German accent, who pops up every now and again to provide suitable exposition. Mitchell remembers that he was not first choice for the part: 'They had cast Anton Diffring in the role and at the last minute he decided to go on holiday. My agent told them I was free and could do the accent so I got the part without even an interview.'

The actor is honest enough to admit that art was not a motivation, 'I did it purely for the money, they paid me enough to put a deposit down on a house and that's exactly what I did. The film was total bollocks.'

Mitchell's scenes were largely confined to the observatory and his comments may well have been inspired by the less than impressive sets; the supposed cutting-edge science facility consisted of a pair of telescopes and a tape recorder with a large dial. Audiences were equally short-changed with the special effects, which left Les Bowie's alien invader, best described as a single, massive eye with tentacles attached, memorable for all the wrong reasons. 'On the whole the effects were a let down,' Baker concedes, 'I remember the alien cloud was created using cotton wool and on screen it looked like…cotton wool. For the most part we focused the action on the characters not the effects'.

'Tempean was a bit like Hammer when it came to spending money,' Sangster wrote in his autobiography, and when he suggested, 'They probably shot their films in the local gravel pit painted white', he was not too far from the truth. Stock footage of the Alps was inserted with haste and with little of the care seen in Richard Gordon pictures, while all the interiors and certain 'exteriors' were shot at Tempean's usual base of Southall, one of the oldest working studios in England. With only two modest sound stages, Southall had been tottering on the brink of administration for some time, surviving on television shows like *Colonel March of Scotland Yard,* but its fragile finances collapsed soon afterwards and *The Trollenberg Terror* was the last feature to be shot there.

Despite its numerous flaws, Lawrence's film met a receptive audience among the less demanding cinemagoers and the critics were generally kind; *Variety* noted, 'The taut screenplay extracts the most from the situations and is helped by strong, resourceful acting from a solid cast.' *Picturegoer* said, 'On a "Boy's Own Paper" level it's uproarious nonsense with plenty of get up and go. But, oh dear, what a hammy monster.'

2: Practising Sadism

This first taste of box-office success on both sides of the Atlantic propelled Tempean on to more meaningful genre efforts, but Forrest Tucker was not so lucky. The American stayed in the UK to appear in another Quatermass-style yarn, also ripped from the small screen and worth no more than a footnote. *The Strange World of Planet X* (1958), based on another Quentin Lawrence serial, offered viewers giant insects, mysterious aliens and an eye-catching tagline—'Every second your pulse pounds they grow foot by incredible foot!' But this micro-budget feature buckled under the weight of its wooden performances, inane dialogue and laughable special effects. The original script, written by René Ray, aka the Countess of Middleton, was mutilated into a feature-length screenplay by Paul Ryder and directed without flair or interest by Gilbert Gunn. The resulting picture belongs well and truly in a bucket marked 'Saturday Morning Kiddie Matinees'.

While Tucker was floundering, Baker and Berman were embarking along what would soon become a well-trodden path for British film producers, towards gothic horror. Engaging Sangster once again to concoct a script, Tempean allocated more money and a bigger cast to what Baker was to describe as 'our first proper "top of the bill" film.'

BLOOD OF THE VAMPIRE
'Nothing like it this side of hell!'

> Bavarian doctor John Pierre is wrongly accused of murder and malpractice and transported to an asylum for the criminally insane, where he is promised a brutal existence. The asylum is run as a private laboratory by a notorious scientist, Dr Callistratus, who when he is not experimenting on the inmates is having them flogged or fed to his dogs. Pierre learns to his horror that Callistratus was 'executed' in his native Transylvania as a vampire but that the fiend cheated death and is now kept alive by regular blood transfusions. Callistratus tells Pierre he has no choice but to assist him in the operations or face dire consequences. Pierre is also given an indication of the appalling experiments the doctor has been conducting in the cellars, eagerly assisted by his hunchbacked servant Carl. While Pierre struggles with his dilemma, his fiancée, Madeleine, enters the asylum in the guise of a housekeeper in an attempt to free him—only to fall victim to Callistratus and Carl.

If imitation is the sincerest form of flattery, then the boys over at Hammer must have felt very smug when *Blood of the Vampire* opened in the UK. 'I make no bones about it,' Robert Baker admits. 'We set out to follow Hammer's formula—it was successful for them and it was successful for us'. To make sure everyone watching knew they were in the realm of Hammer Horror, the film opened with a blood-red caption proclaiming: *'The most loathsome scourge ever to afflict this earth was that of the Vampire. Nourishing itself on warm living blood, the only known method of ending a vampire's reign of terror was to drive a wooden stake through its heart.'* Of course one of the key architects in Hammer's success was writer Jimmy Sangster, who had penned both *The Curse of Frankenstein* and *Dracula*. Sangster was, as Baker asserts, 'an obvious choice'. 'If I went to a distributor and said, "I have a Jimmy Sangster horror picture", they would be interested, no question about that; as a writer he was the "king of the horrors".' Sangster, much to his chagrin, would eventually be billed on posters as Jimmy "Frankenstein" Sangster.

Baker and Berman gave a general indication of the sort of story they wanted, the amount of money they had to spend, and then largely left the writer to get on with it, and all the basic ingredients for *Blood of the Vampire* could have been reheated from

Blood of the Vampire (Victor Maddern, Barbara Burke, Donald Wolfit)

2: Practising Sadism

Blood of the Vampire

Sangster's earlier horrors. The final screenplay so successfully mimics his standard three-act format and general approach that *Blood of the Vampire* is frequently mistaken for a Hammer production. For connoisseurs of that particular *oeuvre*, the producers thoughtfully added unconvincing matte shots, streams of cobwebs and even animated bats.

There was one twist: Sangster's script had no actual vampire—at least not in the accepted sense—although he did create a compelling pantomime villain in the deranged Callistratus, who is dependent on blood transfusions to stay alive and has no compunctions in relation to where the donors come from, or what happens to them afterwards. Tempean could not afford a star so they opted instead for a 'name' and cast Donald Wolfit, a theatrical heavyweight in every sense of the word, who possessed a passing resemblance to a portly Bela Lugosi, complete with deathly pallor and eyebrows that looked like they would squeal if plucked. The soon-to-be 'Sir' Donald was more at home quoting the Bard than lurking about in crypts, but Baker remembers him as being 'very much a stage actor, a gentleman and so forth'; 'He loved to do this larger than life, stagey sort of performance, and one had to sit on him a little bit otherwise he would become too theatrical.'

The job of sitting on the star was allocated to Henry Cass, a former stage actor himself who turned to film directing in the 1930s and whose earlier work had shown an aptitude for light comedy. The director proved equally adept at darker subjects and Tempean had used him previously on the crime thriller *Breakaway* (1955). An interview with the *Kinematograph Weekly* during production revealed that Cass also had a firm grasp of the critical success factors for horror film: 'If you succeed in scaring the girls in the audience into the arms of their boyfriends then you have done your job well.'

In front of the cameras, Baker and Berman had a preference for actors they

53

Blood of the Vampire

knew and Dr Pierre was played by capable Australian actor Vincent Ball, who had earlier appeared for them in *Sea of Sand* (1958). The supporting cast also included a number of regular employees such as John Le Mesurier and Andrew Faulds, both of whom were often to be found in the Baker/Berman repertory company. As was character actor Victor Maddern, who usually played spivs or conniving NCOs but was here buried under some rather unconvincing latex make-up and a cheap fright wig to play Carl. Maddern's character, described in the script as a 'dim-witted one-eyed hunchback', took a central role in the film's advertising but his sole function on screen seems to be restricted to leering at the manacled women. The main object of Carl's attentions was a new name to Tempean, Barbara Shelley, who had essayed the title role in the British-made AIP horror *Cat Girl*, which in turn inaugurated a career as a leading lady in horror films. Shelley would go on to become one of Hammer's most consistent and interesting female stars.

Financing the film required some creative thinking from Baker and Berman, who found themselves victims of a clause in the NFFC charter requiring profits from one film to be invested in the next picture. 'It was called cross-collateralising,' Baker explains, 'and it potentially meant that a run of modest profits over several films could be wiped out by a single loss. The solution was pretty obvious; we put Tempean on the shelf temporarily and set up a new company.' A side effect of the NFFC ruling meant that independent filmmaking in the UK would become a tangled maze of short-lived companies. In this instance, Tempean morphed into Artistes Alliance, but the parent company's distribution deal with Eros for the UK remained in place, with Universal-International stepping in to buy the US rights.

It was these pre-sales that led Baker and Berman to trek into the unfamiliar territory of A features, complete with colour and a relatively comfortable shooting schedule of four weeks. It also marked the producers' first encounter with the

2: Practising Sadism

Blood of the Vampire (Barbara Shelley, Donald Wolfit, Vincent Ball)

tawdry world of alternative, so-called 'continental' versions of films. As well as his regular blood transfusions, the good doctor enjoys some unrestrained torturing of the inmates of his asylum—especially the prettier ones—a pastime which could only be hinted at in the British X certificate print. The more opened-minded Europeans were treated to additional scenes, largely confined to Callistratus's 'private' dungeon, where discarded body parts are on display, the victims of previous experiments are stored, and a number of young women are shackled in various states of décolleté. 'We did that because the distributors could get better prices,' Baker reveals. 'Certain countries would only buy continental versions or else pay more for them; in other words, you could see tits in the European versions and blouses in the British version.'

Baker and Berman's relationship with the censor at this stage in their careers was generally positive, provided they did not go against the BBFC's cardinal rule of juxtaposing sex and horror. 'We didn't need to show him any of the nude scenes,' Baker explains, 'because they weren't going to be used on the British print. We knew what we could and couldn't get away with for the British version and more or less stuck to that.' On the whole, Baker regarded the censor as an ally rather than an adversary; 'John Trevelyan would look at the picture from a filmmaker's point of view and see how it affects another part of the story and he might say, let that stay because the story needs it but take that out because it doesn't affect anything else.' But like many other filmmakers who routinely submitted their scripts to the BBFC for comment ahead of shooting, the duo were old hands at playing the censorship game. 'We would put a few dummy things in the films knowing he wouldn't let them through,' Baker admits. 'If there were half-a-dozen things in the film he objected to, we would agree to take three out provided he let three stay in.'

Even with the BBFC protecting the public from the worst excesses, *Blood of the Vampire* received the obligatory critical drubbing but the producers were far from concerned. 'We never paid any attention to the critics,' Baker concedes. 'They had their own tastes and to some extent they were trying to impose those on the public. The trade papers were slightly different; they guided exhibitors to what films would or would not sell to the public, so that was important. But nothing said by the so-called mainstream critics mattered—not to this sort of film anyway.' Not all the critics were dismissive; *Film Daily* called it 'One of the best films in the horror-fiction category. It ventures into gore and supernatural with a headlong grandeur.' While the *Monthly Film Bulletin* recognised a pastiche when they saw one: 'This essay in hokum has provided the producers with the chance to incorporate every trick of the macabre and the horrific they can legitimately introduce.'

While the British accepted Cass's intent to make *Blood of the Vampire* an out and out horror movie, Universal-International seemed less sanguine and, oddly for the company that banked the lion's share of the profits from Hammer's *Dracula* (aka *Horror of Dracula*), offered exhibitors a two-pronged approach to advertising. The first suggested a science-orientated picture with taglines like: 'From the pages of SCIENCE FICTION'S most SHOCKING tale!' In case that was too subtle, the subtitle promised 'The Strange Experiments of Dr Callistratus.' But those exhibitors who were happy to promote horror movies got to offer patrons, 'From the bottomless pit of hell he came...a nightmare in human form whose unquenchable thirst made every man his victim...whose unspeakable rites made every woman his prey!'

That last line could easily have been the starting point for Baker and Berman's next outing. Jimmy Sangster was afforded temporary respite from middle-European vampires and was given license to re-write British criminal history with the first film directly based on the notorious Whitechapel murderer, Jack the Ripper.

JACK THE RIPPER
'This lady of the night has taken her last walk.'

> It is 1888 and London's East End is in turmoil; a serial killer is stalking the streets of Whitechapel and the police seem powerless to protect the public. 'Look at this street.' Inspector O'Neill says, 'before this Ripper business started, you could hardly move along here. Stalls, barrel organs, people spilling out of the pubs...it was a happy place.' Paranoia and fear soon turn to violence and the mob are prepared to attack any outsider; Detective Sam Lowry of the NYPD and Louis Benz, the crippled assistant to the local doctor, are both singled out. As prostitutes and dancehall girls fall victim to the Ripper, police attention turns to the Mercy Hospital for Woman run by Sir David Rogers, who along with surgeons Dr Tranter and Dr Urquhart seems to be acting suspiciously. It soon becomes clear to the police that the killer is not acting randomly: he is stalking one woman in particular and the race is on to save Mary Clarke.

'Saucy Jack', Britain's most notorious serial killer had already inspired several screen outings, most famously Alfred Hitchcock's *The Lodger* (1927), but none of the previous versions had been bold enough to include his more infamous moniker in the title. 'We were lucky we got to use the title,' Baker explains 'because the censor had banned the use of the title up until then. Many people had tried but the censor had always turned it down. It so happened that we approached John Trevelyan at a period when they were getting a little more relaxed on titles and even allowing a little more action in pictures, and some stuff that you couldn't do before was now allowed.' This more relaxed attitude would be little in evidence when the BBFC received a copy of the script, however.

2: Practising Sadism

Jack the Ripper (Anne Sharp) / INSET: Endre Muller

Baker and Berman were first sold on the idea of a Jack the Ripper film by Peter Hammond and Colin Craig, but the producers did not like their script and promptly engaged Jimmy Sangster to start again. With eight screenplays already to his credit, Sangster was just hitting his stride and was not about to let a little thing like history stand in the way of a good yarn. When the facts failed to fit his narrative structure, he simply invented his own: 'If the writer does his job properly, then it feels right and the audience doesn't notice,' he insisted. Sangster laughs off the idea that he did any research at all but there is enough detail (the vigilante mob; a suspect called Leather Apron, etc) to suggest at least a passing familiarity with actual events; more importantly, Sangster weaves enough local colour into the story to present what feels to be a reasonable depiction of 1880s London, with one glaring exception. The

57

X-Cert

Jack the Ripper (Cameron Hall, Ewen Solon)

producers insisted on having an American leading man so the screenplay introduces a NYPD detective on leave in foggy London and assisting the local bobbies with 'this Ripper business'. Lee Patterson, actually a Canadian, played Lowry, complete with Teddy-boy quiff, who is introduced via a bar-room brawl in 'The Red Goose' pub that could have been lifted intact from any number of Westerns. After establishing his credentials, Lowry launches himself into Shepperton's London backlot, complete with chipper shoeshine boys, giggly dancing girls and assorted Cockneys muttering things like, 'My God, the Ripper, he's done 'er in!'

Once again the producers turned to their regulars for the supporting cast: John Le Mesurier as the taciturn Dr Tranter and George Rose as Mary Clarke's father. Irishman Eddie Byrne, a regular authority figure in horror movies, played to type as Inspector O'Neill, the nominal head of the Ripper investigation, who is soon reduced to scratching his head and looking bemused while Lowry pieces the puzzle together on his own. The script called for another of Sangster's deformed assistants, Louis (Endre Muller), who again menaced the starlets on the publicity stills but emerged on screen as a rather sympathetic character. Despite this veritable shoal of red herrings, the killer will be immediately obvious to anyone who understands how whodunnits work; Sir David (Ewen Solon) is above suspicion and therefore has to be the killer. When Sir David's tenuous grip on reality finally snaps, he reveals a deeply-held grudge against East End tarts in general and Mary Clarke in particular, who afflicted his son with syphillis. 'Like some foul malignant virus,' he rants, 'you and your kind contaminate the gutters you inhabit—the very air you breathe'.

The credits split the directing, producing and cinematographic chores evenly between Baker and Berman; in fact, Bob Baker directed and oversaw the day-to-day production while Berman photographed and handled the business end of pulling the film together under the new banner of Mid Century Film Productions (all the letterheads remained as Tempean Films). The producers had no difficulty raising the £50,000 budget from a combination of pre-sales (to Regal Film Distributors) and NFFC subsidy, but persuading the BBFC to sanction the film was to be more of a

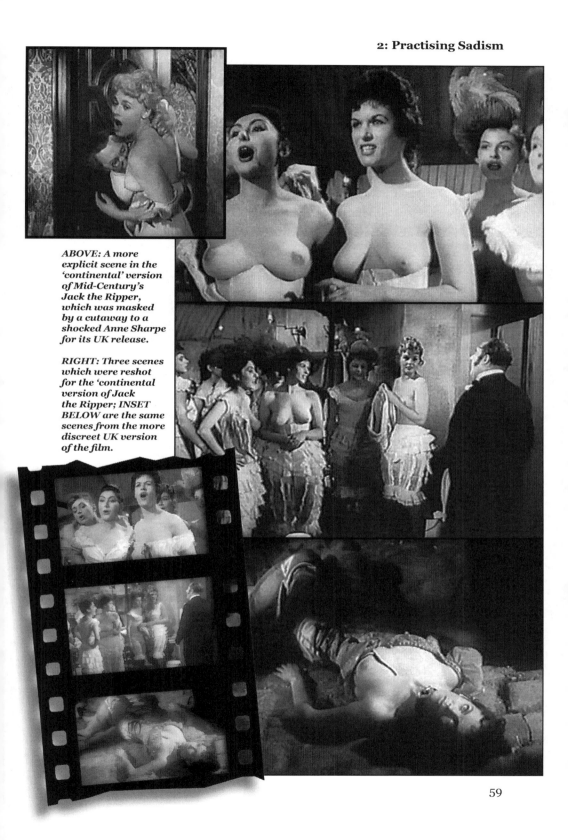

2: Practising Sadism

ABOVE: A more explicit scene in the 'continental' version of Mid-Century's *Jack the Ripper*, which was masked by a cutaway to a shocked Anne Sharpe for its UK release.

RIGHT: Three scenes which were reshot for the 'continental' version of *Jack the Ripper*; INSET BELOW are the same scenes from the more discreet UK version of the film.

X-Cert

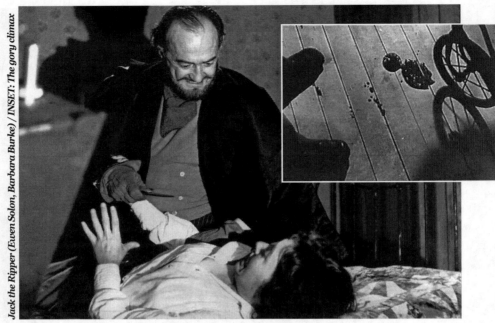

Jack the Ripper (Ewen Solon, Barbara Burke) / INSET: The gory climax

challenge. Sangster's first draft was submitted to Soho Square in December 1957 and provoked the anonymous reviewer to respond, 'This is a monstrous script.' Among the more offensive details were some 'orgiastic' can-can dancing and excessively brutal killings. The reader went on to say that the whole thing was 'too full of sordid and sadistic association to be acceptable.' Tempean agreed to review its approach and submitted a second draft the following July. This time Trevelyan called the producers to Soho Square to discuss the film. The censor's own notes of the meeting confirm that Baker and Berman agreed to have the Ripper kill his victims off-screen 'without unpleasant shots and close-ups.' The censor also records the producers' confirmation that they would shoot their film in black and white.

Baker insists that he had nothing but respect for Trevelyan but concedes that they were all engaged in a game of cat and mouse: 'The censor was important; he could in theory stop the film being released. In practice that wasn't something we really thought about. There were always ways of compromising.' The finished film, submitted in February 1959, provoked outrage at Soho Square and the producers received a shopping list of cuts, including 'the strangling of a prostitute, the attack on a barmaid, champagne over breasts, naked breasts, corpses, shots of weapons...'

Tempean trimmed here and there but kept the film substantially intact, and the resubmitted version was met with similar dismay. Trevelyan's correspondence shows his increasing frustration; in March, he wrote insisting that his suggestions be taken seriously, 'Otherwise we will just have to give the film up.' That threat, to withhold a certificate of exhibition, brought Tempean back to the negotiating table, but there was a lot more wrangling before compromises were finally reached and an X certificate was issued.

Tempean's financial arrangements meant that it could remain relatively relaxed through the months of bickering with the BBFC; its recreation of Victorian London and the mix of saucy girls and mayhem proved particularly appealing to interested American parties and shortly after shooting wrapped, Joe E Levine, the legendary

2: Practising Sadism

showman, stepped forward with £50,000 in exchange for the US rights. *Jack the Ripper* had covered its costs before even being approved by the BBFC.

Levine was not the sort of character to do things by halves and he had a reputation for extravagant promotional campaigns and even more extravagant promises. At a gala dinner for exhibitors in New York, he paraded both Peter Lorre and Gypsy Rose Lee to endorse *Jack the Ripper*, and then he announced to assembled guests that he would be spending $1 million on the film. In case there was any doubt, he then paraded the cash in front of their eyes, carefully shepherded by security guards. He also shot a special prologue, and he removed Stanley Black's music, replacing it with a modern jazz-inspired score. But having banked Levine's cheque, Baker and Berman could afford to be sanguine about the changes. 'He could do what he liked to it,' Baker shrugs. 'Redoing the music meant he could retain the publishing rights which are potentially worth a great deal of money. If you sell the film to a showman you have to let him get on with it; he was going to do it anyway.'

Under the US's more lenient MPAA rating system, Levine was free to use Robert Baker's original 'colour' ending for the Ripper's grisly demise. In the original script, the Ripper fell into industrial machinery and was crushed to a pulp. Trevelyan had vetoed that idea outright and Sangster concocted a new ending where the murderer is crushed under a hospital lift as it descends; the only visible evidence of his death being the blood that seeps through the floorboards. Baker had decided to capture this moment in colour—not as often suggested by colourisation but 'in-camera'; the set was painted monochrome and the scene shot on colour stock.

Levine later boasted that his efforts resulted in a staggering $2 million profit on *Jack the Ripper*, a claim which Robert Baker believes to fall on the side of hyperbole but concedes that the film was easily the most successful of Tempean's cinematic ventures to that point in time. So it is hardly a surprise that the producers decided that their next film should dive back into history for another tale of brutal murder, this time based on the infamous 19th-century body-snatchers, Burke and Hare.

THE FLESH AND THE FIENDS
'Bloody demons of the night sell bodies of the dead for forbidden experiments.'

> Dr Knox, Edinburgh's leading anatomist, has little time for the conventional methods of obtaining fresh cadavers for study, 'Ah yes, Parliament!' he snorts. 'With 500 walking corpses there, you'd think they could spare one!' Determined to continue with his work despite official interference, Knox turns to the city's most successful procurers of fresh corpses, Burke and Hare. These drunken layabouts are more inclined to murder their 'subjects' than go to the trouble of digging them up and in their haste to make money, they kill a well-known prostitute named Mary Paterson. When the body is delivered to Knox, she is recognised by her fiancé, one of Knox's students, but when he raises the alarm, he is murdered. As the killers turn their attentions to simpleton Daft Jamie, their nefarious schemes unravel and Hare eventually turns King's evidence, which sends Burke to the gallows. But the mob is not finished with Hare— or Knox, for that matter.

The task of bringing Burke and Hare's grisly resurrectionis misdeeds to the screen fell to the prolific John Gilling, who was well known to Tempean from its 'quota quickie' days. Gilling brought a strong visual sense and a flair for executing stirrung action sequences but he came with a reputation. 'John was a very forceful director,' Baker said. 'He would upset people but he would get the job done. But he was an abrasive character, particularly with women.' During the making of Tempean's *No Trace* (1950), the director had clashed with starlet Diana Dors and reduced her to tears after only one day of shooting. When Dors retreated to her hotel and refused to continue, she had to be replaced with Dora Bryan.

Gilling's first draft was completed while he was still under contract to Warwick Films, where he was finishing *Killers of Kilimanjaro* (1959), and was basically a retread of his 1948 script for Tod Slaughter, *The Greed of William Hart*, so the final polish was applied by Leon Griffiths and then submitted to the censor's office for consideration. Both writers were instructed to stay as close as possible to the known facts, allowing the producers to squeeze in as much sex and violence as they could under the guise of historical accuracy. To emphasis the point, Baker inserted an opening caption which claimed: '*This is the story of lost men and lost souls. It is a story of vice and murder. We make no apologies to the dead. It is all true.*' In fairness to Gilling and Griffiths, most of the leading characters were pulled from history and the story stays faithful to the record—except for a fictionalised romantic sub-plot between a medical student (John Cairney) and the prostitute Mary (Billie Whitelaw). Mercifully, this intrusion upon historical veracity was kept peripheral and does not intrude too much on the action.

Truth—even a fictionalised version of it—has never carried much sway with the BBFC and the examiners expressed their customary reservations about the subject-matter and added objections to sex, nudity, on-screen murders and so on. Tempean, in turn, offered its own assurances to comply with the BBFC's strictures and the discussion was concluded in time for Gilling to start shooting at Shepperton in May 1959. By then, Tempean had itself slipped quietly into the background in favour of the newly-formed Triad Productions.

Just before shooting got underway, Robert Baker had to deal with a more unusual objection from executives at the Rank Organisation, who thought that the project might impinge upon a copyright of its own. 'Rank had a script by Dylan Thomas on body-snatching which had been gathering dust,' Baker remembers, 'and

The Flesh and the Fiends (Donald Pleasence, George Rose)

The Flesh and the Fiends (Peter Cushing)

The Flesh and the Fiends

they asked to see our script. We agreed if they sent us their script, which they did and it was a beautifully-written piece of prose, not a film though. They read our script and said, "Best of luck".' (The Rank script would find its way to the screen in 1985 as *The Doctor and the Devils,* directed by Freddie Francis.)

In casting the film, Triad pulled off a significant coup by signing Peter Cushing for the role of Knox. The actor was coming off an unbroken run of leading roles for Hammer and at first glance there are similarities between Knox and Cushing's most famous screen role Baron Frankenstein. Both men are obsessive, believe that the end justifies the means and are contemptuous of those in the medical profession who do not share their vision. Gilling's script describes Knox as, 'brilliant, aggressive, provocative and as verbose as ever,' and many of his lines could easily have been written for the Baron: 'If you would be so good as to incline your heads slightly to the right,' he sneers at colleagues, 'you will observe the door. Please use it.' Robert Baker feels the comparison undervalues Cushing and points out, 'He was far better than Frankenstein, as an actor I mean. Dr Knox was a personal portrait of a complex man, something he could get his teeth into.' Cushing did not miss the opportunity to infuse this thoroughly dislikeable man with genuine tenderness, an achievement not lost on his volatile director. 'Tremendously professional, Peter', Gilling told Gilbert Vershooten in *Little Shoppe of Horrors.* 'A little girl runs up to him and he gives her sixpence. She says, "I must not take it. If I do, they'll send me to Dr Knox." And for this scene he shed real tears.'

The supporting cast was just as good. Donald Pleasence and George Rose were both excellent as the grubby sociopaths Burke and Hare, alternating between sly humour, drunken buffoonery and genuine evil. The former was in real life the long-term house guest of actress Billie Whitelaw and the ex-Rank starlet was cast as the prostitute Mary Patterson. The 25-year actress does not quite pull off the Scottish accent but she does create a credible and vulnerable character. The fact that all three

2: Practising Sadism

RIGHT: A bawdy tavern scene in Triad's The Flesh and the Fiends gave exploitation producers Robert Baker and Monty Berman another opportunity to add some nudity for a 'continental' version of the film.

roles are so finely played makes Mary's final encounter with the murderers the more shocking; 'Just the three of us,' Burke coos as he drags her towards the bed, 'as cosy as three bugs in a rug.'

John Cairney, another former Rank player, was Mary's lover, the naive student Chris Jackson. Cairney had played opposite Whitelaw previously in *Miracle in Soho* (1957) but he recalls the actress was especially nervous about their love scenes, particularly dreading the prospect that Gilling would let things go too far. 'She did the scene with two Elastoplasts covering her nipples,' Cairney remembers, 'they scratched my chest like razors and must have been murder to take off but Billie told me, "Otherwise my mother would be affronted".'

If Gilling spared Whitelaw's blushes, he was less concerned about others in the cast. A bawdy-house setting allowed the director to present copious and enthusiastic carousing, plunging necklines and assorted hi-jinks, while the continental version featured the same scenes but with topless harlots positioned strategically around the set. 'There were two scripts, one in yellow and one in white,' Cairney says. 'The UK version was white, the yellow version I never saw, but George Rose told me it played for years in Amsterdam!'

The film's highlights are undoubtedly the murder scenes where Gilling, the

65

The Flesh and the Fiends (Donald Pleasence, Billie Whitelaw)

action director, is in his element. The murder of Esme Cameron's gin-sot Aggie is a fine example of Gilling's work, with Burke suffocating the old woman while Hare dances a grotesque jig. The scene juxtaposes casual brutality with black humour as Burke complains that Aggie bit his hand and Hare retorts, 'Well, you can't blame her for that.' Equally disturbing is the demise of Daft Jamie, slaughtered in a darkened pig-pen with the distraught simpleton staggering around among the squealing pigs.' The effectiveness of these scenes is underpinned by Berman's superb black-and-white photography, which effortlessly evokes the dinginess and squalor of 19th-century Edinburgh. Berman's camerawork is so good that even a famous curmudgeon like Gilling had to express admiration—in his own inimitable way. 'I believe it was the best thing he ever did in his life,' he told *Little Shoppe of Horrors*. 'Being useless with almost everything else, he could be a good photographer when he tried. He really caught the mood and for this I give him full marks.'

2: Practising Sadism

To lend the film greater scope, the producers raided the Rank Organisation's library and bought the crowd scenes created by David Lean for *Oliver Twist* (1948), which they seamlessly matched these to Gilling's original footage. 'We always had to find ways of saving money,' Baker confesses, 'so we paid to get the scenes out of the Rank library...cribbing from the best director in the world! A John Gilling and David Lean film!'

With so much to work from, the distributors still opted to emphasise horror over history, as the plethora of alternative US titles illustrate in particular: *Mania, Psycho Killers, The Fiendish Ghouls*. Baker was philosophical about the distributor's approach, 'I wasn't too bothered what they called these pictures...the distributers knew what sold best in their markets. As long as they paid, they could do what they wanted!' Disappointingly after the success of their previous efforts, *The Flesh and the Fiends* was not picked up by a major distributor in the US and had to wait until 1961 before sneaking out under the auspices of the tiny Valiant Films. In the UK, it fared marginally better in the hands of Regal Distributors and the British critics on the whole were impressed. *The Times* hailed 'a competent piece of work, concisely written with tension, dramatically sustained and well acted.' *Time Out* thought it 'much enlivened by the black-comic capering of Pleasence and Rose.'

The film's British reception could not compensate for the disappointingly-poor performance in the US, and it was enough to convince Baker and Berman that they had mined the horror vein sufficiently. The producers decided that it was time to move on, although they did not entirely abandon the genre: *The Hellfire Club* (1961) explored the wickedly-salacious activities of Sir Francis Dashwood but despite the title, the emphasis was on adventure rather than horror. *What a Carve Up!* (1961) re-united Baker and Berman with Donald Pleasence in a spoof remake of the creaky classic *The Ghoul* (1933), but soon afterwards the partners moved onto the small screen where their considerable energies were gainfully employed on shows like *The Saint* and *The Persuaders*.

While the gothic influence was clearly evident in the Baker/Berman films, two other filmmakers were taking a very different route and following a trail blazed by Roger Corman and his horror/science fiction cheapies for AIP. Charles Saunders was a textbook 'journeyman director', learning his trade with companies like Gaumont British and Gainsborough before branching into directing and, without ever helming an outstanding success, carving out a reputation as a safe and consistent pair of hands. In 1955, Saunders joined forces with Italian-born Guido Coen at Fortress Films to make *A Time to Kill,* the first in a series of routine thrillers the pair churned out over the next three years. These second-rate thrillers are notable now only for featuring a string of leading ladies whose names would become familiar to horror fans, including Hazel Court, Yvonne Romain, Vera Day and Melissa Stribling. In 1957, Saunders and Coen followed the trend away from thrillers and into horror and began their attempt to transplant AIP to the Home Counties with arguably one of most ludicrous films ever to creep out of a British soundstage.

THE MAN WITHOUT A BODY
'*A diabolical dream comes true! Who is his next victim?*'

> *The ageing tycoon Karl Brussard is diagnosed with an incurable brain tumour and travels to London seeking a cure from scientist Phillip Merritt, who has achieved some success transplanting the heads of live animals onto donor bodies. The 16th-century astrologist and apothecary, Nostradamus, whose perfectly-preserved corpse is lying in state in his native France, is selected by Brussard as a donor and he arranges for the head to be stolen, smuggled*

to London and revived in Merritt's laboratory. But Brussard clashes with the newly-revived head and in a fit of temper attempts to destroy the equipment keeping it alive. In a rage, Brussard also attacks and mortally wounds his girlfriend's lover, Lew. Desperate to keep his experiments from failing, Merritt transplants Nostradamus' head onto Lew's body, the operation is successful but the doctor has created a monster bent on destruction.

The film started life as a script by William Grote called *The Curse of Nostradamus* with a basic premise which seemed to have been lifted from Curt Siodmak's twice-filmed novel, *Donovan's Brain*. Where Siodmak had the brain of a dead millionaire kept alive in a jar pending the arrival of a suitable 'donor' body, Grote opted for a more fundamental approach; why settle for a brain when you can have the whole head? The absurdity of the concept attracted the attention of B-movie director William L Wilder, younger brother of Billy, whose CV was dotted with such delights as *Phantom from Space* (1953) and *The Snow Creature* (1954). Wilder found willing backers in the shape of Messrs Saunders and Coen, who were looking for a suitable project to launch their excursion into exploitation. With a meagre budget of £20,000 allocated to the film and the NFFC funding in place, Twickenham Studios was booked and a company called Filmways was established as a subsidiary of Fortress. To qualify for the Eady subsidy, the directing credit was nominally to be shared between Wilder and Saunders, but the latter happily took a back seat when the shooting started, leaving W Lee Wilder well and truly in the driving seat.

The Man Without a Body

68

2: Practising Sadism

With an eye to the American market, Saunders and Coen then engaged Salford-born (and former Mercury Theatre player) George Coulouris to play Brussard, whose munificence when it comes to furthering his own interests sparks the story's descent into horror. After an auspicious start in Orson Welles's *Citizen Kane* (1940), Coulouris made his name playing heavies in Hollywood A pictures like *Watch on the Rhine* (1943) and *California* (1947) before returning to the UK in 1950 and specialising in eccentrics or foreigners in British comedies. In Brussard, he was offered a return to out-and-out wickedness, playing a bully and an unconscionable braggart who surrounds himself with compliant women and sycophantic employees, and whose only motivation is self-interest. The actor relished the return to rampant villainy and delivered a performance the script barely merited—sadly, the supporting cast brought little of that enthusiasm to their own clichéd roles. The pick of a bad bunch is starlet Nadja Regin, who fleshes out a negligée nicely even if the script offers her nothing to do but look concerned. Robert Hutton, a second-string leading man in American pictures, played Merritt, the earnest (but under-funded) scientist, but his performance suggests a complete disinterest in anything but his pay cheque. Money might well have been at the root of the film's problems with a cast and crew totally defeated by the unintentionally hilarious script and Poverty Row budget. The paucity of the budget undermines every scene, most notably in the laboratory sequences where even the sight of Nostradamus's disembodied head is not enough to distract from the distinct absence of scientific equipment.

Shot on a three-week schedule, this confused and confusing tale might just have survived its lack of logical plotting and paper-thin characterisation had Wilder had a dash of the Corman verve with which to pull it off. Unfortunately, he was simply out of his league and what he lacks in pace, he tries make up in bad taste; shots of a transplanted monkey's head, for example, are held far longer than required to give an extra jolt to the viewer. Wilder's film fails to hold the attention, and the sexual shenanigans between Brussard and his mistress, the mistress and the chauffeur, Brussard and his wife, the wife and Merritt's assistant, soon start to get tedious. The relatively compact running time of 80 minutes seems far too long.

Paired for UK release with equally absurd Japanese import *Half-Human* (1958), *The Man Without a Body* managed to slip below the radar of most film reviewers; the critic of *Kinematograph Weekly* was one of the few to brave the experience and noted, 'The few laughs in the wrong place should not prevent it from throwing a scare into the industrial nine-pennies.' The public on both sides of the Atlantic begged to differ and the film sank without a trace.

Wilder continued to beaver away in British B pictures and although he worked again on two further occasions with Coulouris, the horror genre was spared further indignities. As for Fortress Productions, it had already embarked on its second horror picture before the failure of its first became apparent, this time giving Charles Saunders sole control of the direction.

WOMAN EATER
'It's X! It's Sex! It's Box-Office!'

> *From his base outside London, James Moran, a mentally unstable scientist, uses a large Amazonian tree in his experiments to revive the dead. A native boy, Tanga, who accompanied Moran from South America, beats out a rhythm on tom-tom drums as female sacrifices are first entranced by the tree, then ensnared by its branches and finally consumed in the foliage. Despite repeated failures, Moran perseveres, seeking out new victims while*

> the police become increasingly suspicious. The doctor's life becomes more complicated when he develops an attraction to a former fairground dancer, Sally, who comes to his house looking for a job. Moran's housekeeper and former mistress, Margaret, sees the younger woman as a rival and treats her with contempt, leaving the doctor with only one course of action for his next experiment.

Filmed after Lee Wilder's effort on the same Twickenham soundstages, *Woman Eater* found its way on to the circuits long before its stablemate and is frequently mistaken for Fortress's first venture into exploitation/horror. The delightfully batty script by Brandon Flemying is no more than a notch or two above Grote's effort but it serves Saunders well as a vehicle on which to hang as much exploitation as he can get away with. The moment that Moran, up to his sweat-stained armpits in studio plant life, stumbles upon a large and rather agitated tree attacking a scantily-clad native girl, it is clear that he is going to make the most of every opportunity. Later in Moran's makeshift basement laboratory, Saunders revels in the ritualistic sacrifices as young women, dresses fetchingly ripped, are first enthralled and then 'absorbed' by the arboreal menace. How the girls are actually killed or even more fundamental questions such as how an 8-foot killer tree escaped the attentions of HM Customs in the first place, are never allowed to get in the way of cheap thrills.

The entertainment quotient is helped enormously by George Coulouris's star turn as the maddest of mad scientists; the actor plays Moran with a lasciviousness and gravitas that belie the ludicrous plot and flimsy characterisation. Not only is Coulouris convincingly sleazy, he pulls off that rarest of feats and creates a character that is both threatening and vulnerable—even having witnessed his transgressions, one cannot help but feel a degree of sympathy. Seldom has a British screen villain exuded such explicit sexual motivation, whether he is scouring a red-light district for new victims or merely leering at Sally, his pretty new housemaid (Vera Day). Sally's arrival triggers an intriguing triangle when Moran begins to groom her as

Woman Eater (George Coulouris)

2: Practising Sadism

Woman Eater

his next mistress—much to the seething annoyance of his previous paramour, the doting Margaret. 'There was a time when you trusted me,' she whimpers, only to be dismissed with a contemptuous, 'My dear Margaret, I have never trusted you or another woman with anything I didn't want anyone else to know.'

As Margaret, Joyce Gregg shows the all the tight-lipped frustration of an older woman confronted by an airhead blonde with a pert figure and a slightly-used hula skirt. Vera Day, who took second-billing behind Coulouris, was better known as a pin-up model than an actress—which may go some way to explaining why the on-screen tension was mirrored to some extent off-screen. 'George was lovely and we got on very well,' Day remembers, 'but Joyce Gregg wasn't very friendly and I tried not to have too much to do with her. I really don't think she liked me very much and I remember one day she said to me: "You need to lose that cockney accent if you want to get on in this business." Just like that, I was very upset. George would have none of it. "Don't you dare listen to her," he said, "that's what makes you unique!"'

Day quickly bonded with the older man, who shared her anxieties about the quality of the film: '[George] told me not to worry too much about it as no one is going to remember this in a year's time!' The veteran actor's assessment was understandable; Fortress's films suffered from over-ambition and under-funding and in this case, the poorly-integrated stock footage and screen 'monster' were both major disappointments. In truth, the already-tight budget was stretched to breaking-point by an accidental fire just before shooting started which reduced the original tree to cinders and left the prop department a matter of days to construct the unsatisfactory alternative. 'It was very hard to take the tree seriously,' Vera Day admitted, 'Like all these things, you hope they will sort it out in the editing but I don't know how we managed to keep a straight face. It didn't look real when we did it and looking at it on the screen afterwards, it is really obvious there is a hard-working technician in there pushing the arms backwards and forwards.' At a loss over what to do about the tree, Saunders opted for diversionary tactics, as Day remembers: 'He put in so many boob jokes to distract people from the awful monster!' It was a valiant effort, but even the pneumatic Ms Day cannot disguise the fact that the lethal tree is no more than rubber and balsa wood; that victims are required to sashay in to its embrace further undermined any supposed threat.

American drive-ins had been screening this sort of thing for years, but British audiences were completely unprepared and *Woman Eater* received scant attention when Eros released it in April 1958. A year later, it was picked up by Columbia and released in the US with the addition of 'The' to the title and a promise that viewers would 'SEE THE NERVE-SHATTERING DANCE OF DEATH! SEE THE WOMAN EATER ENSNARE THE BEAUTIES OF TWO CONTINENTS! SEE THE HIDEOUS ARMS DEVOUR THEM IN A DEATH-EMBRACE!' As a low budget effort, the film was better than many but faced with the new breed of Hammer horrors and the continued dominance of AIP, it looked like just another cheap-jack monster flick and flopped. The failure of its two films spelled the end of Fortress and the company was wound up soon afterwards. Charles Saunders and Guido Cohen went back to trashy thrillers with titles like *Strictly Confidential* (1959) and *Jungle Street* (1961) before Saunders retired in the early 1960s. Cohen loitered on the periphery of exploitation pictures for the next two decades with only one more foray into the horror genre, Vernon Sewell's *Burke and Hare* in 1972.

For a short time, it looked like two other enterprising producers would suffer the same fate as Saunders and Coen, with their ambitions quashed before they had a chance to hit their stride. New Yorkers Milton Subotsky and Max J Rosenberg are not normally associated with independent British films but in 1956, the future founders of Amicus Film Productions arrived in London to launch themselves as bona fide horror filmmakers. Their first port of call was Hammer House, where Subotsky's script for a retelling of Mary Shelley's *Frankenstein* piqued the interest of James Carreras. Hammer liked the concept but not the script and having suitably reimbursed the Americans, he promptly eased them out of what would become *The Curse of Frankenstein* (1957).

Subotsky and Rosenberg returned to the US and went back to making rock 'n' roll pictures like *Rock, Rock, Rock* (1956) and *Disc Jockey Jamboree* (1957). By 1959, they were ready to have another crack at the genre and returned to Britain with a new company, Vulcan, and a script about New England witches called *Witchcraft*, later retitled *The City of the Dead*.

THE CITY OF THE DEAD
'The thrills, the chills of witchcraft today!'

The New England town of Whitewood has been living under a curse for over 300 years: dragged to the stake by the town elders, the witch Elizabeth Selwyn exalted her master Satan to 'make this city an example of thy vengeance.' The

2: Practising Sadism

buildings have fallen into disrepair, the church is in ruins, and God-fearing folk are warned to stay well away. Nan Barlow, on the recommendation of her college tutor, the sinister Professor Driscoll, books into The Raven Inn to research a college paper on witchcraft and there encounters owner Mrs Newless and the mysterious Jethrow. She also meets the only resident who seems the least bit friendly, Patricia Russell, who runs an antiques store nearby. When Nan mysteriously disappears, it is Patricia who persuades her brother Richard to come to Whitewood to investigate; unbeknown to either of them, Patricia has already been ear-marked by the witches' coven to be its next sacrificial victim.

The script, written by another New Yorker named George Baxt, was intended as a Boris Karloff television pilot and when that project was abandoned, the frugal Milton Subotsky cannibalised the story and fleshed out the spare running-time by introducing a romantic interest for Nan. Max Rosenberg asserts that Baxt hated the revisions and, in an interview for *Little Shoppe of Horrors,* the producer told Tom Weaver that the two men 'hated each other, and got along very badly afterward'; 'I remember Milton calling up and complaining about Baxt, and Baxt calling up and complaining about Milton,' Rosenberg said.

Rosenberg was the deal-maker in the Vulcan set-up and while Sutobsky sorted out his creative differences, he secured finance from successful television producer Hannah Weinstein, which together with the usual NFFC subsidy created a budget of £45,000, enough for a three week shooting schedule. Weinstein insisted her regular producer Don Taylor should oversee the day-to-day production, and it was Taylor who nominated tyro director John Llewellyn Moxey to helm the project.

The cast at this point was largely in place and consisted of relatively young actors in the leading roles and experienced character actors providing stoic support. Dennis Lotis, a cabaret singer by trade, played hero Richard Barlow while Venetia Stevenson is suitability defenceless as his sister Nan, a co-ed with an eye-catching

The City of the Dead (Venetia Stevenson, Christopher Lee)

line in lingerie. The latter, a former RKO starlet and daughter of director Robert Stevenson and actress Anna Lee, comes to a sticky end a mere 45 minutes into the narrative, at which point the mantle of leading lady is taken up by Betta St John, late of *Corridors of Blood*. By far the weakest of the leading characters was Tom Naylor who, saddled with Subotsky's thankless boyfriend role, seems to confuse shouting with enunciation. All the younger members of the cast were, to a greater or lesser degree, overshadowed by two old troupers: Patricia Jessel in the dual role of witch Elizabeth Selwyn and the equally imposing Mrs Newless, and Valentine Dyall as the warlock Jethrow. Dyall's craggy visage peering out of the fog was enough to unsettle the stoutest of hearts, while his doom-laden tones were perfect for pronouncements like, 'In Whitewood, time stands still' and 'To see me is a special privilege, reserved for a chosen few'.

Second-billed, though in no more than a cameo, was Hammer's Christopher Lee, who seemed content at this stage in his career to prowl any cinematic graveyard provided that the producers met his rate. Subotsky, like Richard Gordon before him, knew Lee's appearance as Professor Driscoll was good for marquee value and the actor seemed happy enough to do little more than practice his transatlantic accent and gaze out from under a cowl at the Satanic sacrifices. The one scene in which he seems to be doing something significant, slaughtering a dove in broad daylight, actually goes nowhere and in the absence of something more meaningful, Lee was reduced to barking impatiently at anyone who suggested that the occult is anything other than a serious subject. 'Witchcraft is not nonsense,' he derides. 'The basis of fairy tales is reality; the basis of reality is fairy tales.'

Working to such a constraining schedule, Taylor and Moxey had the enormous good fortune of booking the seldom-used Stage H at Shepperton, the cavernous 'silent' stage that comprised nearly 30,000 sq ft. If one considers the largest stage at Merton Park was less than 5,000 sq ft, then one can appreciate the enormous space that art director John Blezard' had at his disposal to create 'Whitewood'—or at least the half-dozen tumbledown houses that form the doomed 'city'. The controlled environment of the stage allowed cameraman Desmond Dickinson to roam freely through the cobwebbed crypts, tumbledown graves and banks of never-receding fog to give a unique look and feel to the film. It says much for their efforts that *The City of the Dead* would be copied by later British films, notably *Witchcraft* (1964) and *Devils of Darkness* (1965), but with considerably less style.

Predictably, logical plotting plays no part in the narrative; no-one, for instance, seems to have noticed that for 300 years, maidens have been sacrificed twice yearly. But Moxey's assured touch keeps things rattling along at a pace that ensures such inconsistencies and the odd limp performance do not get in the way. By keeping the camera close on the actors, the director maintains a claustrophobic tension, only opening out the action when he is confident that the sets can sustain closer scrutiny or the fog is thick enough to disguise any shortcomings created by budget—or lack of it. The use of shadows and effective staging even invests a throw-away scene such as that in which half-seen figures dance in the hotel lobby, with a latent menace seldom found in exploitation pictures, and it evokes memories of Val Lewton's atmospheric and stylish thrillers of the 1940s.

It is a remarkably confident performance from a debutant director and Moxey has always been quick to acknowledge the contributions of Dickinson and Blezard. The talents of all three combine in some of the film's best set-pieces. Among the outstanding touches is the ancient Reverend (Norman McGowan), the last man of God in a godless city, blinded by the witches and left presiding impotently over a ruined church and an empty parish. 'For 300 years, the Devil has hovered over this

2: **Practising Sadism**

300 years old! Human blood keeps them alive forever!

city,' he groans. 'Made it his own.' Another chilling scene has Nan glimpsing the unsettling residents of Whitewood during a midnight walk through the fog. The inhabitants, presumably un-dead, glower silently at the new arrival. Moxey liked the scene so much that he repeated it when Nan's brother arrives in the town.

This latent sense of dread—what Christopher Lee describes in *The Christopher Lee Filmography* as 'a kind of unseen, indescribable horror'—resonates in the literary works of New England's favourite son, HP Lovecraft, as well as the more recent fiction of Robert Bloch, and modern reviewers often cite the latter as an influence on Subotsky's narrative structure. Hitchcock's *Psycho* (1960), adapted from Bloch's novel, also features the early demise of its nominal heroine (blonde of course) in a remote hotel, and the subsequent arrival of would-be rescuers, unaware that she is already dead. Milton Subotsky always insisted that resemblance was purely co-incidental, pointing out that shooting was underway while Hitchcock was in pre-production and conveniently ignoring the fact that Bloch's novel had been on the bookshelves since the previous year.

Intentional or not, the US distributor, Trans-Lux, played up the similarities when it released the film in 1963, changing the title to *Horror Hotel* and promoting it with the tagline, 'Just ring for DOOM service!' By then the market was becoming saturated with *Psycho*-lookalikes and this half-hearted campaign failed to find an appreciative audience for Moxey's film. Three decades later, Max Rosenberg was still bitter about the film's US distribution, as he told Tom Weaver: 'I love *City of the Dead* but I also hate it because the deal was so bad. We got nothing out of it. But I loved making it. We couldn't get distribution, until finally we distributed it through Trans-Lux...and they were fascist cocksuckers.'

The critics, though, were mildly impressed. The *Daily Cinema* thought it offered 'quite a few thrills for such a cheaply budgeted production', while the *Borough News* hailed 'a classic tale of witchcraft...the sort of picture to send a chill into any heart.' In the UK, the film was regarded as a B-feature and packaged as such by British Lion, making it difficult for Vulcan to turn anything more than a modest profit from the lower half of a double-bill. The disappointing financial return prompted a rethink in corporate strategy for Subotsky and Rosenberg and shortly afterwards, Vulcan was dissolved to pave the way for Amicus a few years later. In 1965, the two producers had their first notable success by reinventing the anthology format with *Dr Terror's House of Horrors*, the formula proving so successful that it became Amicus's stock in trade for the best part of a decade.

At the same time that Moxey was weaving light and shade for Vulcan, another British company was ignoring the fine line between acceptable horror and outright exploitation. Anglo-Amalgamated's Nat Cohen and Stuart Levy, who had already tried their hands at the horror business with *Mother Riley Meets the Vampire,* were best known as film distributors but they soon realised that the closer they were to the production side, the greater the influence they had on the finished product. Expanding its operations, A-A started to sink its resources into independent film production, backing a range of pictures usually shot at its base in Merton Park, from Vernon Sewell's *Ghost Ship* to Peter Roger's *Carry On..* comedies. A key factor in A-A's success was Nat Cohen's natural exuberance and eye for the market, attributes which led critic Alexander Walker to describe him as, 'an impresario, a bon vivant, a racehorse owner with many wins in his stable, he applies the lessons of the turf to the film industry when he affirms that "there is no such thing as playing safe."' Cohen's oft-stated philosophy was to put his money on the line when backing films as he explained to Walker: 'I make a decision on a combination of the project and the individual who brings it to me.'

2: Practising Sadism

In the late 1950s, Cohen and Levy teamed up with AIP in a mutual exchange deal which saw *Attack of the Giant Leeches* (1959) arriving in the UK while the latest *Carry On* flick opened in the mid-West. What the Americans made of Messrs Connor, Williams and Hawtry is anyone's guess but the alliance really started to pay dividends as costs in California soared and AIP looked increasingly to Europe as a production base. Among these early collaborations was the Barbara Shelley picture *Cat Girl*, based on a script by Sam Arkoff's brother-in-law, Lou Rusoff, who also produced.

The joint financing continued into 1959 and included *The Headless Ghost*, an inane horror comedy, and *Horrors of the Black Museum* which starred Michael Gough as a writer who taunts Scotland Yard by staging a series of brutal and bizarre murders. Both projects were brought from Hollywood by Herman Cohen, whose presence in London was not wholly welcomed by the BBFC. Writing in her report, examiner Audrey Field suggested that giving *Horrors of the Black Museum* an X certificate 'would merely act as an umbrella for out-of-the-way sadistic ideas and try the patience of decent people rather too far'. Ms Field's comments proved to be remarkably prescient; the success of the AIP pictures persuaded Nat Cohen that there was money in exploitation and with his subsequent films, he showed that the British could be just as creative as the Americans when it came to 'sadistic ideas.'

The surprising source for the first of A-A's new ventures was Michael Powell, one of the great names in British filmmaking, who approached Cohen with a script previously rejected by the Rank Organisation. The unlikely partnership of would-be exploitation filmmakers and art-house director resulted in what writer Brian MacFarlane has dubbed 'the most notorious film in British cinema history.'

PEEPING TOM
'Do you know what the most frightening thing in the world is...?'

> Mark Lewis is obsessed with films; he works at a film studio and he spends his spare time photographing nude models in a dingy studio. But he has another 'hobby'; he is making a home movie by scaring the wits out of women and recording their reactions as he kills them with a bayonet fitted to the lens of his cine-camera. His first victim is a prostitute, his second an extra at the studio: 'Do you know what the most frightening thing in the world is?' he asks. 'It's fear.' To intensify that fear, Mark has attached a mirror to the camera which allows the victims to share in the experience of their own deaths. Mark's killing spree is temporarily halted when he meets the new tenants in his building, Helen Stephens and her blind mother. The respite is short-lived, however, as Mrs Stephens, sensing something deeply unpleasant about her daughter's new friend, confronts him. As the police close in, Mark embarks on his final, most disturbing project.

The idea for *Peeping Tom* came from Leo Marks, a top code-breaker during the war and regarded in the film industry as something of a deep thinker. Marks and Powell had abandoned a script they were writing about Sigmund Freud when word came through of a rival version being made in Hollywood and, while searching for a new project, Marks suggested a film constructed about the fetish of scopophilia, a condition in which sexual arousal depends on spying on others. Powell, who later identified the film to Bill Kelley in *Femme Fatales* as 'a very special, very personal film', threw himself into the creative process and the two men worked together concocting a screenplay for five months. 'The script very much became a part of my own thinking,' Powell said afterwards.

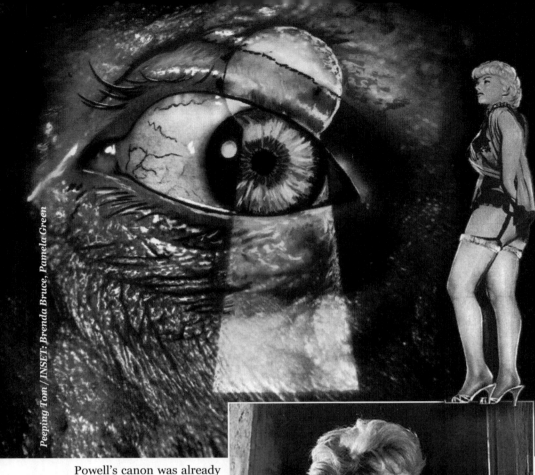

Peeping Tom / INSET: Brenda Bruce, Pamela Green

Powell's canon was already dotted with darkly subversive images and themes: a villain who utilises the cover of the wartime blackout to pour glue into the hair of local women in *A Canterbury Tale* (1944); sexually-repressed nuns conflicted by the presence of a man in their remote Himalayan convent in *Black Narcissus* (1947). Even his most poetic film, *The Red Shoes* (1948), climaxes with the gruesome demise of the heroine. While *Peeping Tom* outdid them all and proved to be Powell's most extreme and disturbing work, it also contains some of his most telling imagery. The paradox of Mrs Stephens is a good example; a blind woman who is the only one to truly 'see' Mark. Powell's dark sense of humour is also evident in the running thread of phallic imagery with keys. Mark distains their use, an allusion to impotency, while Mrs Stephens in talking to Helen makes the point, 'We both have the key of the door—mine needs oiling, yours needs exercising.' Later Mark is handed the key to the newsagents and 'given' a free hand with the sexually-provocative Milly.

Less subtle references abound: the protagonist is named Mark Lewis, a play on Leo Marks, and in a scene surely inserted by Powell, a studio boss called Don Jarvis,

2: Practising Sadism

modelled on the J Arthur Rank supremo John Davis, barks, 'In view of the new economy drive, if you can see it and hear it, the first take is okay.' But the games played by Powell and Marks are generally buried under the more sensational elements and although the BBFC's files on *Peeping Tom* have long since vanished, the accepted view is that Trevelyan deplored the volatile mixture of sexual arousal and murder but was persuaded to let the production continue despite his better judgement.

The man who unleashed *Horrors of the Black Museum* on the British public had no such qualms, although Nat Cohen was uncomfortable with the estimated budget of £150,000—double the average A-A film—and insisted on a reduction to £125,000, which included the NFFC subsidy. Even then Cohen wanted the safety net of a star and suggested Dirk Bogarde, but Rank predictably declined a loan-out of their biggest name for such a tawdry role. Powell managed to interest Lawrence Harvey and the picture was pushed into pre-production only for Harvey to jump ship in pursuit of Hollywood stardom. As the production kept rolling on, Powell worked through a list of names without finding anyone interested and/or appropriate. By the time he settled on the German actor Karl-Heinze Böhm, (billed as Carl Boehm), A-A was in too deep to pull out and Cohen could only register his disappointment.

The rest of the cast reflected similar disregard for the box-office requirements of the film's distributors. Anna Massey, a twenty one-year old redhead (practically a prerequisite for Powell's heroines), was chosen for the role of Helen and the actress is in no doubt she was not cast for her experience. 'Michael had been having an affair for many years with Pamela Brown,' Massey revealed, 'and she and I looked very alike— simple as that'. Theatre actress Maxine Audrey was cast as Helen's mother, the austere Mrs Stephens, while another redhead, Moira Shearer, played the most sympathetic of Mark's victims, Vivian, one of the extras at the film studio. Shearer, a principle dancer with the Royal Ballet, had starred for Powell in *The Red Shoes* and her four-day cameo meant the script was tweaked to include an incongruous dance number.

The last significant female role, Milly the nude model and the most sexually predatory of all Mark's victims, was filled by luck rather than judgement. Powell had a very clear idea of the look that he wanted for the set and took art director Arthur Lawson off to the unfashionable end of Soho to visit the Old Compton Street studio of George Harrison Marks, purveyor of 'adult' photographs and 16mm 'nudie' movies. Marks's most popular model by far was Pamela Green, his girlfriend and business partner, and Powell, as Green recollects, 'took one look at me and announced, "This is the girl I want for Milly." He said he needed someone who could model, appear nude and also act.' Powell was also taken by Marks's set, designed by Green, and had Lawson recreate it entirely on Stage F at Pinewood. Marks himself was engaged as an advisor and unofficial stills man and his studies of Green in character were used as cover stories for popular men's magazines such as *Parade* and *Blighty*.

X-Cert

Peeping Tom (Anna Massey, Carl Boehm)

'In character' from Powell's perspective meant in various states of undress, but the director was frustrated that the censor would not allow Milly to display as much flesh on screen as in Green's magazine shots, and reluctantly ordered her a set of see-through negligées and corsets modified for use on the film. Powell did contrive to shoot a brief nude shot, the scene where Milly reclines on the bed and purrs, 'Are you safe to be alone with? It might be more fun if you weren't'—and in so doing, Green laid claim to being the first nude in a mainstream British feature film.

It was all a bit too much for Nat Cohen. Outmanoeuvred on the cast, tied into Pinewood rather than his preferred (and cheaper) Merton Park and with increasing unease over the subject matter, he displayed none of his usual *joie de vivre*. In a terse conversation recorded by Powell in his autobiography, the executive said, 'I'll tell you frankly, Michael, if I could get out, I would.'

Michael Powell began the six-week shoot in October 1959 with a single-minded determination bordering on tyranny. Pamela Green saw it when Boehm fluffed a line and the director screamed at Karl, 'You are a professional, I would have thought you would have at least known your lines.' The model concluded that Powell enjoyed humiliating actors: 'We were always waiting for an explosion of temper and it always came.' Anna Massey believes it was part of the director's technique: 'Michael Powell always had to have a row before a scene, usually with the camera operator, so there was always tension in the air. He was a complicated man and a great, great master but he was very cruel, no doubt about that; he had his own way of achieving results and he really didn't care if that meant being unkind to other people.' Massey remembers it was an arduous shoot even when Powell was on his best behaviour: 'He shot long takes, 8 or 9 minutes usually, with very complicated camera movements which got on everybody's nerves and just wore us down.'

Powell's capacity for cruelty revealed itself when shooting a close-up of Milly, as he instructed Otto Heller, the cameraman, to remove the protective lens from a

2: Practising Sadism

Peeping Tom (Carl Boehm, Anna Massey)

powerful arc light. 'Otto was very agitated,' Green remembers. 'He told Powell this was too dangerous and it would burn my skin but Powell removed the glass anyway. The heat was like a furnace and my arms and shoulders came up in red blotches. The next day my eyes were swollen shut and the make-up man told me if I had looked into the naked light I'd have been blinded.'

But the cast and crew survived the experience relatively unscathed and Powell completed the film slightly over budget but in time for its world premiere at the Plaza Cinema on April 7, 1960. This was something of a major event for Cohen and Levy, whose films were seldom launched with such razzmatazz. The advertisements in the trade papers promised 'The biggest and most glittering function of its kind ever organised for an Anglo-Amalgamated picture. The five hundred guests will include leading personalities in the trade, top stars, producers and directors, and an impressive list of social celebrities.' Nat Cohen boasted to the press that the film was 'the most intensely dramatic and intriguing thriller ever produced in a British studio'—a description that must have had John Trevelyan holding his breath.

In his autobiography, Trevelyan defended his decision to award an X certificate saying, 'I felt the film would contribute to a public understanding of mental illness,' and he added that 'having accepted the project at script stage we did not feel able to reject the film, so we made extensive cuts and hoped for the best.' Privately, he admitted to Alexander Walker of the London *Evening Standard* that he feared for his job. It is hard to imagine that behind the smiles and posing on the red carpet, Powell and his collaborators did not also sense some of his trepidation.

Disturbing though the murders were, they were not the most serious of *Peeping Tom*'s sins, nor was placing the audience in the camera's eye and thereby making them passively complicit in Mark's sex crimes. Powell went beyond the pale when he depicted the torture that the young Mark had endured at the hands of his father, a doctor supposedly researching childhood trauma and using the boy as guinea pig.

X-Cert

Peeping Tom (Pamela Green) / LEFT: A nude shot cut in UK release

The snatches of home movies recording the child's every tear and scream make uncomfortable viewing for even the most hardened cinemagoer. (Powell added to his own legend by playing the sadistic father, and casting his son as the youthful Mark.)

To offset the discomfiture, Powell injects some comedy; a newsagent whose customers like magazines 'with girls on the front covers and no front covers on the girls', and the reliable scene-stealer Miles Malleson pops up to buy some 'views' from under the counter. But any sense of well-being quickly dissipates as the onslaught begins. The photography, sets, and direction are all top-notch, intensifying the impact, as do the remarkable performances from the leads. Carl Boehm, with such sad eyes and a forlorn expression, is the screen's most vulnerable serial killer, while Anna Massey, whose career would be spent playing plain or repressed women, is excellent as the attractive and vivacious Helen, Mark's only hope of redemption.

2: Practising Sadism

The film's final shots are among the most disturbing, with Powell's off-screen voice admonishing his child—'Don't be a silly boy. There's nothing to be afraid of'— followed by the heartbreaking response, 'All right, daddy; hold my hand...'

It was all too much for the critics, who used their newspaper columns to vent their collective spleens. Dilys Powell told *Sunday Times* readers she had witnessed 'a nauseating emphasis on the preliminaries and the practice of sadism', while Leonard Mosley in the *Daily Express* said, 'Nothing, nothing, nothing—neither the hopeless leper colonies of East Pakistan, the back streets of Bombay nor the gutters of Calcutta—has left me with such a feeling of nausea and depression.' Caroline Lejeune, who boasted that she walked out after the first reel, still reported in *The Observer* that 'It's a long time since a film disgusted me as much as *Peeping Tom*.' And so it went on: 'Amateurishly repellent'— *The News Chronicle*; 'Stinks more than anything in British films since *The Stranglers of Bombay*' — *New Statesman*; '..Shovel it up and flush it swiftly down the nearest sewer. Even then the stench would remain'— *The Tribune*.

The *Monthly Film Bulletin,* an organ of the prestigious British Film Institute, compared Powell to the Marquis de Sade and concluded that 'It is only surprising that while the Marquis' books are still forbidden here after practically two centuries, it is possible, within the commercial industry, to produce films like *Peeping Tom*. De Sade at least veiled his enjoyment under the pretence of being a moralist.' Ian Johnson, writing in *Motion* was one of the few dissenting voices when he described it as 'one of the best British films of recent years... a sad and beautiful film.' Powell described the premiere and its immediate aftermath to *Femme Fatales*: 'They nearly lynched us. Then the reviews appeared in the London papers, and that sealed the film's fate. Nat Cohen pulled the film after five days. I said, "You're pulling it? And over what, bad reviews? You stand by our film. You weather the storm." But he was a coward and his mind was made up.'

Cohen was under more pressure than Powell might have realised. In March 2000, Alexander Walker wrote in *The Guardian* about a meeting he had in 1960 with Robert Clark, a senior figure in Variety, the film industry's official charity and unofficial trade organisation. Clark, who was also head of ABPC, owners of the ABC chain, A-A's exhibitors, claimed, 'We've put Nat in the doghouse until he gets rid of that piece of pornography.' Walker then alleges that Cohen's decision to finance *Peeping Tom* effectively cost him his knighthood.

Anxious to be rid of the hot potato, A-A sold the film to Gala, a second-string distributor, but the controversy did not go away. The *Daily Mail* gleefully reported that Reading Council had banned the film outright, completely glossing over the fact that none of the councillors had actually seen it and that they reacted 'because of the synopsis and the reviews we read in responsible national newspapers and journals which criticised the film.' In a quiet summer for news, the same paper later attacked cinema managers who were using the sensational reviews to promote the film. The *Mail*'s hack opined, 'The fact that their verdicts of nastiness, disgust and beastliness are being exploited to draw customers seemed to me to be one of the most unwholesome gimmicks in film advertising.' Gala's director of publicity, Frank Hazell, was refreshingly candid in his rebuttal, 'Let's face it, this is what we are in the business for, to get people to come and see the films.'

Michael Powell's film career never recovered; his friend and business partner Frixos Constantine insists that the director was effectively black-balled; 'Michael was an extremely tender, reasonable and knowledgeable man but he could be very arrogant and very dismissive...so people turned against him; no-one wanted to work with him. He couldn't get a film made after that.' Powell had the rest of his life to reflect on the film but his most poignant words were delivered three months after that premiere when he told *The Times*, 'I tried to go beyond the ordinary horror film of unexplained monsters, and instead show why one human being should behave in this extraordinary way—it's a story of a human being, first and foremost.'

A-A's unseemly haste in dropping *Peeping Tom* from its schedule created a gap and the only available film it had on the books was just as much of a voyeuristic fantasy. But at least *Circus of Horrors*, written by George Baxt, made no pretence to art—this was unashamed exploitational horror.

CIRCUS OF HORRORS
'One man's lust...made men into beasts, stripped women of their souls!'

> Dr Rossiter, a brilliant but reckless plastic surgeon, is forced to flee to the continent after a botched operation leaves heiress Evelyn Morley permanently scarred. Rossiter, travelling with his acolytes Angela and Martin, assumes a new identity, Dr Schüler, and takes over a ramshackle travelling circus—the perfect place to hide and continue his work. Rossiter builds up the circus by recruiting scarred women, all of them murderers, tarts or thieves, rebuilding their faces, and training them to perform dangerous circus stunts. If one of his women wants to leave or shows attention to other men, they die in bizarre accidents. When the 'jinx circus' arrives in England, Scotland Yard sends in a detective posing as a reporter and arranges for Evelyn Morley to attend a gala performance. Victim to his own arrogance, Schüler/Rossiter insists that the show must go on—even if it means his own unmasking.

According to Tom Vallance in *The Independent*, Baxt's brief from producers Julian Wintle and Leslie Parkyn was for a 'horror script about a circus with lots of gorgeous girls in it' and from the opening scene, those expectations are clearly set out. A beautiful but scarred woman is thrashing around in her underwear, the victim of a fanatical plastic surgeon who operated when 'even God would not attempt a miracle like that.' Then in quick succession, we have a policeman mown down at a road block, a car-crash and a second, somewhat more successful operation on the battered face of the surgeon, Rossiter. Baxt allows the pace to slacken only slightly when he shifts the action to 'somewhere in France' and has the new-look Schüler recruiting busty women with shady pasts. 'Willing subjects for my anxious hands. We hold their safety; they hold their tongues,' he states haughtily.

The concept sounds like a schoolboy's masturbatory fantasy—a circus populated entirely by shapely, compliant women ever ready to serve their 'master', and those who have not yet mastered the trapeze are put on public display in 'The Temple of Beauty'. One 'exhibit' complains about being stared at, only to be told by Schüler, 'Not stared at, my dear, worshipped.' Baxt then takes this caprice and slams it into a rather gruesome horror film without much thought for logic or depth; the girls all need to be punished for one reason or another, and Schüler contrives to have them knifed in the throat, sent plummeting from the high-wire or fed to the lions.

With all of the deaths so brutal, bloody and lovingly-depicted, it's little wonder that the BBFC's Audrey Field wrote in her notes, 'This disgustingly strident script fills me with nausea.' This, of course, was just the sort of reaction that Baxt was being paid to elicit. Wintle and Parkyn were delighted, and they took the project to Anglo-Amalgamated who snapped it up and sold the US rights to AIP—sight unseen. Lynx Films was duly formed and *Circus of Horrors* rolled into pre-production.

Wintle and Parkyn were among the most respected producers in Britain at the

Circus of Horrors (Anton Diffring)

Circus of Horrors (Anton Diffring, Vanda Hudson / ABOVE: Kenneth Griffith, Anton Diffring, Jane Hylton)

2: Practising Sadism

Circus of Horrors

time. They operated out of Beaconsfield Studios and alternated a steady output of mainstream features, usually for the Rank Organisation, with second-feature thrillers such as *Breakout* (1959). Herman Cohen, finishing off *The Headless Ghost* at the time, remembers a certain amount of nervousness in Hollywood about using a production team with no track record in this field. He told Tom Weaver, 'Julian Wintle was a very classy producer for Rank... He was quite the English gent but he did not know horror.' There is no record of Cohen's involvement in the credits but the American insists he was asked by Sam Arkoff to keep an eye on the production, which might explain why the film seems intent on 'out-horroring' *Horrors of the Black Museum*.

Whatever the experience (or lack) of the producers, AIP's investment was in safe hands with its chosen director, Sidney Hayers, a former editor who knew a thing or two about exploitation. Some years later he told *Shivers* magazine: 'I wasn't interested in horror *per se*. It had horrific moments, certainly, though it wasn't what you'd call a horror film in the true sense of the genre; I tried to steer it away.' If Hayers tried to avoid the horror, he certainly knew a money-shot when he saw one and his unflinching camera held onto every glimpse of flesh, every drop of blood, for as a long as possible and then, by delivering a series of gory set-pieces throughout the film, he also ensured that attention was diverted from the rather weak script and lazy characterisations.

87

X-Cert

Hayes was well served by his cast, particularly German-born Anton Diffring who played the autocratic but good-looking Schüler and whose Teutonic bearing lead *The Guardian's* Derek Malcolm to suggest, 'Casting agents became hooked on him as the epitome of the master race'. Diffring plays Schüler with wicked superiority, barely flicking an eyelid as a tart he fancies brutally stabs an elderly customer; later, he is viciously assaulted by a maltreated ape and with half his face torn off, he waves away assistance with a dismissive, 'Purely superficial'.

Donald Pleasence, so good in *Flesh and the Fiends,* essays a brief role as the drunken circus owner with a dodgy French accent who is mauled to death by his own dancing bear. Yvonne Monlaur, with a real French accent, played the only innocent in the whole affair, while Kenneth Griffith and Jane Hylton were the doting brother and sister, both in love with Schüler and both used and abused in that casual off-hand manner that Diffring perfected. Among the girls donning glittery leotards for their art are Vanda Hudson, the love of Schüler's life, who is instantly disposed of when she falls for another man, Erika Remberg (aka Mrs Sidney Hayers), swinging on the trapeze to a bland pop song (and Top Ten hit) by Garry Mills, and Yvonne Romain, late of *Corridors of Blood,* who plays Melina, Schüler's crowning achievement, who is forced to go nervously into a cage of agitated lions. (The actress was doubled by a real male lion-tamer in drag!)

Circus of Horrors: Erika Remberg in a publicity pose

Interiors were shot at Beaconsfield Studios, which had been a staging post for 'quota quickies' since the 1920s, while much of the location footage was actually shot on Clapham Common, where the real-life Billy Smart's Circus provided the glamorous and authentic backdrop, as well as the ringmaster, performers and animals—if not quite the '200 world famous circus acts' that were claimed by the pressbook. The film was photographed by Douglas Slocombe, who had shot Ealing's *Dead of Night* (1945) and who creates some striking images to accompany Hayes's unflinching direction. But despite the polish, one can understand if there was still a certain nervousness at Anglo-Amalgamated after the treatment that only recently had been meted out to Michael Powell.

The critics at least accepted *Circus of Horrors* as an escapist fantasy, albeit a particularly sadistic one, and treated it with the sort of bemused contempt they reserved for films they considered not to be worth the stock they were shot on. *The Daily Cinema* noted 'a grisly no-holds-barred drama, specially geared for the "more gore" customers'. The *Monthly Film Bulletin* thought that 'the film's main concern

Circus of Horrors (Sasha Coco, Kenneth Griffith, Chris Christian, Conrad Philips, Yvonne Monlaur, Jane Hylton, Erika Remberg, Anton Diffring)

is with satisfying those who find mutilation entertaining.' Those were the sort of reviews that distributors could get their teeth into, and more of the same followed when the American Catholic League of Decency condemned its 'excessive brutality, suggestive costumes and situations'.

The success of *Circus of Horrors*, following on from the earlier Technicolor

89

monsters, ensured that the new decade would start on a bow wave of horror pictures. While Hammer pitched into the 1960s at full pelt with the vampiric brides of Dracula, a youthful Mr Hyde, a werewolf, a phantom and more, a whole raft of independent horror producers rushed to follow in its wake.

Michael Powell, A-A's Stuart Levy, Karl Boehm and Pamela Green at the April 7, 1960, Plaza premiere of Peeping Tom.

Chapter 3

Horror and a Dash of Sex

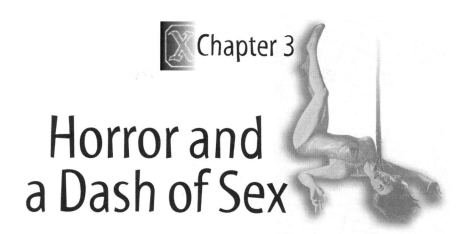

In the late 1950s, Hammer had been given a free rein to plunder Hollywood horror's back catalogue but its success meant that other producers were starting to elbow their way into the revival market. In 1960, Donald Taylor, producer of the modestly-impressive *The City of the Dead*, and his partner Steven Pallos—who collectively operated under the banner of Pendennis Films—announced that they had acquired the rights to Maurice Renard's novel *Les Mains d'Orlac*—last filmed by M-G-M in 1935 as *Mad Love*. The new version, which appropriately enough would be a co-production with the French company Riviera International, would have double the budget of *The City of the Dead*, a major international star and a cornucopaea of British B-movie stalwarts in support.

THE HANDS OF ORLAC
'Saved by the surgeons to play again...or to murder?'

> Stephen Orlac, a famous concert pianist, is seriously injured in a plane crash and, although he survives, his face is burned and his hands have been horribly mangled. Renowned surgeon Professor Volchett manages to save his hands, but Orlac is convinced that the hands of an executed murderer have been swapped with his own. The obsession grows when Orlac is driven by a desire for violence. He attacks the gardener at his estate and is terrified he will strangle his wife, Louise. Believing he needs to flee to protect Louise, he finds himself in a seedy Marseilles hotel where in his confused and paranoid state, he is easy prey for a low-life nightclub magician called Nero and his sluttish moll, Li-Lang. Spotting an opportunity to make money, Nero devises an elaborate plan both to convince Nero that the executed killer has returned for his 'property' and to blackmail him out of his fortune.

Renard's story debuted as a serial in *L'Intransigent* in 1920 and was adapted for the screen four years later, with the celebrated German actor Conrad Veidt as the renowned pianist mutilated in a horrific train crash. The M-G-M version, directed by Karl Freund, took the same premise and introduced the demented Dr Gogol, played by Peter Lorre, who lusts after Orlac's actress wife and seizes on the accident as an opportunity to rid himself of his inconvenient rival. Gogol was very much the central character in that picture but the Pendennis version went back to Renard and switched the emphasis back to Orlac. The new script retained the spirit of Gogol, at

The Hands of Orlac (Christopher Lee)

least in terms of plotting if not characterisation, with the seedy stage magician Nero, whose motivation is greed rather than lust.

The man charged with updating the Renaud story for a modern audience was French-born Edmond T Gréville, a former journalist-turned-film director with a substantial career in mainland Europe and Britain. Gréville's most recent film, the crude teen pot-boiler *Beat Girl* (1960), had featured Christopher Lee as a sleazy strip club owner, so it wasn't too much of a surprise to find Lee attached to the new project in the equally unpleasant role of Nero. Given his oft-quoted admiration for Conrad Veidt, Lee may have felt sleighted not to have been offered the role of Orlac but the production needed an international name and Lee, despite his success as a Hammer's monster, was still seen as a supporting actor rather than a leading man. Nero was another in the actor's long line of self-serving psychotics—Resurrection Joe in an evening suit and with a touch of the theatrics.

To play the title role, the producers opted for Mel Ferrer, a Hollywood actor but hardly a box-office star. Roles in *Scaramouche* (1952) and *War and Peace* (1956) and a much-publicised marriage to Audrey Hepburn had made Ferrer a household name, however, and having recently relocated from California to Switzerland, he was keen to establish his credentials as a European star and had already appeared in *Et Mouriri de Plaisir* (UK: *Blood and Roses*), Roger Vadim's modernist adaptation of J Sheridan Le Fanu's vampire novella *Carmilla*. Traditionally Hollywood stars— even those with no obvious bankability—jealously protected their screen image, and the hiring of Ferrer may well explain why Gréville, writing as Max Montagut, steered clear of the obvious horror potential in the novel and ensured there was nothing unpleasant or inappropriate going on (or coming off) when his leading man was onscreen. Instead, Gréville and his writing partner, John Baines, the creator of *The Haunted Mirror* sequence in *Dead of Night* (1945), use Nero as a vehicle for everything immoral, but even then they go out of their way to ensure that this is kept to an absolute minimum. This decision took the film far away from the contemporary

3: Horror and a Dash of Sex

horror scene in Britain and the US and meant that the 'all new, updated' *The Hands of Orlac* was closer in tone to a 1940s' thriller than a 1960s' horror picture.

Gréville's good intentions were further undermined by the producer's insistence on two completely different versions being shot simultaneously—one in English and the other in French. Christopher Lee, writing in his autobiography remembered, 'We'd do the scene in English, and then the cry *"Version français"* would go up and we'd do it all again in French with rather more expression.' Lee was one of the few versed enough in the language to speak his lines in both versions and seems to have enjoyed the experience, citing his French performance as superior to the English. Predictably, the French version is also a tad racier than its British counterpart and included the briefest flash of a naked breast, courtesy of Nero's sluttish accomplice, Li-Lang. This wasn't exactly two films for the price of one, though; to make the event more interesting, Gréville insisted on different set-ups, sometimes only marginally altered, sometimes from completely different angles, and, by doing so, he increased the shooting schedule and stretched his limited budget.

The cast reflected the international nature of the finance, although most of the British actors offer up no more than cameos. *Blood of the Vampire's* Donald Wolfit is among the most prominent as Professor Volchett, hiding his embarrassment behind a surgical mask for most of his screen time. Donald Pleasence, on the other hand, barely pauses long enough for his presence to be registered. Also featured was David Peel, who played the vampire in Hammer's *The Brides of Dracula* (1960), as well as Janina Faye from *Dracula* (1958)—both reduced to insignificant bit-parts. The Brits were augmented by two French starlets: Dany Carrel was Li-Lang in the smaller of the two roles, who nevertheless gets two full musical numbers in a sparkly bikini and the chance to be used and abused by Christopher Lee, while Lucile Saint-Simon played the more mundane part of Louise Orlac and gets to look fretful, but

The Hands of Orlac (Mel Ferrer)

The Hands of Orlac (Lucile Saint-Simon)

INSET: French theatrical poster / Dany Carroll

apart from a brief and rather mild throttling by her husband, she is given little else to do. In a script notable for lack of imagination, the female roles are particularly clichéd; the promiscuous bad girl is a Eurasian brunette with a tawdry past, while the good girl is a demure Caucasian blonde from a wealthy family.

The Anglo-French *rapprochement* extended to the production chores, which were split between Shepperton and the Victorine Studios in Nice. A number of the crew from *The City of the Dead* reappeared, but while the actors were afforded the luxury of a trip to the South of France, the technicians had to job-share with their French counterparts; cinematographer Desmond Dickinson, for example,

3: Horror and a Dash of Sex

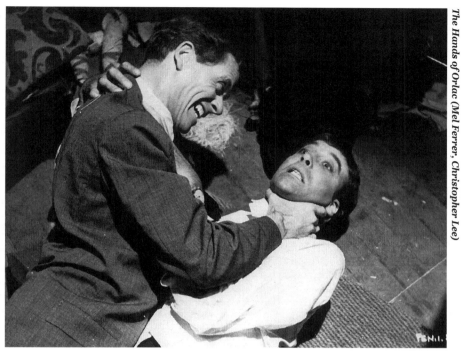

The Hands of Orlac (Mel Ferrer, Christopher Lee)

split his photography credit with Jacques Lemare. It would be nice to report that all this *entente cordiale* was put to good use but sadly, it was not the case. Gréville shows commendable brevity in the film's early scenes, galloping over the crash and the operation to get Orlac into recovery. The ticklish issue of suggesting that he has a killer's hands without anyone confirming it is achieved by the juxtaposition of the two newspaper stories: the execution of the notorious killer and Orlac's accident. In an understandably confused state, Orlac merges the two stories together and then starts to accumulate circumstantial evidence in support of his growing paranoia: a ring does not fit him any more; he struggles to play the piano; he scores far higher than he thinks feasible in a fairground challenge to Test Your Strength. This is all achieved within the first quarter-hour but having established an intriguing situation, Gréville then seems to lose his way.

The pace slows considerably with Li-Lang's unnecessary musical numbers, as well as prolonged scenes of Nero rehearsing, and a number of inconsistencies in Gréville's script only compound the problems and render the plot well-nigh incomprehensible. Nero's cunning plan, for instance, is to drive Orlac mad and <u>then</u> to blackmail him! This ill-thought-out scenario might have passed muster had Gréville not given the game away on the film's elaborately staged 'big fright scene': Nero prowls around Orlac's bedroom, supposedly the guillotined killer who has been resurrected when Volchett stitched his head back on; hidden by a mask and using hooks for hands, the magician achieves the desired effect—only to throw his mask aside and reveal his true identity in the very next shot! That dramatic highpoint occurs some 70 minutes into the film, while the first murder, the potentially gruesome slaying of Li-Lang (which has nothing to do with Orlac), clocks in at the 90-minute mark and involves nothing more disturbing than a discreetly- spreading bloodstain.

This squeamishness sets Gréville apart from most of his contemporaries; even

X-Cert

Terence Fisher, hardly the most extreme of directors, was happily dousing the screen in blood and body parts. Gréville, on the other hand, was more comfortable showing outcomes: the pivotal operation, for example, is a largely anaemic affair with Orlac waking to find his limbs encased in implausibly large plaster casts and without a hint of gore. The flawed logic of the script reaches its overdue climax when the closing scenes reveal Orlac's hands are actually his own—which comes as relief to our hero but does nothing to explain everything the viewer has just sat through.

Saddled with a hopelessly-impaired script, Ferrer sleepwalks his way through the film with almost total detachment. 'Look at these hands,' he pleads unconvincingly. 'They have their own thoughts, their own will. I can't control them!' He aims for tortured artist but struggles to achieve anything above melancholy. Christopher Lee, perhaps sensing that his co-star was underacting, ratchets up his own performance to the level of pantomime, hissing absurd lines like, 'He'll pay through the nose till his eyes drop out' with manic glee and evil cackles—all that is missing is a comic twist of a moustache. Nero's interaction with Li-Lang provides the most entertainment in the film: 'You were born a slut,' he sneers, 'and you'll always be one'. Later he tells her, with total contempt, that she would look a lot less attractive with a scar!

Gréville wrapped his film(s) in the early summer of 1960 and had the British version and its French equivalent (imaginatively-titled *Les mains d'Orlac*) in cinemas within 12 months. Having opted out of crowd-pleasing horror, the target audience was firmly viewed as those who had flocked to see Hitchcock's *Psycho* but even then, Gréville's A-certificate antics looked very bland indeed. *Kinematograph Weekly* called it 'psychopathic poppycock', while *Variety* summed things up with a dismissive 'Old hat'. The film was so out of kilter with the market that the US release was delayed until 1964, but any hopes Taylor and Pallos had for a late revival died when the film opened and promptly sank without a trace. The failure ended Donald Taylor's brief association with the genre although his partnership with Steven Pallos continued and included another international hybrid, *The Devil's Daffodil* (1961), based on an Edgar Wallace novel and also featuring Christopher Lee. Pallos would be tempted back to horror films later in the decade, but with no more success than he had found at *The Hands of Orlac*.

Of course gore is not necessarily a pre-requisite for an efficient horror picture and Gréville might have been advised to cast an eye over the product emanating from Wintle and Parkyn's Independent Artists unit at Beaconsfield studios. Having shocked sensibilities with *Circus of Horrors,* the duo used their contract to supply Anglo-Amalgamated with B features, unleashing some more restrained but no less effective supernatural thrillers directed by veteran journeyman Vernon Sewell. The first of these was *House of Mystery,* which was to reunite two refugees from *Circus of Horrors*, Jane Hylton and John Merivale, as a pair of lovers plotting the demise of an inconvenient husband.

HOUSE OF MYSTERY
'No one's taken it because there's a ghost...'

> *A house-hunting couple, Mark and Stella Lemming, arrive at the seemingly quaint and tranquil Orchard Cottage, somewhat surprised to find it available for a mere £2,000. Inside the house, the Lemmings encounter the housekeeper who is only too willing to tell them something of the property's dark and disturbing past. It seems the previous occupants, Mr and Mrs Trevor, were plagued by apparently random 'happenings'—lights switching themselves off and on, strange noises and ghostly images on their television*

3: Horror and a Dash of Sex

screen. Seeking a rational explanation, the Trevors call in an electrician who suggests that a surge in power caused the problems but the couple are unconvinced. As the occurences intensify, the Trevors experience visitations from an unidentified man who seems to be reaching out to them. Distraught, they call in a medium to help identify the source of the apparitions and, if necessary, to exorcise their home.

Following on *The Medium* (1934), *Latin Quarter* (1945) and *Ghost Ship* (1952), this was Sewell's fourth and final adaptation of the Celia de Vilyars and Pierre Mills play, *L'Angoisse*. Four decades after this 're-imagining', Sewell defended his thrift insisting, 'When you are making low-budget films you have to make a virtue out of poverty. I used my own boat all the time because it was cheaper; I used the (de Vilyars and Mills) play because I owned the rights; I used whatever I didn't have to pay for!' Economy may have been his watchword but Sewell could not be accused of being staid: 'I always liked to try new things, to keep things interesting for me as much as the audience,' he explained. Penning the script himself, he enlivens *House of Mystery* with a complex narrative structure of flashbacks within flashbacks, and maintains no less than three separate plots running concurrently. He also introduces a television as a plot device, playing to an audience susceptible to the idea that the still-novel device sitting in the corner of their living rooms could in some way be responsible for unnatural happenings—pre-empting Tobe Hooper's *Poltergeist* (1982) by some two decades!

The malevolent use of everyday household apparatus was hardly original even in 1961 but Sewell intensifies the threat by his low-key and matter-of-fact approach, which makes the situation

House of Mystery (Peter Dynelely)

97

seem so real—at least for the duration of the feature's trim 55-minute running-time. The policeman who prefers drinking a beer to answering a 999 call; the station receptionist who suggests the apparition was simply a product of the BBC—all add a texture of normality to counteract the air of inexplicability.

The director's efforts are helped by a competent, if relatively-unknown cast: Nanette Newman, the wife of actor/director Bryan Forbes, and Maurice Kaufman, a veteran supporting player, bring credibility to the Trevors. Newman has perhaps the best moment in the film when, struggling in the dark, she manages to get the light working again only to see a man standing in front of her with his hand extended. The real stars are Hylton and Merivale as the lovers with murder on their minds, along with Peter Dyneley as the troublesome spouse. Having also starred with Hylton as husband and wife in *The Split* (aka *The Manster*, 1959), Dyneley plays an electrical engineer who appropriately enough is to be electrocuted in the bath; turning the tables on his would-be killers, he extracts his revenge through the aforementioned household devices. The premise also allowed Sewell to engage in the one unsubtle moment in the film, when Dyneley is seen experimenting with electrical currents on a live dog. If the twist in the tale is transparently obvious, it does not detract from Sewell's efforts and tight plotting and solid execution mark out *House of Mystery* as a compelling ghost story.

The critics on the whole were impressed with Sewell's efforts: *Monthly Film Bulletin* noted, 'The narrative is ingeniously worked out, giving full credit to the supernatural'; while *Daily Cinema* thought it a 'really gripping mystery thriller.' The producers' modest ambitions for the film were realised in May 1962 when it opened a double-bill with another Wintle-Parkyn film, *Payroll* (1961), a gritty and popular thriller directed by Sidney Hayers and released through A-A. Despite its undoubted qualities, *House of Mystery* was always destined for a short shelf life and it was soon relegated to late-night television slots and all-but forgotten.

For his next outing for Independent Artists, Vernon Sewell continued playfully to defy expectations. Working once more with a microscopic budget, a small cast and stark black-and-white photography, he constructed what on the surface appears to be a conventional crime thriller, but it was one which veered into the realms of the supernatural for its startling climax.

THE MAN IN THE BACK SEAT
'This is something new in thrillers!'

> *Two small time hoods, Tony and Frank, out for a quick buck, decide to rob a betting agent, Joe Carter, as he leaves the dog track after a profitable day. However, their plan for a quick getaway is thwarted by his earlier decision to handcuff his wrist to the bag of takings. Things are further complicated when their victim is beaten viciously during the robbery and falls unconscious, leaving his assailants with no choice but to bundle him into the back of their car until they can safely separate him from the cash. Unfortunately, the bookie is more seriously hurt than they thought and they are torn between the need to get away from the scene of the crime and ensuring that their victim does not die in the process. The incompetent crooks' attempts to leave him where he will be found and looked after are thwarted at every turn. They finally abandon any attempt to help him and flee London for Birmingham, only to find that their crime is about to come back to haunt them.*

The tone of *The Man in the Back Seat* was very much in the vein of the Edgar Wallace mysteries which were pouring out of Merton Park Studios and propping

3: Horror and a Dash of Sex

up many an Anglo-Amalgamated double bill; so much so that Sewell may well have deliberately set out to mimic their cost-effective *noir* style. The look and feel were so similar that on some later prints, Wallace's name was added to the title to create the impression that it was adapted from one of his stories. In fact, the script was an original work by Malcolm Hulke and Eric Paice, a writing partnership with limited experience in features but a successful track record on television, working together on shows like *Pathfinders in Space* and *Armchair Theatre*. The writers' small screen experience and ability to establish characters and situations quickly and then get straight to the action played perfectly to Sewell's time and budget constraints, and it is fair to say that the screenplay reads like a superior television play.

Although Wintle and Parkyn are credited as producers, as they had been on *House of Mystery*, they actually had very little influence on the film after the script was approved. 'Julian came on set once, I think,' Vernon Sewell recalls, 'and they would have been around and about at Beaconsfield anyway. But really they had nothing to do with my films. I produced them myself.' Left to his own devices, Sewell engaged 26-year-old Derren Nesbitt for the pivotal role of Tony, the 'Jack-the-lad' who turns from small time opportunist to vicious killer as the film progresses. This would be the first of three films Nesbitt made for Sewell and he remembers his director with some affection; 'Vernon was an actor's director, by which I mean he would

The Man in the Back Seat (Carol White, Derren Nesbitt, Keith Faulkner, Harry Locke)

allow the actor flexibility to build his character and that wasn't something that happened very often in this type of film.' On paper the character, who has his leg in plaster throughout, has an eye for the ladies and an appetite for easy money, and Sewell allowed Nesbitt to fashion some sarcastic humour. Early in the film when the two hoods are in a café and a pretty girl asks what happened to his leg, Tony grins and quips, 'Caught it in a mousetrap'. Nesbitt claims, 'I had to rewrite a lot of my dialogue to bring out that humour and make the character more rounded, otherwise he would have just been a bully.'

As their situation becomes more serious, the likeable wide-boy recedes and Tony transforms into a self-serving thug pushing his side-kick to ever greater extremes. To play the browbeaten Frank, who brings their journey to such a dramatic climax, Sewell cast Keith Faulkner, another competent television actor, and it is the chemistry between Faulkner and Nesbitt that gives the film its emotional core. The two men share most of the screen-time and Sewell liked the partnership so much he repeated it a year later in *Strongroom*, with the pair again playing incompetent crooks.

Carol White, who would achieve fame in the title role of Ken Loach's *Poor Cow* (1967), played Jean, Frank's harried wife who represents his conscience—a nagging voice of reason—as well as the only hope of sanctuary from the wickedness of the outside world. With her dressing gown permanently wrapped protectively around her nightie, White cuts a beleaguered figure desperate to save her husband and return him to domestic normality but unable to counter Tony's corrupting influence.

The script's only other important character was the unfortunate bookie Joe Carter, played by Harry Locke, who, despite having an almost totally passive role, remains the film's most significant plot device. The bookie starts off as a physical burden to Tony and Frank as they try desperately to distance themselves from the scene of the crime but can't seem to rid themselves of the body. When he is not physically in shot or hidden in the back of the car, Carter and his well-being are the sole subject of discussion between the leading players. He becomes a metaphor for their guilt, a Shakespearean ghost silently haunting his murderers, and ultimately he transforms into an avenging spirit for the conclusion—the only moment when Sewell departs from earth-bound but very natural torments of the pair and plunges them into the realm of the paranormal.

Some latter-day reviewers have compared the film's closing scene to the similar scene in the Val Lewton production, *The Body Snatcher* (1945), when the corpse of the murdered Gray (Boris Karloff) seems to return from the dead to exact revenge during a nightmarish coach ride. The notion of revenge from beyond the grave is rejected outright by the film's star, Derren Nesbitt, who dismisses any suggestion of a supernatural ending: 'It's definitely not a ghost; it's all in his mind and that's the way we filmed it. When Keith (Faulkner) sees the body in the back, it's really his conscience playing tricks'. Sewell, on the other hand, was comfortable with the idea of divine retribution. 'I try not to impose views on people,' he said, 'I like to give them something to think about after the film has finished. If you asked me to choose, I'd say that it was a visitation or an apparition, whatever you want to call it.'

The comparison with Lewton's supernatural thriller is not as fanciful as it first sounds, and it can be applied to Sewell's approach throughout the whole film. The catalogue of unrelated incidents could easily have descended into farce but Sewell allows the tension to grow gradually out of the character's frustrations, without the need to impose any outside force or direct threat—although the threat of police intervention is ever-present. Witer David Pirie, an admirer of Sewell's work, called this an 'anxiety dream'—a phrase that neatly encapsulates the awful and irresistible inevitability of Tony and Frank's desperate struggle to be free of Carter.

As in *House of Mystery*, the shortened running time of barely an hour serves Sewell's intentions well and with no need for sub-plots or elaborations, he can allow events to unfold almost in real time, which again helps to build tension. 'That made it a relatively easy film to make,' Nesbitt says, 'but all Vernon's films were. There were not a lot of set-ups or locations and he was an "old school" director who knew his stuff, knew exactly what he was doing, and things went like clockwork.'

The critics seemed to respond to the efficiency of the whole production. *Daily Cinema* said it was 'pint-sized but crisply engineered with plausible characterisation, thrills and acting'. The M*onthly Film Bulletin* liked the 'Mabuse-like finale' and noted that 'Sewell's direction is unambitious but gripping.' Released by A-A on the lower half of a bill with *Dentist on the Job* (1961), a Bob Monkhouse comedy, *The Man in the Back Seat* at least enjoyed a circuit release before, like *House of Mystery*, it slipped into undeserved obscurity. For Vernon Sewell, it was something of a career high. He continued to beaver away in thrillers and horror films without ever quite matching the intensity of his two Independent Artists' Bs.

Independent Artists may have paid the rent at Beaconsfield with these modest exercises but what Cohen and Levy really wanted was an out-and-out horror film to follow on from *Circus of Horrors*. A-A's collaboration with AIP had yielded another Herman Cohen picture, the bizarre *Konga* (1961), which was shot at Merton Park and had the giant ape of the title terrorising London. With Anglophile Herman Cohen in charge, there was no need for Wintle and Parkyn to be involved but that situation changed in 1961 when the American decided to part company with his benefactors and strike out on his own as an independent. With a screenplay newly-arrived from Hollywood and no producer, Julian Wintle and Leslie Parkyn were summoned to Anglo-Amalgamated's Wardour Street offices to discuss AIP's proposed adaptation of Fritz Leiber's 1943 novel, *Conjure Wife*.

NIGHT OF THE EAGLE
'Witch or woman, what was it?'

> *Professor Norman Taylor, rising star of Hempnell Medical School, provokes a certain amount deal of jealously among his colleagues and Tansy, his wife, becomes convinced that one of them is using black magic to harm him. She fortifies their cottage with a number of charms but Taylor, disgusted at her superstitious attitude, destroys them. Almost immediately, things start to go awry in Taylor's once-perfect life and he experiences a series of seemingly-unrelated incidents, including an accusation of rape by one of his students. Tansy becomes obsessed with the idea she needs to sacrifice her life in order to save her husband and flees the cottage, intending to drown herself. Beside himself with worry, Taylor pursues her and with the help of a black magic ceremony, he manages to save her life—but it comes at at a price. Tansy, in a state of shock, is no longer responsible for her actions and Taylor realises that if he is to free his wife and save his career, he needs to confront the forces that are rallying against him.*

Leiber's novel had been filmed in 1944 by Universal Pictures as *Weird Woman*, but this rather limp 'Inner Sanctum' vehicle for horror star Lon Chaney was not enough to put off two of America's most renowned fantasy writers, Richard Matheson and Charles Beaumont. 'Chuck and I wanted to do a script together,' Matheson says. 'We loved the book and wanted to do something with it. We knew that Universal had the rights but we went ahead with it anyway—it was for fun, really.' Coming from a literary background, both men had enjoyed success with television productions, but their real claim to fame was with the big screen—in Matheson's case with *The Incredible Shrinking Man* (1957) and a crypt-full of Poe adaptations, and Charles Beaumont most recently with the Roger Corman film *The Premature Burial* (1962). Both men also had a close relationship with AIP's Jim Nicholson, who encouraged them to collaborate on the screenplay.

In adapting the book, the writers retained the New England setting—'Where else would a witch operate?' Matheson asked rhetorically—but they abandoned Leiber's original concept of a full-blown coven on campus and opted instead for just two witches, one on either side of the black/white magic divide. Crafting an intelligent and literate script, they removed all the novel's references to possession and spirit transference and went for the more subtle and chilling suggestion of psychological control. Leiber's stone dragon was also changed to a less cinematically-challenging (and less expensive) ornamental eagle. The Americans could also take the credit for introducing a strong sexual angle; far from being a stuffy academic, their hero is something of a sex-object to his female students, with unfortunate consequences in the case of one impressionable young lady.

The Matheson/Beaumont screenplay, under Leiber's original title, appealed to James Nicholson and after negotiating the rights from Universal, he paid its authors $5,000 each for their efforts. Seizing on a line from the script, he then re-titled the project *Burn, Witch, Burn* (a title which it would retain for the American market) and despatched the whole to Messrs Cohen and Levy as a suggestion for their next collaboration.

A-A set the film's budget at £50,000, spelled out a requirement for a star name acceptable to AIP and left Independent Artists to get on with the detail. Wintle, who was fully occupied with a bustling production slate, brought in Albert Fennell as producer and Sidney Hayers to direct and, perhaps aiming to recreate some of that *Circus of Horrors* verve, he commissioned George Baxt to re-draft the script—a decision that was to lead to considerable acrimony over the years. Richard Matheson, who had no direct involvement in the film after it was sold to AIP, has been at pains to minimise Baxt's contribution, insisting, 'I didn't see any scenes in that movie that I didn't recognise.' Baxt, who is credited as co-writer on the British but not the US print, told *Scarlet Street*, 'I did a complete re-write from top to bottom! I mean they couldn't go on the floor with the script they [Matheson and Beaumont] wrote. I wrote scenes he never heard of!' Among the scenes that Baxt claims credit for are a bridge game and a chase, as well as the transference of the story to its English setting. Sidney Hayers, the closest we have to a neutral in this authorship dispute, told *Fangoria*, 'George didn't have a lot to do with it. If he did anything it was very, very small because the (Matheson-Beaumont) script was hardly changed at all.'

While the stages at Beaconsfield were being prepared for a relatively generous six-week shoot (supplemented with some location work in Cornwall), Fennell was looking for a star to appeal to the Americans, which in a 1960 horror film meant just one person. It was hardly a surprise, therefore, when the press announcements were issued that Peter Cushing, one of the few bankable names in British horror pictures, was attached to the project. After a rash of monster films, it is easy to see why Cushing would have been attracted to such a clever and subtle script, which had the added bonus of allowing a rare outing in a contemporary setting. It was still a horror film however, and Cushing would soon jump ship in favour of the title role in the Hammer adventure romp, *Captain Clegg*.

The inconvenience of losing their male lead was overcome for Wintle and Parkyn when AIP signed Janet Blair to play the role of Tansy, with the Hollywood studio guaranteeing her salary as part of its financial commitment. Best known for

3: Horror and a Dash of Sex

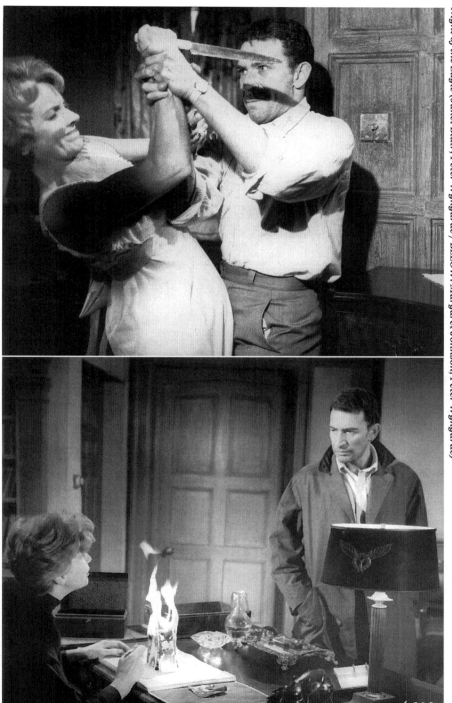

Night of the Eagle (Janet Blair, Peter Wyngarde / BELOW: Margaret Johnson, Peter Wyngarde)

musical comedy—including a massive 42-month Broadway run in *South Pacific*—Blair was thought a sufficient box-office name to allow the British producers some latitude in casting the role of Taylor, and the part was offered to Peter Finch. The Australian prevaricated before turning the role down, which left Fennell without a lead once more as the production deadline approached. Peter Wyngarde, an English television actor who had played the small but crucial role of Quint in Jack Clayton's masterful ghost story *The Innocents* (1961) was approached but, like Finch, he was also less than impressed. The actor told his fan club, 'When my agent sent me the original script…I didn't like it very much. It was very much in the not-so-good-as-a-Hammer-film category and frankly I threw it out of my window!' Wyngarde changed his mind when Independent Artists returned with an increased offer—a figure he puts in excess of £5,000.

Wyngarde was not a star but he did have sex appeal and he would later send many female hearts fluttering in the role of the androgynously-camp *Jason King* in the television series of the same name. Even in the early sixties, he had a curious effect on women; *The Times*'s correspondent Irene Roper returned from an encounter with the actor and reported somewhat breathlessly that he was 'a man who clearly

Night of the Eagle (Peter Wyngarde, Janet Blair)

3: Horror and a Dash of Sex

Night of the Eagle

had this mysterious thing known in show business as "star quality"... a mantle of magic which is there whether they are on stage or in the bath.' Hayers, recognising the 'magic', exploited Wyngarde's exaggerated machismo throughout the film. In front of his admiring students, Taylor positively struts, while at home he is very much the alpha-male, barking orders while stripped to the waist and flexing a toned torso for the benefit of his doting wife. Sexual tension runs hand-in-hand with professional jealousy in the relationship between the Taylors and Flora, the villain of the piece, who is a far cry from the shrew-like matron depicted in Leiber's novel. As played by Margaret Johnson, the character runs from coquettish to, in Tansy's words, 'a middle-aged Medusa' as Taylor initially welcomes her support and ultimately rejects her in favour of his wife. Johnson, a stage actress described by *The Independent* as 'a striking and elegant presence', brings a mixture of menace and neurosis to the part but, like Wyngarde, it was a role the actress had sought to avoid. 'I hated that,' she told writer Brian McFarlane, 'even though it was a good part. It wasn't the sort of film I enjoyed doing.'

Whatever the misgivings of his cast, Hayers had no intention of recreating the Eastmancolor excesses of *Circus of Horrors* and went instead for a far more subtle approach, building the suspense by layering on a series of apparently unrelated incidents which gradually ratchet up to a terrifying confrontation in the closing scenes of the film; Hayers starts the process in the opening shots, when the camera pans past an ominous stone eagle and into Taylor's classroom. The emphasis from the outset is on everyday reality, rather than anything paranormal. In a sequence of short scenes, we then learn that Taylor is something of a pin-up to his class; he drives a sports car, has an adoring wife and his job prospects are stratospheric. But beneath this veneer, things are not quite so rosy: he and Tansy are, and always will be, outsiders in a tight-knit and waspish academic community.

Taylor is unshakable in his conviction that the supernatural is a figment of fevered imaginations; the opening words in the film are his emphatic: 'I...do...not... believe!' which he has scrawled on the blackboard, adding, 'Four words necessary to destroy the focus of the supernatural. Belief is vital!' He is aghast when, rooting around in his wife's undies drawer, he finds a perfectly-preserved spider, and a subsequent search of the house reveals a veritable treasure-trove of charms and totems. 'Ridiculous—it's stupid' he storms, 'I can't believe it: a woman of your intelligence...' Tansy, in obvious distress, cries, 'I will not be responsible for what happens to us if you make me give up my protection!' The script does not dwell over much on Tansy's conversion to the dark arts, which has occurred after a trip to the West Indies, apparently, nor does it explain how Taylor has failed to notice that his wife is a practicing witch. Jettisoning unnecessary exposition, Hayers starts to pick up the pace with a tape recorder blasting out hostile noise, followed by a thunderous banging on the front door. Throughout everything, Taylor sticks to his assertion that it can all be explained away.

The credibility of the film rests largely on Wyngarde's performance; the weight of evidence is clearly running against Taylor, but he still needs to be stubborn and dismissive without alienating the audience through his arrogance. This is a difficult balancing act when the actor is handed lines like, 'If we were to investigate the strange rituals performed by women on their intuition, half the women in the country would be in an asylum.' Likewise, his behaviour over the alleged sexual assault was probably acceptable within the context of a 1960s' male-dominated society, but it does rely on bullying the clearly-traumatised girl. 'You phoned me on Saturday night, with a very disgusting proposition!' he bawls, 'When I threatened to hang up, you used vile language—VILE AND FILTHY!' However, Wyngarde does manage to elicit sympathy by being so devoted to Tansy, and their commitment to each other provides the impetus for the narrative.

Some of the execution is hackneyed; thunder and lightning heralds an onslaught of the supernatural while a clock chimes midnight, and Hayers stresses Flora's malevolence during her climactic speech by lighting her from below. But even such clichés as these do not detract from Margaret Johnson's powerful performance as she descends into scorn and hatred. 'I knew you were naïve' she spits at Taylor, 'but I didn't know you were as naive as all that. You are behaving like a frightened schoolboy, frightened of being wrong!' The few weaknesses of Hayers's direction are more than offset by the positives and among the highlights is the chase sequence, which climaxes in a car-crash followed by a midnight pursuit to a graveyard. This genuinely chilling passage is underpinned by stunning photography and subjective camera angles.

Taking delivery of the film, Wintle and Parkyn decided to drop the catchpenny *Burn, Witch, Burn* and replace it with the more understated *Night of the Eagle*, in a possible attempt to evoke memories of Jacques Tourneur's earlier masterpiece of witchcraft and paganism, *Night of the Demon* (1957). The two films are not that alike, but they do have one commonality; in Tourneur's film, the 'curse' is transferred from donor to recipient care of ancient runes inscribed on a scrap of paper. Hayers's equivalent of the runes is a modern tape recorder, which when played provokes the demonic attack and is, at the climax of the film, inadvertently directed from Taylor to Flora—resulting in the grisly death of the latter.

Picking up an X certificate from a British censor notoriously prickly about the subject of witchcraft, the film was received with mixed reviews from the critics. *Time* thought it 'not much of a movie but it goes to show what can happen in a community that fails to pay its teachers a living wage.' The *New York Times* was more impressed, hailing 'perhaps the best outright goose-pimpler dealing specifically with witchcraft since *I Walked with a Zombie* in 1943.'

Independent Artists had always maintained a broad portfolio of films, spanning comedies, thrillers and social drama, and its efforts in the fantasy genre showed a similar diversity. For its next outing, it would retain the low-key black-and-white photography that had been *de rigueur* for its B pictures but rather than follow-up on *Circus of Horrors* or *Night of the Eagle*, it crafted a film that was to be reminiscent of the best of 1950s' science fiction—naturally Wintle and Parkyn treated this tale of alien invasion in a distinctly British way.

UNEARTHLY STRANGER
'Terrifying, weird...macabre! Unseen things out of time and space!'

> Dr Munro, who leads a team of British scientists experimenting with the projection of material objects through time and space, is found dead in mysterious circumstances and Major Clarke, the security officer in charge of the ensuing investigation, reveals that the American and Russian scientists engaged in similar research have also been killed. When Mark Davidson arrives to take over the project, Clarke is particularly interested in his wife, Julie, a foreign national, who displays a number of disturbing physical characteristics. Davidson continues with the experiments but Clarke has aroused his suspicions and he becomes convinced that his wife is not all she seems. Confronting Julie, Davidson forces her to reveal the truth—an act that costs her her life. Distraught at losing the woman he loves, Davidson discovers that she was not working alone and has to act quickly to preserve the secret data before it falls into the wrong, unearthly hands.

Unearthly Stranger started life as a screenplay written on spec by actor Jeffrey Stone, better known as d'Artagnan in the popular 1950s television series, *The Three Musketeers*, and for brief spell as a Universal contract artist in forgettable films like *The Thing that Couldn't Die* (1958). By 1962, Stone had left the Hollywood lifestyle behind him and was in New York trying out a number of avenues of employment, including writing. 'A friend of mine mentioned that he knew a producer who was looking for a low-budget script,' Stone remembers. 'I said I had one and gave him *A Left Handed Marriage*. A few weeks later Rex called me from London and made me an offer of $10,000, which I accepted right away. I never heard from him again.' The 'Rex' mentioned was Rex Carlton, sometime film producer whose chief claim to fame was mounting his own production of *The Brain That Wouldn't Die* (1962). By swapping out Stone's beguiling title for the much more marketable *Unearthly Stranger* and adapting the script to an English setting, Carlton was able to sell the script to Wintle and Parkyn, who were ever on the lookout for films to feed into A-A's distribution maw. Independent Artists then engaged John Krish, a BAFTA-nominated documentary filmmaker keen to break into features, to direct.

Krish later claimed that when he arrived at his Beaconsfield production office, Carlton's script had been rejected outright by A-A. Independent Artists was already committed by then and handed its new director the not-inconsiderable challenge of getting a script acceptable to the money men while at the same time getting the actual production up and running. Given a free rein, Krish slimmed down the cast list, simplified the narrative and injected a vein of black humour. 'She's an alien, isn't she?' Major Clarke inquires of Davidson's wife. 'She was born in Switzerland,' Davidson retorts, the implication being that anyone born beyond Britain's shores was already beyond the pale.

Such xenophobia was an echo of the paranoia-fuelled science fiction that had come out of Hollywood a decade earlier, and the plotline of *Unearthly Stranger* has direct parallels with the likes of *I Married a Monster from Outer Space* (1958), with just a hint of *Invasion of the Body Snatchers* (1956). Lacking the money to create

X-Cert

Unearthly Stranger: US theatrical poster

complicated special effects or monster make-up pushed Krish into more creative solutions: the aliens travel to earth by means of thought transference—a considerably cheaper option than a spacecraft—and they look and act more or less like us, except that they do not blink their eyes and have an unnatural tolerance to pain. The low

3: Horror and a Dash of Sex

Unearthly Stranger (Philip Stone, John Neville, Gabriella Licudi)

budget also meant that Krish and his team were not in a position to stage elaborate set-pieces, and one of the key sequences in the film involves nothing more elaborate than a casserole dish!

This minimalist approach was to bring about one of the most unsettling scenes in the film, entirely without any overt threat or graphic violence. Julie is walking past a school playground when she is noticed by one of the children, who instantly stops playing and starts to back away. The other children then do the same *en masse*. By developing a growing sense of unease rather than relying on action sequences, the Stone/Carlton/Krish script successfully focuses on the human side of the drama, pulling out subtexts on gender, class and, unusually for a film about aliens, compassion. When Mark finally accepts that his wife is an alien he bleats, 'I don't care where you have come from... you are what I love! I have only ever seen you as a woman, not as anything else!'

Albert Fennell, who had done such a reliable job on *Night of the Eagle,* once again took on the production chores, but it was Krish who came up with a suitable choice for leading man: John Neville. The leading light of the Royal Shakespeare Company was a reluctant screen actor, although much later in life he would discover the joys of television through a recurring role in *The X Files*. On stage, Neville was considered to be *the* leading man of his generation; second only to Richard Burton in terms of box-office clout. The actor's gaunt face and somewhat ungainly physique made for an unusual screen hero, but he carried an air of integrity and sensitivity that perfectly suited the role of Davidson, a man devoted to his work and deeply in love with his wife. To play opposite Neville, Krish found raven-haired Gabriella Licudi, whose Moroccan background and Spanish/Greek extraction lent her a distinctly un-English air and physically set her apart from the rest of the cast without overstating the point. The fact that she was uncommonly beautiful also helped to rationalise, at least in the minds of male viewers, Mark's reluctance to admit the truth even when it becomes glaringly obvious.

X-Cert

Patrick Newell, who would later play the cherub-faced 'Mother' of *The Avengers* television series, joined the cast as the prying Major Clarke, while Philip Stone was cast as doubting scientist John Lancaster, who becomes Mark's confidante. Another familiar face but killed off far too early, is *The Trollenberg Terror's* reliable scene-stealer Warren Mitchell, whose gift for accents had established him as a cut-price Alec Guinness and who once again essays a scientist, only this time with a music-hall Scottish accent. Mitchell remembers a certain amount of disorganisation on the film: 'I was called in at the last minute, I think, or at the last minute they decided that they wanted a Scottish accent. Normally you would get time to practice these things but here it was a question of hitting the ground running.' Mitchell's role as Davidson's predecessor was important only in the establishing of an air of mystery surrounding the laboratory and his early demise allowed an acceptable amount of exposition to be speedily passed to the audience. 'Like all the films I made at that time, I did it for the money,' Mitchell concedes. 'We all did. Art didn't come into our thinking.'

For once, the scientific mumbo-jumbo is kept to a minimum; the boffins, we are informed, want to 'harness the power of concentration', which will apparently allow them to transport people and objects through time and space, using a power called 'TP91'—and that's about as technical as it gets. Inevitably, inconsistencies crop up between the re-writes; the business of the aliens stealing Warren Mitchell's body and replacing it with bricks, for example, appears terribly important at the time but goes nowhere. Sections of dialogue also feel like they might have been rushed in at the last minute, and even seasoned pros like John Neville struggle to bring any life to some of their lines: 'John, in a little while I expect to die,' Davidson gasps at the opening of the film, 'To be killed by something you and I know is here. Invisible... moving unseen amongst us all. Even if I had known what I know now, could I, or anyone, have held back...the terror?' But these are minor quibbles; the cast, on the whole, offer credible performances, particularly Newell's odiously bluff Major Clarke, whose timely interventions ensure that the film manages to stay well clear of sentimentality. At the same time Krish's crisp and efficient direction, particularly his use of tilted angles and 'fish-eye' close-ups, sees to it that the whole is greater than any sum of its parts, aided by an atmospheric score by Edward Williams, tight editing and moody photography from Reginald Wyer, who had lensed the earlier Independent Artists films, *The Man in the Back Seat* and *Night of the Eagle*.

The *Monthly Film Bulletin* found plenty to like and concluded that *Unearthly Stranger* was 'the best British SF-film since Wolf Rilla's *Village of the Damned'*, but like all of Independent Artists' B pictures, the film had been made to order and when it fulfilled its function of supporting whatever A feature required it, it disappeared from sight. John Krish went on to direct a number of feature films, including *The Man Who Had Power Over Women* (1970), as well as reuniting with Wintle and Fennell on *The Avengers* television series, but he never attracted anything like the attention he deserved and today is known almost exclusively for his award-winning documentary work.

Unearthly Stranger marked the end of a short but memorable association with the fantasy genre for Independent Artists and despite a stream of successful films, like Lindsay Anderson's *This Sporting Life* (1963), the company was struggling to stay afloat. Julian Wintle's wife, Anne Francis, wrote in her biography of her husband that his guiding principle was to make films which were 'artistically satisfying and commercially profitable.' The cornerstone of the company's success was the careful management and planning which had ensured Beaconsfield's sound tages were kept fully utilised with a continuous stream of product. But the pressure to maintain this

3: Horror and a Dash of Sex

level of output while remaining commercially viable proved too much and Wintle and Parkyn eventually decided to dissolve their partnership.

The last film from Independent Artists, an innocuous comedy entitled *Father Came Too*, was completed in 1964, after which Leslie Parkyn decided to retire from the industry while Wintle took on the onerous task of mothballing Beaconsfield. 'The firings were as awful as the hush of an empty studio,' he told his wife, 'the few of us creeping around like ghosts.' Then, like Baker and Berman before him, Julian Wintle found a productive niche in television series, working on *The Human Jungle* as well as *The Avengers*.

The small screen's gain was definitely a loss to independent filmmaking but at the time, the defection of such creative producers to television seemed to do little to stem the growth of British films and it would be almost a decade before their absence was truly felt. In the meantime, there was a gap that the Americans were rushing to fill—and much vaunted British expertise in horror pictures ensured the genre was getting its fair share of Yankee dollars. M-G-M had backed *Village of the Damned* in 1961 and in 1963, as part of major push in the UK, it mounted the supernatural shocker *The Haunting*, while Hollywood rivals 20th Century Fox had bankrolled Jack Clayton's classic, *The Innocents* (1961). Given this migration of talent and money to this side of the Atlantic, it is perhaps not too much of a surprise to find the name United Artists providing finance for a brace of low-budget horror pictures. What *is* a surprise is that the company best known for big budget mainstream movies like *The Magnificent Seven* (1960) and *West Side Story* (1961) would ally themselves so closely with two films that would have given even Hammer pause for thought.

DOCTOR BLOOD'S COFFIN
'Can you stand the terror...the awful secret it contains?'

> Dr Peter Blood, expelled from the Vienna Medical Academy for his unethical experiments, arrives in the small Cornish village of Port Carron to take over his father's practice and continue his fiendish work. Utilising the network of abandoned mines that riddle the hillsides, Dr Blood builds a secret laboratory and sets about acquiring 'donors' for his heart transplant operations. Blood starts to abduct members of the local community by using the tropical drug Curare to induce total paralysis and then, while the 'patient' is still conscious but unable to move, he removes their beating hearts. Blood forms a romantic attachment to recently-widowed nurse Linda Parker, but when she realises that her employer is up to no good, she tries to dissuade him from continuing. They quarrel and the increasingly-unbalanced Blood decides to prove that his process works by reanimating her deceased husband, Steve. When he shows Linda his handiwork, she flees in terror, calling her revivified spouse 'a creature from Hell.'

Nathan Juran, who wrote the screenplay under the name Jerry Juran, concocted *Doctor Blood's Coffin* as an American horror movie, set in and around a western gold-mining town. Juran, better known as the director of stop-motion features like *20 Million Miles to Earth* (1957) and *The 7th Voyage of Sinbad* (1958), then sold the screenplay to Canadian director Sidney J Furie, who saw immediately the potential for a low-budget assault on Hammer's horror territory. Setting up under the banner of Caralan Productions Ltd, Furie concluded his distribution deal with UA and hired James Kelly, later the director of Tigon's *Beast in the Cellar* (1970), and Peter Miller to rework the script and transfer the action to rural Cornwall.

X-Cert

Dr Blood's Coffin (Hazel Court)

Furie had never made a horror film before, but he knew where his market lay and he fashioned a film that was one of the most 'Hammer-esque' horrors since *Blood of the Vampire*. The director rams home the analogy from the opening credits—blood red, of course—and continues the theme throughout the whole film, from the suitably pounding soundtrack to a title character clearly modelled on Jimmy Sangster's view of Baron Frankenstein. This hand-me-down characterisation is most apparent with Blood's cynical disregard for human life in the cause of the greater good. 'He was no good to anyone, hanging around the pub all the time instead of making something of himself,' the doctor says. 'I am going to take this heart and put it into a dead body. I am going to give life to someone who is dead.' Like the Baron, he rages against the medical establishment that banned his experiments and drove him into exile while demanding that medical science be 'ruthless and unafraid.'

To play this ersatz Peter Cushing, Caralan engaged Irishman Kieron Moore, a good-looking actor who had been groomed for stardom by no less a luminary than Sir Alexander Korda. The Irishman peaked early with his spectacular miscasting as Vronsky opposite Vivian Leigh in *Anna Karenina* (1948), and the critical mauling that followed robbed his career of its momentum. His later performances ranged from the 'interesting but unsuccessful' to the 'perfunctory and unsuccessful'. By the time he signed for *Doctor Blood*, Moore had slipped down to supporting roles in the likes of Disney's *Darby O'Gill and the Little People* (1959).

To provide the doctor with some brief respite from the horror, Furie brought in Hazel Court, who since her earlier trip on Sewell's *Ghost Ship* had been chased by the Hammer monsters in *The Curse of Frankenstein* (1957) and *The Man Who Could Death* (1959). As nurse Linda Parker, the actress more or less carried on from where she had left off in previous efforts, providing the voice of reason, the prospect of romance and ultimately the potential victim of despicable deeds. Solid British character actor Kenneth J Warren played the policeman doggedly trying to make sense of it all, while Paul Stockman, buried under latex as the late Mr Parker, was at least offered the satisfaction of throttling his tormentor.

3: Horror and a Dash of Sex

Dr Blood's Coffin (Hazel Court, Paul Stockman)

Dr Blood's Coffin (Paul Stockman, Kieron Moore)

Behind the camera, the Hammer connection extended to special effects wizard Les Bowie and to Phillip Martell, musical supervisor on countless Hammer films. Furie also called on the services of art director Scott MacGregor, who would go on to be a regular on Hammer's horrors in the late Sixties and early Seventies, including *Scars of Dracula* (1970) and *Vampire Circus* (1972). MacGregor's contribution to *Doctor Blood's Coffin* is evidenced in its crumbling tin mines and the most successful scenes in the film are set in a series of tunnels and caverns created on the stages at Nettlefold Studios, Walton-on-Thames. It was a sign of the times for these smaller British studios that Furie's film was one of the last to be made at Nettlefold before the 60-year old film facility opened its doors for the last time to admit the property developers.

MacGregor's interiors were nicely complemented with some excellent exterior photography, shot in and around the idyllic village of Zennor, which stood in for the film's fictional Port Carron. Sidney Furie recognised the cinematic value of the rugged landscape, and the coastline has seldom been as well-served as it was here by cinematographer Stephen Dale, who counted future director Nicolas Roeg among his camera crew. Cornwall, of course, proved a particularly popular setting for genre movies, including *Night of the Eagle*, *City in the Sea* (1965) and the later *Crucible of Terror* (1971). The cinematic value of abandoned tin-mines was also recognised by one of Hammer's more stylish 'quickies', *The Plague of the Zombies* (1966), but director John Gilling had to make do with the far less evocative landscapes available in the Home Counties.

With so much expertise on both sides of the camera, one might have hoped for a more polished effort, but *Doctor Blood's Coffin* falls way short of expectations. The acting is a distinctly mixed bag. Court looks fetching in her nurse's uniform and tries her best with the sort of one-dimensional role that she could do in her sleep. When she admonishes Blood with, 'You can't let a man die so you can discover something. It doesn't matter how important it is, that is murder,' one can almost believe that she means it, which is more than can be said for Moore. The film's lead tries hard to match Cushing in conviction but despite some wide-eyed intensity, there is no real belief, and his delivery of lines like 'He's going to help me prove I can give life where there was death' is purely perfunctory. Caught by the coroner *in flagrante delicto* by removing a heart, Blood is drawn into committing increasingly desperate actions to cover for his mistakes and his character becomes increasing unstable; Moore's performance ranges from the merely twitchy to the manic, without establishing anything remotely like credibility.

For the most part, Furie seems content to allow the visuals to unfold onscreen without the need to build tension and, like the victims, the film struggles to overcome an inherent lethargy; there is simply too much talk and not enough action. The few interesting set-pieces which could have pepped things up are allowed to slide into tedium: when a victim, the curare coursing through his veins, drags himself across a hillside in an effort to escape, Furie allows the sequence to linger too long and the impact soon dissipates. The director does introduce some low-brow humour—Blood is shown having a slow, languorous look at Court's derriere—and the director was no slouch when it comes to exploiting bad taste. His camera lingers on the agonised eyes of his still-conscious victims as Blood hacks into their bodies to remove their organs. With no attempt to cut away at the crucial moment, Furie is effectively offering up an early rendition of 'torture porn'. These scenes would have been enough to get the film its X certificate from the BBFC and the fact that the censor grumbled about the climatic tussle between Dr Blood and the newly-resurrected corpse is more a tribute to Freddie Williamson's make-up than Furie's staging.

Perhaps surprisingly, UA was happy enough with the finished product to rush it into cinemas at the start of 1961, less than six months after the start of filming, though it had to endure some decidedly mixed critical reaction: 'Lacks style, suspense and imagination and will scarcely satisfy even the most naïve necrophiliac,' sniffed the *Monthly Film Bulletin*, while *Time Out* thought it a 'surprisingly grisly low budget British exploitation effort.'

In the US, where the market was now becoming flooded with low-budget horror movies, *Doctor Blood's Coffin* waited for 18 months before finally sneaking out for a handful of play-dates, and by then the UA experiment with British horror had already yielded its second effort.

THE SNAKE WOMAN
'Weird! Supernatural! Horrifying! Serpent-girl terrorises town!'

> *Dr Adderson's wife is in the advanced stages of pregnancy and fearing that she will succumb to a hereditary madness, he has been injecting her with concentrated snake venom. Unfortunately, she dies in childbirth and the midwife, Aggie, notices that the newborn girl, while appearing healthy, is icy cold and has no eyelids. Aggie announces that the baby is pure evil and incites the locals to burn the laboratory to the ground and kill the doctor. The child, subsequently named Atheris, is saved by Adderson's colleague Dr Murton and raised on the moors by a shepherd. As Atheris grows to womanhood, the country is plagued by a series of deaths, seemingly from snakebites, and a Scotland Yard detective, Charles Prentice, is sent to investigate. Prentice is immediately attracted to the beautiful woman and only when she starts to behave oddly does he realise that something is very wrong.*

The story was written by an American, Orville H Hampton, who had turned in some interesting work for Robert Lippert, including the early Hammer *noir*, *Lady in the Fog* (1952), but he also has to take responsibility for the dire horror movie *The Alligator People* in 1959. His screenplay was purchased by Caralan but having no

The Snake Woman: US theatrical poster

money left in the pot for a new writer, the chore of transplanting Hampton's original to its new English setting—Northumbria to be exact—fell to Furie. The director, still with his sights aimed well and truly at Hammer Horror, pushed the time-frame back to 1890 to cash in on the current fad for period pieces. Intended only as the lower half of a double-bill, the perfunctory re-write left *The Snake Woman* looking

3: Horror and a Dash of Sex

The Snake Woman (Susan Travers)

like it was constructed with the sole intention of making the A film look better. Production values were rock bottom, the black-and-white photography was functional at best, and even the revised script was barely able to sustain interest for more than a fraction of its already-truncated running time of 68 minutes.

While the crew were largely held over from *Doctor Blood's Coffin,* including Stephen Dale on cinematography, Antony Gibbs as editor and Phillip Martell overseeing the music, the cast was definitely a rung or two down—no room for Hammer starlets here. Amongst the relative unknowns was Susan Travers, who had a brief role in *Peeping Tom* and was promoted to star, and John McCarthy as Charles Prentice, as wooden a hero as it is possible to imagine. Arnold Marlé, who had played an octogenarian doctor in *The Man Who Could Cheat Death,* popped up as the octogenarian Doctor Murton, but even he struggles with some truly trite dialogue. 'Can you imagine the excitement,' he says flatly, 'when the scientific world learns that a cold-blooded child was born alive? It is of the utmost importance to human knowledge that your child's life be preserved at all cost!'

Dr Adderson declares that venom has been used to treat 'haemophilia, epilepsy, rheumatism, hypertension—even cancer', which may contain an element of truth but the lines are delivered so functionally by John Cazabon that the assertion sounds implausible. If the logic of administering such venom to a hysterical and very pregnant woman is hard to grasp, suspension of disbelief is rendered unattainable by lines like, 'Now, Martha, there's no sense in your carrying on like this. There's no use screaming. Let's get this over so that I can return to my work!'

In the face of improbable characterisations, the leading players simply give up and deathlessly intone their lines. The notable exception is Elsie Wagstaff, playing the aged crone Aggie, who certainly can't be accused of underperforming. She rants, raves, mutters and cackles and then launches herself into outbursts like, 'It is evil! It has the eye! It is the devil's offspring!' Wagstaff continues in this fashion more or less for the duration, which at least makes her memorable, if for all the wrong reasons. None of the other support stands out. The local villagers, when not marching torch-in-hand, are given to sitting in the pub peering suspiciously at strangers.

That *The Snake Woman* fails on every conceivable level can largely be attributed to Furie who, having set up a vaguely interesting conflict between ancient cults and Victorian sensibilities that mixes paganism, voodoo and herpetology (the study of snakes), just as quickly loses interest and resorts to a run-of-the-mill monster flick. There is some atmospheric use of locations, and every now and then some tension threatens to build, only to be negated by an illogical plot twist and leaden dialogue. If Furie had been a little more engaged, he might well have fashioned his material into something at least watchable; after all, Hammer did just that in 1966 when the basic premise was reused for *The Reptile*—but then again, that had the irrepressible John Gilling bulldozing his way through a limp script.

A trade screening prompted general sneers from the critics, including the *Daily Cinema*, which called it 'ripe horror hokum with a few well-contrived thrills...more likely to get unintentional laughs than chill spines.' *Films and Filming* scoffed that 'the producers' best hope is to offer £10,000 to the first spectator to die laughing', while the *Monthly Film Bulletin* opined, 'Set in the 1890s...direction, acting and script are all so painfully inept and primitive that the film might well date from the same period.' With *Doctor Blood's Coffin* already on the circuits, *The Snake Woman* was somewhat surplus to requirements and UA was at a loss as to what to do with it. It was briefly associated with the imported curiosity *The Split* (1959), and over the next few years, it was hauled off the shelf to make up various double-bills, including a re-release of UA's *The Vikings* (1958).

Furie survived the disaster of his first two horror films and his name attached to a number of significant films in future years, including the high-grossing poltergeist picture *The Entity* (1981). His first port of call after *The Snake Woman*, however, was a more improbable one: the Cliff Richard musical *The Young Ones* (1961).

By now, Hammer's influence on British horror pictures was all-pervading and companies which had been in business for years without showing any inclination towards the genre suddenly embraced this new wave. In June 1960, the inexhaustible Danziger brothers, Edward and Harry, abandoned their usual diet of micro-budget thrillers and threw their limited resources into a period horror picture based on the works of a certain Bostonian writer named Poe.

THE TELL-TALE HEART
'From the terrifying pages of Edgar Allen Poe!'

> Edgar Marsh, a timid Parisian librarian, lives alone except for his housekeeper and spends his evenings in an alcoholic haze looking at pornography. When he catches sight of his new neighbour, Betty Clare, undressing, he senses the opportunity to escape from his drudgery and asks his friend Carl for advice on how to court her. Edgar is totally smitten but Betty has eyes only for Carl, who out of respect for his friend offers her no encouragement—at first. When Edgar is alerted to the betrayal, he attacks Carl in a murderous rage and beats him to death with a poker, hiding the body beneath the floorboards. The police assume Carl has fled because of his gambling debts but Edgar is given little opportunity to enjoy his triumph. Tortured by guilt, he becomes obsessed with the idea that Carl's beating heart is haunting his rooms and, as his mind starts to unravel, Betty begins to suspect the truth.

The Tell-Tale Heart (Laurence Payne, Dermot Walsh)

Director Roger Corman and AIP would soon claim a virtual monopoly on screen adaptations of Poe's works but at this point, the Danzigers appeared to have a clear run at what would prove one of the most lucrative franchises in the horror film canon. *The Tell-Tale Heart*, one of Poe's best-known short stories, was published in 1843 and tells how an unnamed narrator plots and then executes a plan to murder the old man who lives in his building. The motivation for the crime is put down to revulsion of the old man, in particular his clouded 'vulture-like' eye. The body is then dismembered and hidden under the floorboards. When the police arrive to investigate the crime, the narrator is initially calm and collected, although his demeanour is soon unsettled by what he imagines to be the incessant drumming of his victim's still-beating heart.

The Tell-Tale Heart had made it to the screen on a number of previous occasions, usually as a short, and it is easy to see why the copyright-free tale with its limited scope and grisly dénouement would appeal to Danziger Productions Ltd. New York businessmen by trade, Edward J and Harry Danziger arrived in Britain in the early 1950s to make television films but they found that they could just as easily apply their

The Tell-Tale Heart (Laurence Payne / INSET: Adrienne Corri)

assembly-line principles to film production. Establishing their own production line at New Elstree Studios in Hertfordshire with a staff of some 200, the brothers churned out films with titles such as *Devil Girl from Mars* (1954), *The Depraved* (1957) and *A Woman Possessed* (1958). At their height, the Danzigers would boast that a film a month was passing through their five soundstages, but the focus was very much on quantity rather than quality. Brian Clemens, one their most productive writers, told Andrew Roberts of *The Independent*, 'I'd receive a phone-call on the Monday telling me to write a script based on twelve nuns' outfits, a nuclear submarine and a double-decker bus by Friday.' Two factors remained common to all Danziger movies: the budget was practically non-existent and what appeared on the screen was nowhere near as interesting as the title suggested.

Having decided to make a horror film, the Danzigers did not see the project as a radical departure from their usual formula; Brian Clemens was once again engaged, reworking a script by Eldon Howard, with the directorial reins handed to another regular, Ernest Morris, who had been directing their cheap-jack potboilers since 1957. The modest increase in their usual budget (averaging £15,000) was eaten up by the period setting, leaving Morris to work in the far more economical black-and-white film stock, a decision that stymied the release of the film for nearly two years and prevented it from making any serious in-roads into AIP's success. Corman's version

3: Horror and a Dash of Sex

of *The Fall of the House of Usher* opened in the States shortly after the Danzigers started in production and it was to provide AIP with a staggering box-office return on its $100,000 investment.

With so little material to draw upon in terms of plot, Clemens needed to be on inspired form to spin Poe's story into a feature film, and he almost pulls it off. The writer expands on the tale by introducing a love triangle and transforming the murder into a *crime passionnel*; he also takes the liberty of setting the film in Paris, presumably to summon vague echoes of Poe's other well-known tale, *The Murders in the Rue Morgue*. Sex is important to Clemens's story and he positively rams it into the narrative, including having Edgar gaze on Betty in her underwear—basque and stockings—the essential undergarments for British horror movie heroines; we have already watched Edgar look longingly at a prostitute and show a proclivity for dirty postcards. The writer also mixes in references to Norman Bates, both in the voyeurism and the suggestion that Edgar experienced a not entirely healthy relationship with his mother, absent and presumably dead (though this is never made clear). The least successful innovation from Clemens was a rather clumsy twist-ending which reveals the foregoing to have all been a dream—or possibly a premonition? Either way, it was more suited to one of his television productions.

There are other weaknesses with the screenplay, particularly in the early stages of the film where, unusually for a Danzigers production, the pace is too slow and the dialogue contrived. Things improve considerably as Edgar careers towards the murder; a very graphic scene for its time, which may well have elicited a stronger reaction from Trevelyan's office had Morris been able to shoot it in colour. From that point on, Morris's skill comes to the fore with a cacophony of sound underpinning Edgar's escalating paranoia, which includes dripping taps, ticking clocks and the rolling back and forth of a chess piece (the two friends played chess together).

Essentially a three-hander, Morris's film is well served by his lead performers, particularly Laurence Payne, who is excellent as the shy librarian in a fragile mental state at the beginning of the picture and a total wreck by the end. 'You know! You know, don't you?' Edgar screams, 'I can hear it, can't you? The beating of his infernal heart!' Adrienne Corri, too intelligent an actress to be shoehorned into anything as straightforward as a clichéd heroine, lends Betty a more knowing and sophisticated air than the script intended and creates a far more sexual character out of her as a result. Of the three, Dermot Walsh, who had starred for Vernon Sewell in *Ghost Ship* and countless B movies since, has the least interesting role but he also delivers an involving performance.

With such a strong sexual overtone running through the narrative, the censor's office was understandably nervous when it saw the script and Morris's visualisation of it did nothing to ease the concern. To secure their X rating, the producers had to trim shots of Edgar's pornography collection and request that Adrienne Corri's smouldering be considerably dampened down. Despite the cuts, the scenes involving sex and bloodletting, though they were not allowed to exist simultaneously in John Trevelyan's world, were still strong enough to impress the critics. *Kinematograph Weekly* said the film 'excites the imagination and steadily works up through sex and horror to a salutary and showman-like climax.'

The distributors thought Poe and sex were a sure thing at the box office and the publicity campaign was a heady mix. The pressbook and newspaper advertisements were liberally scattered with fictionalised quotes attributed to the author, including: 'He had the pale blue eyes of a vulture...so horrible, it chilled the very marrow in my bones' and 'The beat of his deathless heart...ripped into my tortured brain.' Neither line features in Poe's short story (or the film for that matter). The US poster played up the voyeurism angle with the teasing 'There in the window I saw my beloved... framed in the betraying shadow of my best friend!' And the producers also stole a gimmick from William Castle by tacking on a title-card advising squeamish patrons to look away from the screen whenever they heard the beating of a heart!

Both UK and US releases (as second-feature to *Live Now, Pay Later* in Britain but on a double-bill with *Black Zoo* in America) were held up until 1962, by which time the template for Poe had been established by Corman and it looked nothing like the Danzigers' product. As a consequence, the American press-pack was far less impressed than its British counterpart, the *New York Times* summing up the mood when it dismissed Morris's efforts as a 'terrible little British job...Poor Poe.'

In 1962, American quickie producer Robert L Lippert made a welcome return to Britain to embark on a series of films made in collaboration with UK company Parrish-McCallum Productions. Lippert had been prolific in the country a decade earlier, providing Hammer with the script, star and US distribution to make films like *Stolen Face* (1952) and *Spaceways* (1953); he was also instrumental in setting up *The Quatermass Xperiment* (1955), the company's biggest success prior to the gothic horror boom.

The Fox producer was much more than just an opportunistic financier. Born in

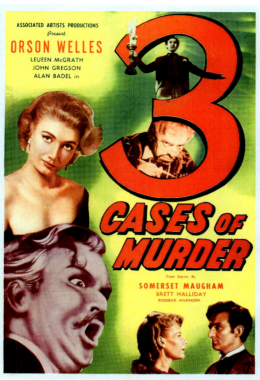

Three Cases of Murder/Grip of the Strangler - US theatrical posters

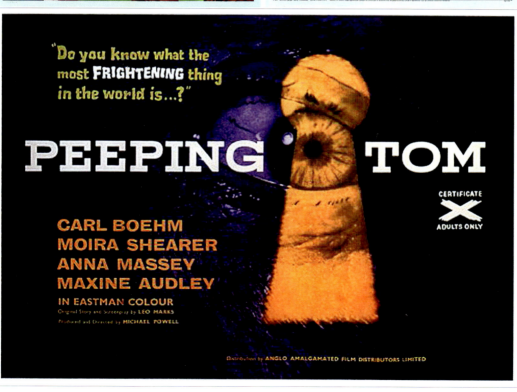

Peeping Tom - UK theatrical poster

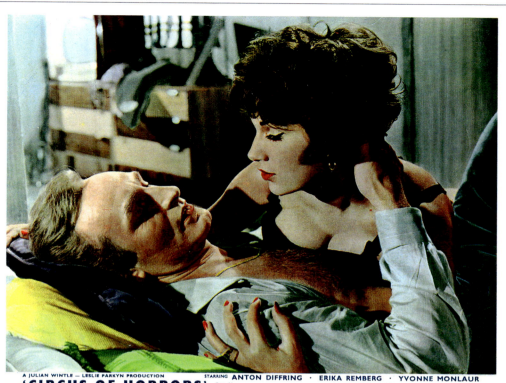

Circus of Horrors (Anton Diffring, Yvonne Romain)

Circus of Horrors (Vanda Hudson, Jack Carson)

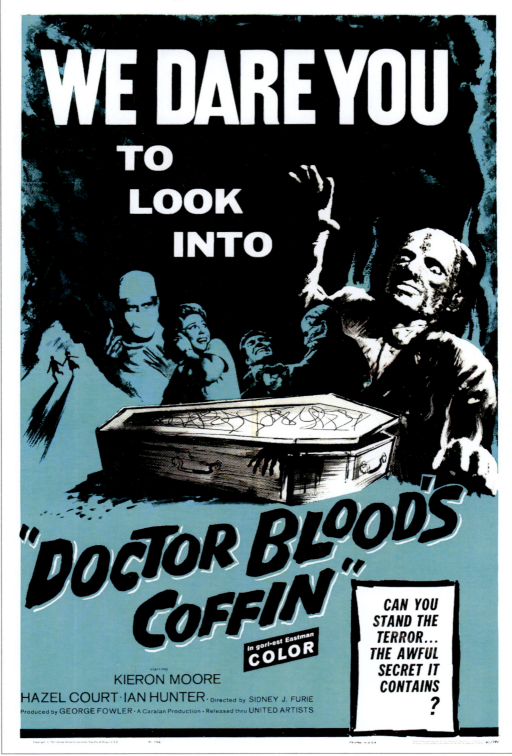

Theatre of Death (Christopher Lee)

The Frozen Dead (Dana Andrews, Anna Palk, Alan Tilvern, Edward Fox)

Berserk! (Diana Dors)

Berserk! - US theatrical poster

Trog (Geoffrey Case, John Hamill)

Incense for the Damned (Peter Cushing, Patrick Mower)

3: Horror and a Dash of Sex

California, he had developed an almost inexhaustible appetite for the film business, building and managing a chain of cinemas on the West Coast and using the profits from his exhibition empire to launch into film production. Specialising mainly in westerns and thrillers, Lippert churned out over 120 features between 1946 and 1955, an impressive achievement in numeric terms at least. It was enough to win him a long-term contract with 20th Century Fox to supply their burgeoning distribution arm with supporting features and by the early 1960s, Lippert was in a position to boast to the *Daily Cinema* that 'I've made the second most pictures in the world!'

Lippert's films rarely rose above adequate (and for many that would have been considered a stretch) but occasionally he turned out a gem, if more by luck than judgement. *The Fly* (1958) was one, a gruesomely-effective sci-fi/horror film with Vincent Price that became a solid box-office hit for Fox, spawning the inevitable sequel (*Return of the Fly*, 1959). By 1962, Lippert's operation was producing six films a year, many written by Harry Spalding, at an average cost of $100,000. When the rising production costs in California threatened to tip over his delicately-balanced financial model, the producer joined the migration of American filmmakers to Italy but his stay in Rome was short-lived and he quickly decamped for more familiar territory at Shepperton Studios. Some years later, Spalding summed up the attractions of Britain in an interview with Tom Weaver as 'the Eady Plan money', and that Lippert could rid himself 'of a good deal of the responsibilities, because English producers were basically in charge of shooting.'

In late 1963, gothic horror was once again *en vogue*; Hammer was shooting *The Evil of Frankenstein* at Bray, while over at Compton, Robert Hartford-Davis was trying to out-Gainsborough Gainsborough with *The Black Torment*. Lippert looked to be following the trend by recalling the director of many of his 1950s efforts, Terence Fisher, thought of by some to be the father of the British gothic horror film. Sadly, the inaugural feature of this new generation of Lippert films, *The Horror of It All*, was a far cry from Fisher's best work—despite the presence of such notables as Dennis Price, Valentine Dyall and Andree Melly, whose fanged appearance was a

The Horror of It All (Pat Boone)

memorable highlight of Fisher's earlier success, *The Brides of Dracula* (1960). The tagline from the British posters, 'When boy meets ghoul...it's laughs at first sight!!!' gives the game away. Fisher told the trade press, 'It's a musical-comedy, or rather a musical parody of horror films... For me it was a sort of experiment and I am not sure whether or not I did a good job with it.' The director had every reason to doubt, as this ill-conceived entry in the horror-spoof sub-genre emerged as clumsy and boring and the low spot of Fisher's career.

At the same time that Terence Fisher was putting the finishing touches to *The Horror of It All*, a British producer named Jack Parsons was also at Shepperton making *Catacombs,* a Hitchcock-style thriller directed by Gordon Hessler. Parsons's reputation was built on crime thrillers like *Strangers' Meeting* (1957) and *Model for Murder* (1959)—the latter starring Hazel Court and Michael Gough. Although he was a full-time film producer, Parsons, like Lippert, had a lucrative sideline in film exhibition and he and his wife owned a chain of seventeen cinemas scattered throughout the English provinces. The two men appeared natural allies and when Lippert established a semi-permanent production office at Shepperton, he invited Parsons to take charge.

The first outing for the new partnership was a return to more traditional horror fare and was inspired by a newspaper article that Spalding had read, outlining the attempt by a city authority to sell off a cemetery to a property company. The only proviso to the sale was the ghoulish requirement for the purchaser to exhume all the graves and relocate the remains to a new site. Re-jigging his original concept for an English setting, Spalding managed to weave the reanimated spirit of long-dead witches, blood-feuds and Devil worship into a tale of property re-development in contemporary Britain.

WITCHCRAFT
'After 300 years in the grave...they returned to wreak blood havoc!'

> *The Lanier and Whitlock families have been at each other's throats for generations, ever since the Laniers convicted Vanessa Whitlock of witchcraft and had her buried alive. Three centuries later, the Laniers have bought the Whitlock cemetery with the intention of redeveloping the land into a housing estate. Against the wishes of their respective families, Amy Whitlock and Bill Lanier have fallen in love but their union holds no prospect of reconciliation between the feuding families. Morgan Whitlock, the patriarch of the clan and Amy's father, is particularly outspoken in his hostility to the Laniers. Morgan intends to summon up the forces of the 'old religion' and avenge himself on the hated Laniers. He gets his opportunity when the bulldozers dislodge Vanessa's grave and free the witch to walk the earth once more.*

The 1960s' love affair with urban renewal may have provided the starting point for Spalding's tale, but any social comment was pushed firmly into the background of what amounts to a hillbilly-style family feud but with witchcraft instead of shotguns. With the Shepperton soundstages booked for a shooting schedule of thirteen days, Don Sharp, who had helmed Hammer's well-regarded *The Kiss of the Vampire*, was brought in to direct. On paper Sharp was allocated nearly double the regular Lippert schedule of seven days, but the director would struggle to shoot even this relatively modest film on time. Part of the problem lay with the British crews who were subject to stricter union rules than their American counterparts and stuck rigidly to more structured working days. Even then, as a number of Hollywood filmmakers found, the British were slower at setting up than their US colleagues. Roger Corman, who

Witchcraft (Yvette Rees)

Witchcraft (David Warbeck, Diane Clare, Lon Chaney Jr)

was working for AIP in Britain around the same time, estimated that twenty days production in England was the equivalent of fifteen days in the States.

Shooting under the title *Witch and Warlock,* Sharp was allowed the luxury of a day's filming at Oakley Court, the country house on the banks of the Thames that provided Hammer's studios next door with one of its favourite locations. The 19th-century gothic folly-style architecture of the Court was seldom seen in either daylight or a contemporary setting, but it is rather wasted in some throwaway shots which could have been filmed almost anywhere.

This day trip aside, the cast and crew were based at Shepperton, a studio in crisis at the time. Having been among the busiest in Britain, Shepperton's soundstages had been empty for the two months prior to Don Sharp's arrival. The parent company, British Lion, had experienced a rollercoaster ride of boom-and-near-bust for years and by the time that *Witchcraft* made it into cinemas, the company would be on the brink of financial collapse. In the meantime the management, desperate to impose austerity measures, was facing off against unions equally desperate to resist; the archaic work practices remained in place but morale around the studio floor was at rock bottom.

If working in such an environment was not stressful enough, Sharp's difficulties were exacerbated by Lippert's decision to cast a genuine horror heavyweight, Lon Chaney Jr, in the role of Morgan, the warlock so violently opposed to the new housing development. Chaney, the son of the silent movie legend, had achieved something approaching screen immortality with the title role in the popular Universal horror picture *The Wolf Man* (1941), but the almost unbroken run of second-rate vehicles that followed gradually eroded his star-status. To squeeze value from its contract, Universal kept the actor busy and when there were no horror films available, and he was pushed into whatever B western happened to be shooting on the lot. Bitter

3: Horror and a Dash of Sex

Witchcraft (Diane Clare, Lon Chaney Jr)

over the treatment he had received and unable to shake off the shadow of his famous father, Chaney started drinking and soon acquired a reputation for being 'difficult' on set. When Universal declined to renew his contract, he struggled to get roles even in the cheapest horrors. Over the years, the marquee value of his name diminished but was never quite extinguished; AIP shoehorned him into *The Haunted Palace* (1963) opposite Vincent Price, but it failed to spark a career revival and talk of a contract was quietly forgotten. Spying an opportunity, Lippert stepped in, paying him a pittance for five days work, and despatched Chaney to London for what was effectively a cameo role. As Sharp discovered, the actor came with a lot of emotional baggage. 'He did drink a lot,' the director told Chaney biographer Don G Smith, 'but he was a very lonely man. He was such a nice man; kind, friendly. He was almost grateful when someone would spend ten minutes talking with him...I didn't know what happened in his life, but he was terribly lonely.'

In order to accommodate Chaney's difficulties, the script was altered to keep the actor to the periphery of the action; entering a scene, barking at his co-stars and then exiting with unseemly haste. Sharp could rework the schedule to ensure that Chaney's scenes were shot in the forenoon when he was still *compos mentis* but there was little opportunity to indulge in retakes to get things perfect and most of these scenes have the look and feel of a dress-rehearsal. The actor himself, appearing bloated and puffy-eyed, delivers a bombastic performance, making up in volume what he lacks in screen time.

By contrast, Jack Hedley gave Bill Lanier a solidity lacking in Spalding's lightly-sketched character. An ex-Royal Marine who turned professional actor in the early 1950s, Hedley became a popular star in the BBC television series *The World of Tim Frazer*, going on to become a jobbing actor, playing heroic or authority figures in any number of films, including *The Crimson Blade* (1963). The cast also included

Diane Clare, playing—with no real conviction—the lovesick Amy Whitlock. She is perhaps best remembered for *The Plague of the Zombies* (1966) and would become something of a fixture in low-budget horror movies of the period. Prominent among the supporting players was Welsh-born actress Yvette Rees who played the striking (but seemingly mute) Vanessa, the visual appearance of whom looked to have been inspired by horror icon Barbara Steele's long-dead witch in Mario Bava's *Mask of the Demon* (1960).

Onscreen, the cast take the whole thing as seriously as one might expect, but there is something distinctly unsettling about the great bear that is Chaney crashing into a sitting room where a contingent of very English character actors are taking tea and hollering at them in his distinctive Californian accent. The film's problems do not lie only with the performances—Spalding's script also plays fast and loose with trivialities like logic and plotting, which left its director struggling valiantly to rise above his material. In at least a couple of sequences, Sharp manages to suggest a better film trying to get out—one of which has Vanessa, funeral-shroud billowing, picking her way through the broken gravestones of a rain-soaked cemetery. Other highlights include Tracey's moonlight walk into the clutches of the coven and the aged and crippled Helen alone and stalked by Vanessa. The film's fiery climax is also well-staged, with the filmmakers purchasing and then destroying a house already scheduled for demolition. But despite these teasing hints, nothing more meaningful emerges and *Witchcraft* remains an interesting but minor effort.

To promote the film, Lippert took the unusual step of tying the fictional theme to genuine witchcraft practices. Claiming that England alone had as many as 30,000 practicing witches, he wheeled out occult expert TC Lethbridge, author of the book *Witches*, to endorse the feature: 'The Witch cult still survives as an organised belief today. I have talked to numerous members of witches' covens,' the writer insisted. The makers of *Rosemary's Baby* would play this 'authenticity card' to perfection in 1968 but for a film like *Witchcraft*, it seemed a preposterous assertion, not helped by the inclusion in the US screenings of 'witch deflectors'. Mr Lethbridge's view on how these one-inch diameter polystyrene buttons, decorated with skull and crossbones, might protect viewers from the 'the eerie web of the unknown' is not recorded.

Nevertheless, the witch deflector, or perhaps the witch expert, seemed to work their magic. The *Variety* critic certainly seemed to be under a spell when he praised the 'eerie music, low-key photography, competent acting and a gimmick-filled plot,' then went on to assert that *Witchcraft* was a 'good example of its kind...and should attract audiences addicted to horror films.'

By now, the Lippert/Parsons operation was hitting its stride. While Bob Lippert criss-crossed the Atlantic to keep an eye on his American businesses, track down properties and identify stars to send to London, the day-to-day production chores were delegated to Parsons. Stanley Morgan, who appeared in two of these Lippert films, remembers Parsons as a 'somewhat Hitchcockian figure, though less rotund; a very easy-going producer and thoroughly nice man who exuded quiet authority but never, to my knowledge, contributed anything but positive, paternal interest to the atmosphere on set.' Parsons himself seemed to accept his role as Lippert's 'man on the ground' somewhat reluctantly, telling *Kinematograph Weekly* that he preferred the business side to line production. 'If you spend too much time in the studio you get out of touch with the world and over concerned with artistic matters—lighting, camera angles and so on.'

For their next outing, the partners decided to recall Terence Fisher, even though he had floundered so badly on *The Horror of It All,* with the offer of a science-fiction horror film which held out an opportunity to explore more challenging territory.

3: Horror and a Dash of Sex

THE EARTH DIES SCREAMING
'Who...or what were they...who tried to wipe all the living creatures off the face of the Earth?'

> The streets of Britain are devoid of human life, cars are abandoned and bodies are strewn everywhere. Only a few have survived including Jeff Nolan, an experimental test pilot, Taggart and his 'wife' Peggy, and Mel and pregnant girlfriend Lorna. When the group is attacked by robotic creatures, they flee to an inn to consider their plan of action. They discover to their horror that the robots are capable of taking over the dead bodies of their victims and using the animated corpses to attack the survivors. Conflict within the group grows as Taggart insists that they need to flee while they can but both Jeff and Mel want to launch their own attack and destroy a transmitting station that seems to control the robots. Taggart flees while the others mount their attack, but they are forced to leave behind Lorna who is in labour. When the robots return, Lorna is trapped in the inn with a newborn baby and no way to escape.

Promoting his British pictures to the *Kinematograph Weekly*, Lippert boasted, 'I make what we call commercial pictures; they're low-cost pictures but every so often one of them becomes a big picture. We're producing this picture on a modest budget but giving it quality. We'll take advantage of anything they leave lying around.' This philosophy of reuse could certainly be applied to Harry Spalding's script, which had a distinct sense of the familiar about it. The writer had dabbled in this territory before with *The Day Mars Invaded Earth* (1963), which has invisible aliens infiltrating the bodies of unsuspecting earthlings as the prelude to a full-blown invasion. *The Earth Dies Screaming* took this premise to the next step and postulates what would happen to humanity if that invasion had actually taken place. Spalding's basic premise is intriguing but the writer adds nothing that had not already been seen in numerous

The Earth Dies Screaming (Vanda Godsell, Virginia Field)

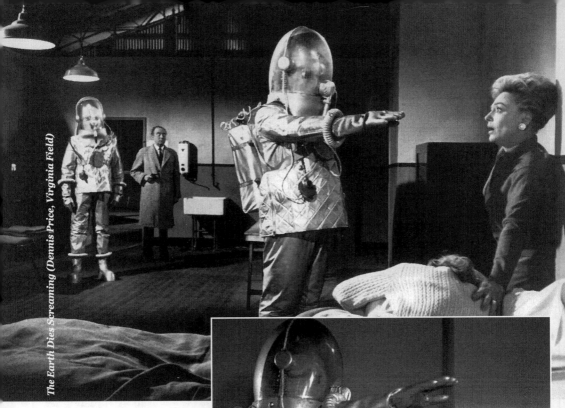

The Earth Dies Screaming (Dennis Price, Virginia Field)

previous genre pieces, thereby placing the weight of fashioning something more worthwhile out of the material once again onto the shoulders of the cast and director.

Topping the cast-list was an ageing Willard Parker, the action star of countless B westerns who had worked for Lippert in *The Great Jessie James Raid* (1953), as well as the more recent and less successful *Air Patrol* (1962). As part of his deal with Parker, Lippert secured the actor's wife, Virginia Field, to play his onscreen love interest, the one and only time the couple appeared on screen together. The British-born actress had at one time been under contract to David O Selznick and although she never became a major star, she had featured in a number of significant films including *Waterloo Bridge* (1940). By 1963, the screen careers of both Parker and Field were in terminal decline and they would soon give up acting entirely to pursue other interests. Sadly, the opportunity for a last hurrah did nothing to motivate the players and neither contributed anything more than a perfunctory performance. In fairness to Parker, he was at least ten years too old to pull off a convincing 'Boys Own adventure' type hero and Field was saddled with a badly underwritten role that left her with nothing to do beyond look bemused in a Joan Crawford hairstyle.

Given the freedom to fill the supporting cast from the ranks of British character actors, Terence Fisher engaged one of his favourite performers, the permanently-befuddled Thorley Walters, who had just featured for the director as Dr Watson in

3: Horror and a Dash of Sex

The Earth Dies Screaming (Virginia Field, Willard Parker)

Sherlock Holmes and the Deadly Necklace (1962) and who played to type here as the bumbling drunk, Edgar. Vanda Godsell played Violet, with relative newcomers David Spenser and Anna Palk as the young lovers. Pick of the bunch was undoubtedly Dennis Price, one of the few to emerge from *The Horror of It All* with his dignity intact, who played Taggart, a self-serving opportunist vying with alpha-male Jeff for the leading lady's attentions.

Even in his gothic horror pictures, Fisher always seemed more interested in the human drama than shocks, and the early sequences with civilisation—and civilised behaviour—collapsing show the director at his most engaged. Overcoming the twin handicaps of poorly-edited stock footage and robots that would have been laughed at in kiddie-matinees, Fisher uses his disparate group of survivors to paint a sombre and disturbing picture of a world in meltdown. 'Whoever did it has won the war,' says Taggart balefully. 'All they have to do is move in and take over.' Taggart then turns his vitriol on Jeff, deriding his attempts to bring organisation and leadership to the group: 'There aren't any rules; there isn't any order,' he sneers. 'We can make any world we like.' These sequences, which contrast the external threat with internal friction, are played out in the claustrophobic atmosphere of an abandoned hotel—a standing set at Shepperton. The moral ambiguities raised lend Spalding's script a layer of complexity that is usually lacking in films of this type, and the relationship between Taggart and Peggy is particularly intriguing: 'You and I made a bargain,' he says without further elaboration, clearly regarding the woman as some kind of possession and casually issuing orders to her; later, abducting her at gunpoint.

Away from the tensions between Jeff, Peggy and Taggart, Spalding's writing slips back into cliché and all of the characters can easily be summed up in single words: 'hero', 'girlfriend' etc. Fisher recaptures some of his old form with the first appearance of the now-undead Violet, and he even manages to generate suspense when the painfully slow-moving zombies trap Peggy. Unfortunately, the film starts to fall apart after the disappearance of Taggart and our heroes decide to mount an attack on a radio-mast. Suddenly, Fisher is directing—with no great conviction—an action movie. The carefully established atmosphere is lost among the poorly-staged gung-ho stunts and even the well signposted but chilling reappearance of Taggart fails to get things back on track.

Few critics bothered to see the film but those who did tended to side with the *Kinematograph Weekly's* dismissive 'juvenile nonsense.' Suggestions by subsequent reviewers that *The Earth Dies Screaming* was an influence on George Romero's *Night of the Living Dead* can be dismissed, despite a few superficial similarities.

Critical failure was hardly new to Lippert's operations and the production line was soon in full flow with a re-working of the producer's greatest success, *The Fly*. Once again Jack Parsons was left to oversee what would prove to be the third and last screen outing for the Delambre family, with Don Sharp again asked to craft the proverbial silk purse out of Harry Spalding's sow's ear of a script.

CURSE OF THE FLY
'What made them half-human creatures from the fourth dimension?'

> For three generations, the Delambres have experimented with teleportation and they have finally succeeded in teleporting human beings between their laboratories in Canada and London. Martin Delambre, the eldest son, meets and falls in love with Patricia Stanley, a fugitive from a mental institution. To evade the authorities, he brings her to his father Henri's house. Unbeknown to Patricia, the victims of the family's previous experiments, now reduced to a half-human state, are being kept in cells in the gardens. The police are anxious to return Patricia to the 'safety' of the asylum and start to investigate the Delambres' activities in more detail. Henri plots to escape to his youngest son Albert's lab in London using the teleporter, but things do not go to plan. Henri's atoms become lost in the fourth dimension, while Martin's unstable metabolism also starts to unwind. It is left to Albert Delambre to try to save what remains of the family.

George Langelaan's original short story, which first surfaced in *Playboy* magazine in 1957, was set in France and concerned the attempts by Andre Delambre to transport living matter using a 'disintegrator-reintegrator'—with tragic and grotesque results. Lippert had co-produced the 1958 film version under Fox's own banner, with Kurt Neumann directing and Vincent Price starring—not as the misguided scientist but as his brother Francois. The superior cast, better script and far larger budget than usual (circa £175,000) rewarded Lippert with a rare mainstream box-office success, which in turn ensured a sequel the following year. Price returned and Lippert took a back seat and left the production chores to Bernard Glasser, but with significantly less resources and a budget hacked by nearly two-thirds, *The Return of the Fly* (1959) had all the hallmarks of a poorly-organised cash-in.

Given the length of time between the first and second sequels, one might have hoped for a more considered approach and certainly Harry Spalding had aimed high and fashioned a protagonist in the image of Claude Rains. The writer later claimed that the producers had the veteran scene-stealer of films like *Casablanca* (1942) and *Notorious* (1946) in their sights for Henri Delambre, and the septuagenarian actor would have invested Delambre senior with an appropriate air of faded elegance and charm. But Lippert's funding model would have discounted Rains, even if the actor had been attracted to the role, and when the cast list was eventually announced, it included the more economical figure of Brian Donlevy.

Irish-born but a star in Hollywood since the 1930s, Donlevy's first trip to Britain was in 1938 to appear in the Gracie Fields vehicle *We're Going to be Rich*, but the

3: Horror and a Dash of Sex

Curse of the Fly (Brian Donlevy, Carole Gray)

former Fox contract star made his most memorable contribution to British cinema in 1955, when Lippert exported him to play rocket scientist Bernard Quatermass in *The Quatermass Xperiment* (1955). By then he could count over 75 films, numerous radio shows and an Oscar nomination (for *Beau Geste* in 1939) on his CV. Generally cast in the role of a hard-drinking, hard-talking tough guy, Donlevy was mocked in some quarters over his expanding girth, dentures and toupee, but he remained a household name throughout his long career, albeit in decreasingly-worthwhile films. Soon after appearing in *Curse of the Fly*, he furnished the dreaded AIP cameo for something called *How to Stuff a Wild Bikini* (1965), after which his career petered out and he died in 1972.

The supporting players all reflected Lippert's budgetary constraints, although they did include a genuine aristocrat and a former matinee idol among them. Rachel Kempson, aka Lady Redgrave, making a rare film appearance as Madame Fournier, the supervisor of the asylum, gets to adopt a convincing French accent in lieu of a characterisation. Fournier's chief value is to shed some light on Patricia's dubious past and to initiate the police inquiries into her new benefactors. Patricia, the latest recruit to the Delambre family, was played by West End stage-star Carole Gray, who was introduced to the press as a 'singer, ballerina, professional ballroom dancer, musical comedy star and straight actress'. The South African actress opened the film in eye-catching but preposterous fashion by escaping from a lunatic asylum in slow motion, clad only in designer bra and panties. The understandably-smitten Martin Delambre was played by George Baker, who had enjoyed a passing brush with fame in the 1950s as the swashbuckling star of *The Moonraker*, subsequently spending the rest of his career in conventional leading men roles. Further down the cast list was *Witchcraft*'s Yvette Rees as Tai, the spiteful housekeeper with a grudge against the new mistress; unfortunately, Rees's performance is undermined by some quite awful 'oriental' make-up and her own clipped delivery. Tai's on-screen husband, Wan, a sort of butler-cum-lab assistant is played by Burt Kwouk, and this lame Tai/Wan joke is the closest Spalding comes to wit.

The script on the whole is weak, bordering on nonsense. The central premise—scientists pushing at the boundaries in the name of humankind, irrespective of the consequences—is as old as cinema, but rarely has it been done with less conviction. When Henri, who has been complicit in the most heinous of crimes, declares, 'I am not some kind of monster, I am doing this because this machine could be a great and wonderful gift', it is almost a laugh-out-loud moment. Equally absurd is Martin, knowingly engaged in immoral and illegal activities, blithely marrying a woman he has bumped into while she was running semi-naked through the woods. 'I'm sorry, it's none of my business,' he says, and the subject is never mentioned again. In the blink of an eye, he has booked her into his hotel, lent her some money and, after a long walk in Black Park, popped the question—all this in the knowledge that he is already married to a woman who is locked in a cell and in a state of cellular mutation! If that was not enough, Martin, having inheriting his grandfather's genes, has the limited life-cycle of a tiny insect and is dependent on regular injections to prevent sudden ageing and gruesome death. Thrust into this bizarre concoction is a slice of Daphne Du Maurier's *Rebecca*, wherein the housekeeper, out of some sense of misguided devotion, tries to drive the present Mrs Delambre insane.

That *Curse of the Fly* remains among the more entertaining of Lippert's later films is almost entirely due to the direction of Don Sharp. From the opening scene of a window exploding outwards in slow motion, he establishes a mood of the surreal that makes the film if not credible, at least watchable. Nothing much can be done with the laboratory scenes, which are perfunctory at best, replete with the expected arrays of equipment, lots of flashing lights and flickering guages, but in which none of the scientific byplay makes any sense whatever. But Sharp is far more comfortable with Patricia's midnight prowling through the sprawling Delambre estate. Through a clever use of shadows and sound—thunder rumbling off in the distance and wind whistling through the trees—the director creates an atmosphere of ominous dread. Add in a haunting piano, familial secrets and a glut of locked doors, and Sharp has turned a clichéd science-fiction pot-boiler into Gainsborough gothic! Basil Emmott's excellent cinematography and the eerie music of Bert Shefter underscore the mood to perfection.

On the downside, the production values are not high, the make-up is particularly poor and the performances are mixed. Carole Gray, when she is allowed to put on some clothes, gives a reasonable account of herself as the vulnerable and troubled Patricia; George Baker, on the other hand, is wooden and charmless, and he takes a curiously detached view of the family's previous failed experiments—particularly when Patricia stumbles into the cells by accident and Martin says to her blandly, 'I hoped you wouldn't go there. I meant to warn you.' The victims, including his first wife, are then dismissed as 'animals; part of a research experiment'. Brian Donlevy is even less convincing. He hits his marks and avoids bumping into the scenery but his performance is robotic and his delivery pedestrian. When Patricia, on the point of hysteria, informs him that she has seen a nightmarish 'woman-thing', he replies, 'There's nothing like that in our house. You better pull yourself together.' Nor is there any sign in either Albert or Martin of the madness that has supposedly gripped successive generations of the family; when Donlevy decides to teleport the victims to London, aware that their bodies might fuse together, he dismisses protests with a casual, 'We're scientists—we have to do things we hate, that even sicken us.'

Only Henri's youngest son, Albert (Michael Graham), shows any humanity and when he is confronted by the pulsating mass that arrives in his teleporter, he looks suitably nauseous as he reaches for an axe. The killing is conducted off-screen but the sight of the merged bodies was too much for the censor, even with an X certificate, and he insisted that the scene be trimmed to all but the briefest of shots.

Released in the US in 1965 on a double-bill with another British film, *Devils of*

Curse of the Fly (Carole Gray / INSET: Stan Simmons, Mary Manson)

Darkness, and with a typically hyperbolic tagline—'The Screen's Great Scream-and-Fright Show!'—it nevertheless failed to incite much interest among filmgoers. The film's British release, held up until 1966, was also poorly received and generated some withering commentary from the critics. The *Kinematograph Weekly* thought it had 'some moments of suspense and excitement' but summed the picture up as 'mediocre', a view endorsed by the *Daily Cinema* which at least praised Don Sharp's 'deft way with interesting shock effects'. The lame box-office performance on both sides of the Atlantic effectively ended the on-screen saga of the Delambre family. In 1986, the franchise was revived by David Cronenberg in a big-budget, effects-laden epic that shared its title but little else with Lippert's films.

Lippert and Parsons's British operation found that it was enjoying more success with thrillers such as *Night Train to Paris* (1964), an espionage yarn starring Leslie Nielsen, and the relative failure of *The Earth Dies Screaming* and *Curse of the Fly* signalled a move away from horror pictures. The duo made a half-hearted attempt to revive another dormant Fox franchise with *The Return of Mr Moto* (1965), in which Henry Silva replaced Peter Lorre as the second-rate Charlie Chan. Then they took a stab at science fiction with *Spaceflight IC-1* (1965) before returning to thrillers with Sidney Salkow's T*he Murder Game* (1965), which marked the end of Lippert's contract with Fox after ten years and over 120 films, taking his career-total to over 240. Still in his mid-fifties, Lippert was in no mood to retire and although he still dabbled in film production, he devoted most of his time to his exhibition business, including the building of what is generally accepted to be the first multiplex in the US. Jack Parsons made only one more film, *The Last Shot You Hear* (1968), directed by Gordon Hessler and partly financed by Lippert, which turned out to be a ham-fisted Hitchcock lookalike, hardly worth the time and effort involved.

While Lippert was establishing his home from home at Shepperton, another survivor from the 1950s was checking into Merton Park Studios to start work on *his* latest horror film. Richard Gordon was back in England to make his first film since the relative disappointment of *Corridors of Blood*; he brought with him a script that had been acquired five years earlier for Amalgamated Productions but was now the vehicle by which he was to launch Gordon Films Inc as a production entity.

DEVIL DOLL
'The devil doll—It walks. It talks. It kills.'

> The Great Vorelli's hypnotism/ventriloquism act is the talk of London, but there is something unsettling about his performances: the dummy, Hugo, seems almost too real. American journalist Mark English is determined to expose what he believes is a clever charade and takes his fiancée Marianne to see the show. Marianne is hypnotised by Vorelli and later forced to invite him to a charity ball, where he uses his powers to seduce her. Soon afterwards she falls into a trance. That same night, Mark is visited by Hugo who pleads, 'Help me. Find me—in Berlin, 1948. Find me'. A subsequent search into Vorelli's past convinces Mark that the hypnotist performed an obscene experiment on his assistant years before and transferred his spirit into the body of the dummy. Marianne, unable to resist the hypnotist's will, calls off her engagement to Mark and announces that she will marry Vorelli instead. It is then that 'Hugo' decides to take matters into his own hands.

Frederick E Smith's story first appeared in the *London Mystery Magazine* under the title of *The Devil Doll*, where it caught the eye of John Croydon, then on the lookout for new properties for Amalgamated Productions. The story is often linked to the famous ventriloquist sequence in *Dead of Night* (1945), which also featured a dummy called Hugo, but the author shied away from the suggestion that he was

3: Horror and a Dash of Sex

influenced by the Ealing picture. Croydon, on the other hand, almost certainly was—according to Richard Gordon: 'John had been a producer on *Dead of Night* and I am sure it was that connection that attracted him to the story in the first instance.' Of course, the premise of ventriloquism had been unsettling cinemagoers for decades, as Gordon recollected, 'I had seen *The Great Gabbo* and I always had an interest in ventriloquism as a suitable subject for a horror film. I had also seen a Lon Chaney film called *The Unholy Three* which also dealt with the subject, so I was very pleased when John came up with the project.' The story's author was not involved in any of the negotiations: *London Mystery Magazine* had contracted for all subsidiary rights, so Smith was unaware that the film had even been made until it turned up at his local cinema!

A first-draft script had been written in 1957 by Gil Winfield, who had appeared in *Fiend Without a Face*, and it was later refined by Ronald Kinnoch, who had been the production manager on *Fiend* and who wrote under the name of George Barclay. Kinnoch was also slated to direct the film while Chuck Vetters wrote a third draft under his Lance Z Hargreaves pseudonym. By then, the title had lost the definite article to become merely *Devil Doll*, thereby avoiding confusion with M-G-M's Tod Browning/Lionel Barrymore picture of 1934, *The Devil Doll*—even though that had nothing whatever to do with ventriloquism.

The demise of Amalgamated Productions had put *Devil Doll* on the back burner, but Richard Gordon retained the rights and early in 1963, he was ready to re-launch the project. After his earlier dealings with M-G-M, Gordon was understandably shy of involving another Hollywood major so he approached his friend Ken Rive of Gala Film Distributors, a small UK outfit that specialised in art-house films, including the works of Ingmar Bergman, Federico Fellini and François Truffaut. Rive was eager to move into film production and he had established Galaworld Film Productions to carry his ambitions forward; *Devil Doll* would now be the first under this banner, with parent company Gala distributing it in the UK. Rive's partner in Galaworld

Devil Doll: US lobby card

Devil Doll (Bryant Haliday)

was Sidney J Furie, the director of *Doctor Blood's Coffin*, who also signed on to direct the film.

Financial contributions from Gordon Films Inc, Galaworld and the NFFC still did not quite meet the budgetary requirements for a full four-week shedule, but the final element of the package fell into place when Gordon signed his star performer. 'We couldn't afford a big star to play Vorelli,' Gordon says, 'but I knew an actor called Bryant Haliday personally and had seen some of the films he had made in France. I knew he was very keen to act in English language films and when *Devil Doll* came along, I thought he would be ideal and he was very keen to do it.' Haliday was so committed to the project that he not only volunteered to put up his own portion of the budget but he also agreed to defer his salary in exchange for a percentage participation in the profits.

Bryant could not be termed a conventional leading man; he was a classics scholar who taught Latin and Greek and trained for the priesthood before studying law at Harvard, where he developed an interest in the performing arts. After a flirtation with his own stage troupe, he established a film distribution company serving the US art-house circuit, which brought him into regular contact with Messrs Gordon and Rive.

Opposite Haliday, Furie cast William Sylvester, an American-born actor who had arrived in Britain in the late 1940s and appeared on stage at the Old Vic and in a number of films including *Gorgo* (1960). Sylvester's contract guaranteed him top billing in the UK, with Haliday enjoying the same status in the US. Gordon recruited two of his favourite performers from *Corridors of Blood*, Francis de Wolfe

3: Horror and a Dash of Sex

as the kindly Dr Keisling and Yvonne Romain, who had since made appearances in *Circus of Horrors* and Hammer's *The Curse of the Werewolf*, where her Latin looks were ideally suited to the role of a Spanish servant girl. Another decorative part had followed for Hammer in the less gruesome *Captain Clegg*, before Richard Gordon called to offer her the part of sexy socialite Marianne Horn.

Also in the cast was former pin-up girl Sandra Dorne, as Vorelli's past-her-prime assistant Magda, who dotes on her employer but is treated with barely-concealed contempt. Dorne's generously-proportioned frame and platinum blonde mane had enlivened a number of British B pictures in the 1950s, but her career had faded as she approached middle age and by the time she came to make *Devil Doll*, Gordon was one of the few to remember her earlier outings.

Having overseen preproduction, Sidney Furie found himself in something of a dilemma. The director had been offered the reins of Rank's *The Ipcress File* (1965), the film that would confirm Michael Caine as a major box-office star, and although he could still have accommodated *Devil Doll* in his schedule, he was understandably reticent to become too closely associated with another low-budget effort on the eve of starting such a crucial film. Furie offered Gordon a ready-made replacement in the shape of fellow Canadian Lindsay Shonteff, whom he had met while working in Canada. When Shonteff struggled to find work in North America Furie invited him to London with a promise to help out. 'Sid did just that,' Shonteff told Allan Bryce in *The Dark Side*. 'It took maybe six or seven months of knocking around in cheap hotel rooms but when you are young it's no problem. In fact it's quite enjoyable.' *Devil Doll* represented the breakthrough that Shonteff was looking for, though his mentor did not entirely fade into the background. 'Sidney didn't want his name on it,' Richard Gordon explains, 'Which is understandable. But he oversaw the film as much as he could and he kept an eye on Shonteff, who was making his first film in England. The finished film was very much Lindsay's work though.'

By now, even the lowest budget horror films were being shot on colour stock and monochrome was only being used for *Psycho*-style thrillers or art films. Shonteff's budget stretched to nowhere near that required for colour, so the fledgling director had to make a virtue out of the constraint. The sequences with Vorelli performing in the theatre illustrate just how successful he was, with the unseen audience hidden by a smoke-filled gloom which engenders a cold and unsettling quality in keeping with the general tenor of the script. The director extenuates the strangeness of the place by employing extreme close-ups and low angles (the former also helped the exploitation aspect, with frequent close-ups of the buxom Ms Romain's enthusiastic gyrating in a low-cut blouse). Shonteff also enjoyed a piece of serendipity here by finding the Metropolitan Theatre on the Edgware Road unused and scheduled for demolition. Gordon had fond memories of the theatre from seeing Tod Slaughter perform there during the 1940s and although it was empty, the building was still in a reasonable state of repair. As the last residents before the bulldozers moved in, Gordon's crew used not only the stage but also the dressing rooms and interiors to provide authentic locations for their film.

All told, it was a remarkably confident effort for a tyro filmmaker, with Shonteff not afraid to experiment and employ negative imagery and freeze-frames to create a genuinely jarring effect. Not all of the director's ideas worked so well, however; after some 75 minutes of running time in conventional mode, for example, he suddenly introduces a wholly inappropriate voiceover to articulate the thoughts of the hero! For the most part, Shonteff succeeds in creating a disquieting feel to the film and this mood is reinforced on the soundtrack, which features a pulsating rhythm that came about by chance when the producers realised that they did not have the funds available to pay for a musical score and had instead to fall back on that old standby, the music library. The uncredited tracks that Shonteff cobbled together at random add considerably to the power and intensity of the film's shock sequences.

The director's handling of the cast is less polished. William Sylvester is competent enough as the square-jawed Mark but he essays the role with a detachment bordering on disinterest. The girls, in the main, were hired for their looks rather than their talent and Romain is the only one who is given anything remotely challenging to do, though even she displays little of the promise of *Corridors of Blood*. As far as the acting is concerned, the real success is Bryant Haliday, who creates a disconcerting screen persona ideally suited to Vorelli. He is effortlessly frightening when berating Hugo: 'You've been in your little wooden body so long, you've become an individual again,' he says with sadistic relish. 'I think I must teach you a little lesson.' But the real coup was in being equally as chilling when not being overtly threatening. 'Hugo, she said you were ugly,' he purrs through the bars of the cage, egging the dummy on to do mischief to his inconvenient assistant. Moments later, with a murderous glint in his glass eyes, the little fella appears next to Magda, who is reclining on the chaise longue. 'I shall miss her in many ways,' Vorelli sighs.

Shonteff also deserves credit for the fact that Hugo the dummy emerges as a character in its own right. With its regulation fixed grin, Hugo starts off as menacing but then becomes sympathetic to the point where it is almost like watching a caged child being tormented by a sadistic adult. Hugo was in fact played by a female circus midget, Sadie Corre, who went on to enjoy a career in cinema ranging from *Chitty Chitty Bang Bang* (1968) to *Return of the Jedi* (1983).

Wisely, the script avoids too much analysis of how Vorelli managed to achieve his devilish feat. 'I tell you he has robbed this man's soul. I don't know how,' Mark says, before adding, 'I can't give you any scientific explanations but I tell you that's what's happened.' The climactic battle between the diminutive Hugo and his tormentor, a rapid-cut melee of flailing arms and grimaces, was shot using a hand-held camera and is both bizarre and effective. It is a considerable improvement on the scene as scripted, which envisaged a set-to across the stage, ending with Vorelli's fall from the gantry and the real Hugo, who has lain comatose in a Berlin hospital, suddenly reviving. The new ending was much closer to Smith's original concept and allowed Shonteff one last turn of the screw: a close up of Hugo overlaid with Vorelli's plea to 'Get me out of here!—I am the great Vorelli!'

In Gordon's previous films, hero and heroine had to content themselves with meaningful looks or a chaste kiss, but with cinema starting to mirror the increasingly liberated views of society at large, Shonteff felt free to introduce all manner of saucy behaviour, including Mark and Marianne engaging in passionate love-making in the front seat of his car. The location of this coupling attaches a vague suggestion of casual promiscuity to Marianne, but it was entirely dictated by a budget that did not allow for a bedroom set! These scenes, relatively tame as they are today, quite vexed the British censor who insisted that they were trimmed before he granted the film an X certificate. Shonteff turns a good deal more coy later in the film when Marianne is 'summoned' from her bed by Vorelli and she is dressed a nightgown that would have been acceptable to any 1940s' heroine. The subsequent seduction is achieved with nothing more provocative than a naked shoulder—the implications of rape are left completely unexplored by the script, which glosses discreetly over the material potential of Vorelli's power.

Ms Romain's blushes in both scenes were spared by the 'no nudity' clause in her contract and it was left to Sandra Dorne, spilling out of her tight-fitting basque and fishnet tights, to show some flesh. Gordon remembers, 'She was a sort of Diana Dors

3: Horror and a Dash of Sex

Devil Doll (Bryant Haliday, Yvonne Romain)

type and used to this sort of thing,' and Dorne provided more overt titillation with the briefest flash of nudity in the British print and a slightly longer version of the same scene in the overseas version. European audiences were also treated to more explicit nudity in two specific sequences involving professional models, rather than actresses. The first of these is a straightforward alternative version of the scene in a Berlin bedroom where a token floozy (Pamela Law) is shown in her underwear in the British version but topless in continental prints. The second sequence is slightly more distasteful: Vorelli calls a mousy girl onto the stage and under hypnosis has her perform a strip in front of the leering audience, after which she ends up naked. Trixie Dallas, a professional stripper, mumbled through her lines before stripping down to lace underwear, but Shonteff's camera lingers a little too long for the scene to make comfortable viewing. Gordon accepted the need to move with the times: 'I didn't have any problem with making these films slightly sexier,' he insists, 'and there was nothing offensive in *Devil Doll*, but I don't think they add anything to the film. They were there for overseas distributors to add if they wanted. It only became less attractive later on when the market demands were becoming quite explicit.'

With Gala releasing the film in Britain, Gordon was free to sell the worldwide rights on an *ad hoc* basis. Joe Solomon's Associated Film Distributing Corporation, a grand title for a company specialising in films like *The Playgirls and the Vampire* (1960), another Gordon release, picked up the North American rights. AIP was then among the distributors leasing the film for various overseas territories.

Critical notices generally reflected the flair that was shown by Shonteff and his crew. The *Monthly Film Bulletin* considered that 'a strong dose of horror and a dash of sex make *Devil Doll* a good bet for exploitation pay-off', while *Motion Picture Daily* called it 'a first rate little horror film of the sort that used to be made by bright young directors in the Forties.' *Variety* was one of few that felt short changed: 'slow-paced pic never comes up to its title in the way of shocks, thrills, scares, sex or other dividends... has been done before and better.'

X-Cert

Satisfied with the results of *Devil Doll* and convinced that Bryant Haliday had both the talent and the presence to become a major horror star, Richard Gordon set about tailoring a vehicle specifically to promote the actor's screen ambitions. With Lindsay Shonteff amenable to a second outing for Gordon Films Inc, the producer considered remaking *The Hounds of Zaroff*, the Richard Connell short story of 1924 which had previously been filmed by RKO as *The Most Dangerous Game* (1932). But this tale of a psychotic hunter bent on stalking human prey was unavailable, so Gordon turned his attentions to a story which stayed within a broad hunting theme, albeit from a very different perspective.

CURSE OF THE VOODOO
'Blood sacrifice of the Simbaza!'

Mike Stacey, a renowned white hunter, and his companion Major Thomas, are tracking lions in the African bush when they fall foul of the mysterious and isolated Simbaza tribe—who hold the lion sacred. Thomas warns Stacey that the Simbaza 'are further from civilization than Stone Age men,' but he laughs off the idea that they can invoke the dark arts to protect their gods and blithely leads his expedition into the heart of their forbidden territory, determined to finish off a wounded lion. Stacey is attacked and badly injured but he manages to kill the lion. However, his shots alert the Simbaza to the presence of the expedition. Members of the tribe turn up at the camp but Stacey laughs off their threats and completes his expedition before returning to London. Trying to pick up the threads of his life with wife Janet, Stacey develops flu-like symptoms and in his feverish state is tormented by visions that range from being chased by a lion to encountering a Simbaza warrior in full tribal gear on a London bus! In desperation, Janet consults an African expert and discovers that her husband's only hope of survival is to return to the land of the Simbaza and kill the witch doctor.

Curse of the Voodoo (Dennis Price, Bryant Haliday)

3: Horror and a Dash of Sex

The script, originally called *Lion Man*—a title used throughout the filming—came from the pen of the inexhaustible Brian Clemens, who took time off from working with the Danzigers to concoct this tale under the *nom de plume* of Tom O'Grady. At first glance, Clemens's screenplay is a more ambitious project than the writer's usual work, promising, as the press book succinctly puts it, 'the horror and bestialities of voodoo in a story that reaches across four centuries and continents...' The writer's opening narration continues in the same vein: 'Africa! Where the primitive tribes still practice evil religions which weave a dark web of death around those who sin against their gods!' This was heady stuff for a B picture and a dose of budget reality soon left only a passing nod to such primordial terrors in the film itself. Shonteff was afforded the same four-week shooting schedule and around £35,000, so there was no question of shooting on the 'Dark Continent'. After all, Richard Gordon was the man who transformed the English Home Counties into New Mexico, so recreating the African bush in Regent's Park was all in a day's work! The weather unfortunately was far from kind and rain played havoc with the schedule. The film would finally complete a full week late and some £15,000 over budget. African skies have never looked quite so cloudy and gray, and the rain-sodden 'location' sequences quite mar the credibility of the end-result.

With Bryant Haliday playing great white hunter Mike Stacey, Dennis Price, now a familiar face in poverty-row pictures, was drafted in to lend the film some box-office appeal. 'Dennis was still a well-known name in Britain,' Gordon insists, 'and Bryant Haliday wasn't. I thought that Dennis would help to sell the film to the circuits in Britain.' The British actor, shoehorned into the 'African' sequences, was there to offer exposition and little else as he manfully offered up lines like, 'The Simbaza are a tribe that worships lions. They also practice a very potent form of black magic...' Despite a generous second-billing credit, Price's screen-time is limited and there is not much opportunity for him to be anything other than a cheerful foil to Haliday's taciturn expeditionary.

The rest of the cast have about them that air of anonymity commonly associated

Curse of the Voodoo

with cut-price productions. Lisa Daniely, a regular on British television, was the best known of them but hardly a familiar face and her presence as Stacey's long-suffering wife did nothing to launch a film career. The others are capable and play their roles with straight-faced solemnity but are largely there simply to populate the landscape. The crew at least had something of a track record in this sort of thing and included Gerald Gibbs, who had been the cinematographer on Hammer's *X The Unknown* (1956) and *Quatermass 2* (1957). Art director Tony Inglis had perhaps the biggest challenge, to make contemporary interiors look interesting without the funds to do anything interesting with them, and *Curse of the Voodoo* was not his finest hour. The cramped sets that he delivered could have allowed the director to ramp up the tension as the increasingly desperate Stacey starts to mentally unravel; instead, they look bland and somewhat seedy, and the flat lighting and unimaginative camerawork only compound the impression of watching a rather dull TV drama.

Not surprisingly, given the tight shooting time and forced rescheduling, the film exhibits a rushed and amateurish feel. Only in the book-ending African sequences, particularly at the cat-and-mouse climax when Stacey runs out of ammunition, does Shonteff create any sense of urgency. When the story switches to contemporary London, the director seems to lose all interest in both the leading character and his self-imposed predicament, and he struggles to imbue *Curse of the Voodoo* with any of the qualities of its predecessor.

Scenes that should have injected some energy into the story, such as the frenetic voodoo-inspired dance routine, are allowed to go on too long and become tedious. A sub-plot involving Stacey's marital difficulties exists purely to introduce Ms Daniely into the film and flesh out the running-time further. The obligatory appearance of an expert in Simbaza folklore is a clumsy and poorly staged segueway into the film's climax, although one has to admire actor Louis Mahoney for being able to cope with some cringe-making lines: 'A curse, seeking out across continents, hounding and haunting a man no matter where he might hide—the gradual destruction of mind and body and spirit...'

Curse of the Voodoo might just have passed muster on a dramatic level if the viewer genuinely cared about Stacey and his desperate efforts to avoid his strange fate. But the character as written is a thoroughly unpleasant bully and drunk, totally lacking in any redeeming qualities that might have evoked sympathy. If there were any hints of compassion and humility in the script, then Haliday was not the actor to bring them out. He had demonstrated in *Devil Doll* that he was more of a screen presence than a competent actor, and playing Stacey pushed his talent beyond its limitations; his delivery is stilted and his acting wooden. Looking back at the film some four decades later, producer Gordon remained faithful to his star. 'Bryant was an extraordinary talent who could have been a major star,' he insisted, 'had he not chosen to go his own way.' Haliday's future would include two further outings for Gordon, where he would be seen to much better effect.

Of the supporting cast, Dennis Price stands out, effortlessly cultured and totally watchable in what was the first of three films he would make for Richard Gordon. 'Dennis was in good shape—physically I mean,' Gordon says, 'and although he had been a big star, he had no pretensions about himself. He was grateful to be working and totally committed to the part.'

Despite this commitment from the cast, the finished film was less than the sum of its parts; the stock footage, for example, a positive feature of Richard Gordon's earlier films, is poorly integrated and reinforces the slap-dash feel of the production. Its producer was under no illusions about the quality of the film and he describes the effort as 'my least favourite of the pictures I worked on.' There were few dissenting voices among the critics; *Variety* thought the acting was 'robotic' and concluded a damning review with 'suspense, flat acting and trite story add up to soggy thrills, and as a shoestring production it's pretty threadbare.' *Curse of the Voodoo* lived up to the low expectations that its makers had of it and proved a minor and forgettable entry in Richard Gordon's canon.

It was not just US-based producers like Richard Gordon and Robert L Lippert who saw the potential in British-made fantasy films, local producers were also aware of the potential market that had opened up. Two entrepreneurs elbowing their way into the horror genre were former assistant director Tom Blakeley and producer Bill Chalmers, who initially teamed to form Planet Film Distributors and then expanded their operations into the area of film production. Blakeley's father John had been something of a 'mini mogul' in the North West of England, where he owned and ran a cinema chain based in Manchester. In the 1920s, Blakeley senior branched into film production, eventually establishing the Mancunian Film Corporation to launch a series of cheap and cheerful pictures starring comic Frank Randle. Tom Blakeley's induction into the industry came through serving in his father's distribution business and gradually easing himself into production proper. In 1963, Planet produced their inaugural feature, *The Marked One,* a forgotten B directed by veteran journeyman Frank Searle. A year later, Blakeley and Chalmers mounted what they hoped would be a successful entry into the horror film market with something of a rarity in the British horror canon, a contemporary vampire tale.

DEVILS OF DARKNESS
'Mystic evil from beyond the grave!'

> *Paul Baxter, holidaying in rural France during All Saints Eve, is alarmed when one by one, three friends die in mysterious circumstances. The cause of death in each case is ambiguous and Paul believes that the local police are complicit in a cover up, although he has no proof. The local aristocrat, Count Sinistre, while friendly enough on the surface, seems also to be involved in the conspiracy, which appears to revolve around an ornate medallion in the shape of a bat. Paul returns to London with the bodies and insists on proper autopsies; he is particularly concerned about a mark on the corpses' necks. But he is unaware that Sinistre has pursued him to England, determined to retrieve the medallion. Now disguised as a portrait painter, Sinistre inveigles himself into Paul's circle of friends and selects Paul's girlfriend, Karen, to be his next 'bride'. When Paul discovers that the Count is actually a long-dead vampire, he realises that he is in a race against time to prevent Karen from joining the growing ranks of the undead.*

Shot at Pinewood in May of 1964, *Devils of Darkness* is a potent mix of paganism, witchcraft and vampirism set in deepest, darkest Brittany. It also introduces to the screen the latest in the long line of decadent aristocrats created by British studios in the form of Count Sinistre, aka Armand du Moliere, a sixteenth-century nobleman whose misdeeds were so grievous that he was sentenced to be buried alive. The film's prologue, and easily its best sequence, is pure Hammer: a suitably grave narrative introducing the Count's 'infamous and barbaric crimes' is overlaid on the sight of a red-robed figure placing a black candle on Sinistre's seemingly-impregnable stone tomb. No sooner has the stone cracked open than a poorly-animated bat is preying on the local gypsies and in particular, a raven-headed wench named Tania who has been singled out as a future consort to this new 'Lord of the Undead'. One moment Tania is flouncing around the campsite, twirling her underskirts and banging her

X-Cert

Devils of Darkness (Carole Gray, Hubert Noël)

tambourine with gusto; the next, she has been laid to rest on a carpet of red flower petals—only to be wrested from the grave and informed that she will be required to follow Sinistre until 'the end of time'. Cue the blood-red opening credits.

From that spirited opening, former *Movie-go-round* film critic Lyn Fairhurst's script is all downhill. Opting to place her protagonists in modern Britain dilutes much of the appeal of her tick-list of horror staples, which includes rhubarbing peasants, duplicitous foreigners, gypsy curses and dead but still predatory aristocrats. The very familiarity of the clothes, sets and manners weakens the Count's other-worldliness and renders him just another serial killer. Incidentally, this was the first British film since Bela Lugosi's unfortunate encounter with Mother Reilly to place the Undead in a contemporary setting—although technically Von Housen was just a common or garden madman.

If the setting undermines the dynamic of the story, the script is fatally flawed by its failure to stage anything remotely interesting after the Count has vacated his rustic domain; he simply moons about London in much the same way as he had in France. Even the involvement of the Metropolitan Police fails to generate any sort of dramatic momentum, although they do seem to take the prospect of a vampire stalking pre-Swinging London rather seriously. 'Don't you think it's about time you told me everything,' Scotland Yard's finest says, 'tangible and otherwise.' After a great deal of pointless meandering, the film finally arrives at a climax that appears to owe its inspiration to Don Sharp's *The Kiss of the Vampire* (which was released by Hammer two years before), in which the scarlet-cloaked figures of the vampire cult are summarily dispatched by a *deus ex machina*. The Count himself, attempting an escape, stumbles into bright sunshine and mercifully ends it all by immediately crumbling into the obligatory skeleton.

The love triangle, which could have generated some heat, is also a half-hearted affair, with no electricity at all between the main characters. Steely-eyed Frenchman

3: Horror and a Dash of Sex

Devils of Drakness (William Sylvester)

Hubert Noël injects some swarthy charm into his somnolent presentation of Sinistre but he cannot match Christopher Lee for animal sexuality and physical presence. 'If only I could do something to lessen your grief,' he purrs to Rona Anderson. 'Let me help you erase this unhappy memory.' What threat he poses comes from his swordstick (a handy substitute for fangs), rather than anything inherent in his biological makeup. Nor are the ladies who compete for the Count's favours particularly evenly matched. Tracy Reed, niece of Carol Reed and cousin of Oliver, plays the free spirit Karen Steele, who subsidises her bohemian lifestyle by stripping off and posing for Sinistre's latest masterpiece. Reed has the looks of a Barbara Steele but little of her screen presence and she remains a passive and wan figure throughout. Carole Gray, from *Curse of the Fly*, plays the feisty, green-eyed Tania who, after the exertions of the opening sequence, is left fuming from the sidelines as the smooth-talking Count canoodles with Karen. Both of them dwarf the diminutive Noël, so it is probably a blessing that fisticuffs did not break out. Sinistre's feebleness is further emphasised by the machismo of William Sylvester, who makes up for his passive turn in *Devil Doll* by playing the rather unlikeable Paul with gusto.

The whole thing is directed at a leisurely pace by Lance Comfort, a graduate of Ealing studios, who seems to be completely at sea with the notion of exploitation. The 'swinging' party, for example, has nothing racier than a few middle-aged drunks and a couple of lesbians dancing discreetly in one corner. As a measure of how tepid the whole affair was, the BBFC had nothing more than an unnecessarily-prolonged bout of snake-dancing to complain about, though Trevelyan still insisted that it was suitably trimmed. Aside from the opening sequence, Comfort does occasionally hint at better things, as in the death of an 'occult expert' played by Eddie Byrne, who is attacked in his laboratory by unseen forces and expires amid the frenzied hollering of caged animals. A portrait that 'weeps' blood is another striking visual image, but it ultimately adds nothing to the narrative.

The film does look good. Reginald Wyer, Wintle and Parkyn's cinematographer,

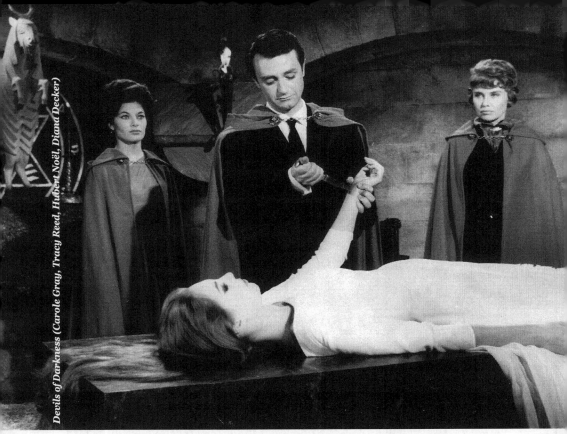

Devils of Darkness (Carole Gray, Tracy Reed, Hubert Noël, Diana Decker)

does a splendid job and art director John St John Earl makes full use of the Pinewood stores to give it a polish lacking in many of its contemporaries. But even with a free run of the Pinewood backlot, Chalmers's claim to *Cinema Today* that the budget topped £100,000 appeared to verge on the side of hyperbole. At any rate, the film struggled to find a place on the national circuits in the UK and had to endure a spotty release; it fared marginally better in the US, where a double-billing with *Curse of the Fly* at least had the backing of a Hollywood major, 20th Century Fox.

The mixed reception for *Devils of Darkness* did little to dampen the enthusiasm of Blakeley and Chalmers, although it did restrict their financial resources and in preparing for their next assault on audience sensibilities, they started to seek out a suitable partner to share in the risk.

Chapter 4
Excruciating Bad Taste

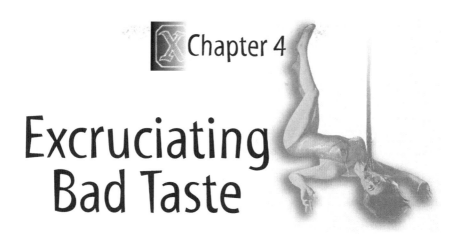

The mid-1960s was not a good time for the British economy as a whole but the film business was enjoying something that could loosely be termed a 'boom'—despite the closure of cinemas and audience numbers dropping at an alarming rate. American interest rates had hit a forty-year high and production costs in California had gone through the roof. While Britain's finances were in equally poor shape, the generally lower production costs and Eady Levy made the UK seem a very attractive option to filmmakers. In 1965, Columbia joined rivals M-G-M and 20th Century Fox in the setting up of a British production office and Universal quickly followed suit. Smaller companies also joined the rush and despatched their brightest and best to London to sniff out new filmic opportunities. Among the 'mini-moguls' taking leases on West End flats were Joe Levine of Embassy and Martin Ransohoff at Filmways. In April 1966, *Time* magazine coined the expression, 'London: the Swinging City' and even ultra-cautious British companies started to get in on the act; Anglo-Amalgamated announced an ambitious £3M programme and British Lion issued a press statement promising 'about a dozen features over the next year or two.'

The big money went into big mainstream films, of course, and stayed well away from the independent sector, although the success of fantasy films from Hammer, Amicus and Tigon reinforced the perception that British horror films could be sold anywhere in the world. While M-G-M and Fox pumped their millions into the likes of *The Yellow Rolls Royce* (1964) and *Those Magnificent Men in their Flying Machines* (1965), a steady flow of dollars and talent trickled through to the horror genre.

Richard Gordon was among the producers benefiting from the 'feel good' factor and soon after completing work on *Curse of the Voodoo*, he teamed up with fellow Englishman Gerry Fernback to form Protelco, specifically to mount new horror and science fiction films. Reviving the spirit of his earlier Amalgamated films, Gordon was out to secure modestly-budgeted double bills of similarly-themed films which could be packaged together for the North American market and distributed individually elsewhere. He already had the first of these films, a science-fiction shocker entitled *The Projected Man*, financed and ready to shoot, and the second piece fell into place when he was introduced to Messrs Blakeley and Chalmers and read their script for *The Night the Silicates Came*. In exchange for providing co-production finance on what would become *Island of Terror*, Protelco took the US rights and left Planet to distribute the film separately in the UK.

The two features were to be shot more or less back-to-back; the *Island of Terror* co-production would be produced by Tom Blakeley while Protelco's *Projected Man* was put in the capable hands of Gordon's old business partner John Croydon.

THE PROJECTED MAN
'The human laser beam with enough power in one hand to destroy a city.'

> At the Faber Research Foundation, Professor Paul Steiner and his assistant, electronics expert Christopher Mitchell, have invented a means of projecting matter over distances. Steiner has successfully projected a live rat via his system of Light Amplification by Stimulated Emission of Radiation (LASER) and transformed it back into solid form again; the professor is undisturbed by the fact that the animal later died an agonising death. Dr Blanchard, a director of the Foundation supporting Steiner's work, is less impressed and announces that he is closing down the facility, leaving Steiner to call in old friend Dr Patricia Hill (nicknamed 'Piggy') to help him stabilise the process. But time is running out and, faced with corporate obstinacy and sabotage, Steiner decides to experiment on himself in an effort to save his research. The experiment goes wrong and a horribly scarred and deranged Steiner is let loose as 'the projected man'.

Hollywood writer Frank Quattrocchi wrote his screenplay for *The Projected Man* in the 1950s and touted it round a number of Hollywood companies before it ended up on the desk of Alex Gordon at AIP. Unable to interest Arkoff and Nicholson, Alex passed the project on to Richard Gordon, who took up the rights and commissioned Peter Bryan to write a redraft suitable for shooting in England. At that stage veteran journeyman Francis Searle was pencilled in as director. Unable to secure finance after the demise of Amalgamated Productions, *The Projected Man* languished in a

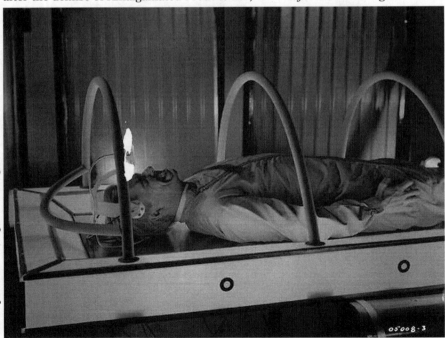

The Projected Man (Bryant Haliday)

4: Excruciating Bad Taste

The Projected Man (Bryant Haliday, Norman Wooland)

cabinet in Gordon's office until the launch of Protelco presented an opportunity to get the project back onto the drawing board.

Leaving Fernback and Croydon to tweak the screenplay into a shooting script, Gordon concluded a 50% funding deal with Michael Klinger and Tony Tenser at the Compton Group, purveyor of such gems as *The Black Torment* (1964) and *The Pleasure Girls* (1965). Compton's investment bought it the UK rights and took the total budget up to £100,000—a generous figure by Richard Gordon's standards, but the producer still felt he had no room for complacency. 'The main expense would be on the special effects,' he explained. 'They needed to look good. On a film such as this there was no point in trying to save money there, and it just wouldn't work.' John Croydon had stressed the same point to the *Daily Cinema*: 'Horror films have always been a dead cert. I feel it's because horror is always visual and visuals have no boundaries. The audience reaction in London to a science fiction-horror movie would be repeated in Bangkok.' The man who was given the job of provoking that reaction was Ian Curteis, a novice director making what would prove to be his one and only feature film.

By the time Curteis came on board, the casting was already complete. Richard Gordon had toyed with the idea of Bryant Haliday headlining both co-features, which would have proved something of a challenge to the respective schedules. The idea was shelved when Peter Cushing became available for *Island of Terror*, leaving Haliday confirmed as Professor Steiner, a basically well-meaning but misguided scientist meddling in things best left alone. Opposite Haliday as Patricia 'Piggy' Hill, Protelco signed Mary Peach, a minor star in Britain who, despite having a smaller and less important role, was guaranteed top billing in the UK and secondary credit in the US. The supporting roles went to established character actors Norman Wooland

and Derek Farr, while Ronald Allen played the romantic lead, Dr Mitchell. Sam Kydd, the only actor who would appear in both *The Projected Man* and *Island of Terror,* had a small but eye-catching cameo as a petty thief who has an unfortunate encounter with the titular character.

With so much resting on visual impact, Gordon recalled Flo Nordhoff, who had worked on *Fiend without a Face*, to design the impressive 'projected man' makeup. The German worked from a cast of Haliday's face—far cheaper than sending the star to Munich—to generate an impressive mask of sinuous tendons, creating the impression that Steiner's face had literally been turned inside out. As a mask it was relatively straightforward to apply and saved Haliday the discomfort of long hours in the make-up chair. The special effects, which accounted for approximately 25% of the budget, were far less straightforward. The effects team, under the direction of Mike Hope and Robert Hedges, was required to create a series of spectacular laser sequences on the Merton Park soundstage and their execution proved particularly problematical, partly because they were so ambitious. 'Special effects in those days were very often a matter of trial and error,' Gordon says. 'You tried something and if it didn't work you did it another way. The crew was doing their best but a lot of it wasn't working and needed to be re-done.' As the production fell behind schedule, the pressure mounted on Curteis, a situation that was exacerbated by the decision to shoot in Techniscope. The process was at that time more associated with Italian spaghetti westerns, and it created the effect of widescreen (by 'cropping' the frame) without necessarily reflecting the quality—although in expert hands, the result could be impressive (Sidney Furie's *The Ipcress File*, for example). Curteis's inexperience meant that the benefits of the process were being lost which, added to the slippages, left the producers with no alternative but to intervene. 'Curteis was struggling and towards the end of the shooting, John Croydon and I spoke and we agreed to take him off the picture,' Gordon revealed. 'John then stepped in and finished the last week or so of filming.'

The film that emerged shows no obvious signs of this disruption; *The Projected Man* looks polished and professional, even if the script lacks any real ambition and belongs very much to the era in which it was written. The characters, situations and style all hark back to films like *The Fly* (1958) or *The 4D Man* (1959), without adding anything especially new. But the technical aspects of the piece do combine well—the laser sequences are particularly effective—and music and sound effects complement the action perfectly. As Gordon and Croydon expected, it is Nordhoff's work that commands centre-stage and Haliday's make-up is an undoubted highlight, equally convincing in both shadow and light, its impact only diluted by overuse.

Haliday, playing a rather clichéd role, makes Steiner a cultured and sympathetic character, but not above the odd wry comment: he casually dismisses concern for a 'projected' laboratory rat with the flippant, 'It's gone wherever good rats go.' By contrast, a disinterested Mary Peach struggles to offer any conviction to dialogue such as, 'No human being could survive a time transition of that kind—not without fearful consequences!' The actress's uneasiness extends to her love affair with Dr Mitchell, which is perfunctory rather than passionate, and it is left to starlet Tracey Crisp to raise temperatures by stripping down to her undergarments before being attacked by the titular character. If things are a little lightweight on the side of the angels, the villains more than make up for it and add tremendously to the humour. At one point a mysterious and uncredited, Blofeld-like cat lover threatens Norman Wooland with, 'Oh no, Dr Blanchard, it's not finished. Don't forget I still have those photographs...' The overall quality of the film is underscored by the final scene, in which Steiner's haunting, disembodied cries offer a genuinely chilling climax.

The Projected Man (Tracey Crisp, Bryant Haliday)

X-Cert

Predictably Ms Crisp's vulnerable state featured heavily in the film's publicity in both the UK and US, but pride of place went deservedly to Nordhoff's make-up in a campaign that played down the science in favour of the monster—a policy which found favour with both public and critics. *Kinematograph Weekly* liked the 'clever trick photography and the special effects' and thought the make-up man had 'done a good job'. 'It's a pity about the X certificate,' it went on, 'for there is nothing in the horrors to harm the average, hard-boiled child of today.' But the *Monthly Film Bulletin* was conflicted: 'An odd mixture this. It begins well...but begins to go gradually downhill'.

While, Curteis was struggling at Merton Park, *Island of Terror* was rolling over at Pinewood under the watchful eye of Terence Fisher, fresh from his triumphant return to form in Hammer's *Dracula-Prince of Darkness* (1965).

ISLAND OF TERROR
'How could they stop the devouring death...that lived by sucking living human bones?'

> A research establishment on a remote island is experimenting with a cure for cancer, but something goes horribly wrong and soon afterwards a local resident is found dead, his body apparently drained of bone. With animals dying in the same manner, the authorities call in an eminent pathologist, Dr Stanley, and a bone specialist, Dr West, who arrive in a helicopter along with West's new girlfriend, Toni. Working with the local GP, Dr Phillips, the scientists trace the source of the outbreak to the scientific laboratory but while investigating in the basement, they are attacked by mutant creatures with snake-like appendages. When they discover that these mutated monsters are reproducing at an alarming rate and will soon surround the village, Stanley and West try to arrange a trap involving cattle poisoned with Strontium 90. Powerless to intervene, the islanders barricade themselves into the village hall and await a final confrontation with the 'silicates'.

The screenplay for *The Night the Silicates Came*, written by Edward Andrew Mann and Allan Ramsen, was acquired for Planet by Bill Chalmers, who then sent a copy on to Protelco. The premise, with its echoes of *Fiend without a Face*—an isolated community is threatened by man-made creatures—had instant appeal for Croydon and Gordon. 'It had the potential to be a great picture,' Gordon enthused, 'and without exaggeration, I think it was one of the best science fiction screenplays I have ever read.' The project received the green light, and with a budget similar to that of *The Projected Man* and split between Protelco, Planet and the NFFC, it was enough to secure Pinewood studios and the woodlands of nearby Black Park.

With Peter Cushing contracted for the role of Stanley, Gordon wanted Barbara Shelley, who had just essayed a rapacious vampire in *Dracula-Prince of Darkness*, as Toni. Toni's contribution to the narrative, aside from introducing a little sex appeal, is largely confined to putting herself in danger and waiting to be rescued and when Shelley declined the unchallenging role, it was handed to Carole Gray who had just performed a similar duty in *Curse of the Fly*. Edward Judd was the man entrusted with the heroics, and the star of Val Guest's *The Day the Earth Caught Fire* (1961) offers up a rugged, good-looking bone-marrow expert, with a taste in fine wine and an eye for the ladies. The ubiquitous Eddie Byrne provides solid support as the country doctor who spends most of his time scratching his head in disbelief, while Niall MacGinnis played the genial 'Head of the Island'—a title that apparently required no further explanation. MacGinnis, who was such a memorable villain in

4: Excruciating Bad Taste

Island of Terror (Edward Judd, Carole Gray) / INSET: A silicate

Tourneur's *Night of the Demon* (1957), is reduced to modelling a nice line in chunky knitwear and peering through his binoculars, leaving Cushing and Judd to do all the hard work.

Despite Gordon's passion for the script, the picture does not get off to the strongest of starts with some laboured exchanges of dialogue emphasising a number of plot contrivances, including the nuggets of information that the last boat is about to leave and will not be back for a week and that the long-promised telephones are yet to be installed. The ensuing isolation from the mainland is such a crucial point that the locals feel the need to mention it several times in subsequent scenes! If that was clumsy, then the pseudo-scientific gobbledegook is quite absurd. 'The potential of the cell membrane must be maintained during the radiation of the nucleus,' opines one white-coated scientist,

155

who then also feels a need to inquire, 'Is the tri-tem stage complete? And the paper applicator..?'

Clearly the paper applicator was not in place, resulting in, as one astute local observes, 'Some peculiar goings-on going on on this island...' Things start to pick up when the scientists are wiped out and Fisher is allowed to move away from this soulless world of white-coated boffins, into the woods and caves where the newly formed creatures, dubbed 'silicates', stalk their victims. The director, shrewdly, does not give much away in these early encounters but the local policeman (Sam Kydd) paints a pretty vivid picture for us in his inimitable way: 'His body is all like jelly,' he exclaims, 'It's like nothing I've ever seen. There was no face—just a horrible mush with eyes sitting in it!' Later, when the intrepid heroes are trapped in the basement lair, Fisher creates tension by concentrating on the actors' reactions and keeping the creature's onscreen appearance to an absolute minimum.

The silicates, as designed and operated by John St John Earl and his team, look like giant turtles with a probing tentacle and are at their most convincing when they remain more or less static—or better still, unseen. The creatures are far less effective when they are required to move and are clearly being powered by stuttering motors or in some cases, pulled by wires. The film's weakest moments come when they mount what are supposed to be mass attacks; the pitched battle between 'hundreds' of silicates (barely double figures, in truth) and dynamite-throwing locals is cringe-worthy. One could forgive Fisher if he felt frustrated and years later, he told Harry Ringel in *Cinefantastique*, 'Personally I detest most science fiction films.'

By contrast, Cushing seemed to be enjoying his time away from Hammer in a run of science-fiction films, having just completed the title role in Gordon Flemyng's *Doctor Who and the Daleks* (1965), to whom he would soon report back for a sequel. While shooting *Island of Terror* at Pinewood during the day, Cushing was appearing on the West End stage in the evenings but far from being fatigued, he seems to have been invigorated by the challenge and brings humour and easy charm to a role that he could have played in his sleep. Gliding over the dullest of dialogue, he essays a nice line in gallows humour: watching West bandage what remains of his arm after an encounter with a silicate, he quips, 'Watch it boy or I'll sue you for malpractice!' He also humanises Stanley by indulging in moments of unease or indecision. When Toni refuses to be left behind in the car, he says, 'Oh, let her come. I wouldn't want to stay out here alone, either. It's too damn creepy.' When West says, 'Let's not take any unnecessary risks,' Stanley retorts, 'Yes, especially with me!'

The ease with which Cushing was able to rise above his material brought some inevitable comments from the press about squandering his talents. In an interview with the *Evening News* in 1966, Cushing said, 'A lot of people have accused me of lowering my standards but I have never felt I'm wasting myself. You have to have a great ego to want to play Hamlet all the time, and I just haven't got that ego. Challenge me on this and I'll say: "well, I've kept working".' The actor's natural modesty belies a talent for realism that is exemplified in one of the most effective scenes in the film: when Stanley has his arm hacked off to prevent the contamination from spreading. Cushing's agonised writhing makes for uncomfortable viewing—so much so that the censor also required cuts to ensure that the film obtained its X.

With a large proportion of the budget consumed by elaborate special effects, the remainder of the production, notwithstanding the cast, is left with a threadbare feel. The one extravagance seems to have been the helicopter, a novelty that pleased the director so much that he deemed it worthy of several close-ups of its own. Later, Cushing and Judd are reduced to examining scientific documents in a corner of a pub so as to negate the need for a whole new set. The climax—supposedly hundreds

4: Excruciating Bad Taste

Island of Terror (Peter Cushing)

of silicates descending on a barricaded town hall—is realised almost entirely with a third-party description of what is going on!

The shortcomings of the budget aside, *Island of Terror* offers a workmanlike programmer enlivened by good performances and several good sequences, and it was enough to convince critics and the public alike. The *Motion Picture Exhibitor* summed up the general view with the thought that 'audiences should be well scared and well entertained.'

Extremely pleased with the commercial outcome of their first two features, Gordon and Fernback pressed on with their third, one that continued Protelco's policy of working with a variety of local producers. *Naked Evil* (aka *Exorcism at Midnight*) took Richard Gordon back into the world of voodoo and marked a return to the genre of Steven Pallos, the producer of *The Hands of Orlac*.

NAKED EVIL
'The few that survive would be better off...dead!'

> Violence erupts in an English city when a hood named Lloyd starts to use voodoo against a rival gang led by the nightclub owner, Spady. A series of mysterious deaths forces the police to intervene and they start to investigate the staff and pupils at the local hostel for Commonwealth students, in particular Danny, who has been having a relationship with a former hostess at Spady's club. Benson, who runs the hostel, has been given an 'obi', a bottle of graveyard dirt topped with feathers, which transfers a death curse to the recipient. Having spent time in the West Indies, he knows about the terrifying effects of voodoo and calls in his old friend Father Goodman to neutralise its power. Benson remains under attack from supernatural forces

and the strain begins to take its toll as he becomes increasingly erratic; by the time he realises that the school's caretaker, Amazan, is somehow implicated, it is too late. Dick Alderson, Benson's assistant, decides that the only hope of defeating the Obeah magic lies with a confrontation between the powers of good and evil in the basement of the school.

Naked Evil fits into a sequence of voodoo-inspired films that originated in Britain in the 1960s and includes Gordon's *Curse of the Voodoo*, an episode in the Freddie Francis antholgy feature *Doctor Terror's House of Horrors* (1965) and the later AIP/Poe film *The Oblong Box* (1969). What makes *Naked Evil* unique is the positioning of Christianity and Obeah—West Indian magic—on diametrically opposite sides of the faith divide. The plot of *Naked Evil* is, aside from its foray into gang violence, essentially a battle between Father Goodman, representing the Church of England, and Amazan the West Indian witch doctor. Given the sensibilities of the filmmakers and the audience they were targeting, it would not be too much of a surprise to learn that the Christian God vanquishes his upstart rival in the closing reel.

The screenplay was drawn from a teleplay by Welshman John Manchip White, a writer of both fiction and non-fiction who had turned his hand to the film business, working as a script doctor for Samuel Bronston on his European-based epics like *El Cid* (1961). Closer to home, White had written *The Camp on Blood Island* (1958) for Hammer, as well as a number of scripts for the BBC, including *The Obi*, which became *Naked Evil*. Steven Pallos saw the potential for a big screen adaptation and sold the idea to Columbia on the understanding that he could find a partner to contribute to the budget. Knowing that Protelco were actively looking for projects, he sent a copy of the play to Richard Gordon, whom he knew from their mutual distribution interests. Gordon liked it and was keen to make a deal but was concerned that the budget, pegged at £60,000, precluded the use of colour. Believing the days of black-and-white B features to be coming to an end, Gordon suggested that they commit additional funds and shoot the film in Technicolor but Columbia, which saw the film purely as a supporting feature and therefore of limited shelf life, declined. Accepting this enforced constraint, Gordon agreed to provide 50% of the budget, his intention being to package the film with a future Protelco feature.

With Gerry Fernback as producer, the director's chair was assigned by Pallos to Stanley Goulder, who had helmed the well-regarded thriller *Silent Playground* (1963) and had earlier served as Robert Day's assistant director on *First Man into Space*. Goulder's first task was to rework White's television script, adding several new characters and opening out the action—at least as much as the restricted budget allowed.

Limited resources were also the defining factor in casting the film, although it gave Gordon the opportunity to indulge in his love of using old-time professionals wherever possible. 'I have always preferred casting such actors in my films,' he explained, 'both for the pleasure of meeting them and because I considered them good value for money.' The role of Benson went to 60-year old Basil Dignam, who had appeared in *Corridors of Blood* and had been active in films and on the stage for several decades, usually playing authority figures such as diplomats and barristers. The romantic leads, Dick Alderman and Janet Turrell, were to be played by relative unknowns Anthony Ainley and Suzanne Neve; the former was making his feature debut and had a solid theatrical background while the latter had played some minor parts in films but was very much a television actress, having a recurring role in the BBC-TV series, *Smuggler's Bay*.

Behind the camera, the crew reflected considerably more experience, as well as familiarity with the genre. Geoffrey Faithful had been the director of photography on *Corridors of Blood* and *First Man into Space*, as well as Gordon's non-horror

4: Excruciating Bad Taste

films *Kill Me Tomorrow* (1957) and *The Secret Man* (1958). Faithful had also shot the highly-regarded M-G-M science-fiction thriller *Village of the Damned* (1960). Peter Musgrave, who had been sound editor on Amalgamated's productions as well as *The Innocents* (1961), had been promoted to editor on *Silent Playground* and he returned to this film in the same capacity. Even the art director, the ever-reliable Denys Pavitt, had worked at Amalgamated.

Gordon may have been unable to persuade Columbia to upgrade the piece to colour but that did not stop the talented crew under Goulder's direction rising to the challenge and producing a film that has moments of genuine quality. The pre-credits sequence is a good example of a director making use of limited resources to draw the audience into the story. A clearly agitated black man, O'Neill, scurries through a grubby tenement block, avoiding the attentions of his obstreperous landlady and locking himself into his sparsely-furnished apartment, only to be confronted with the dreaded obi—as static a menace as it is surely possible to conjure. By focusing on the man's reactions, Goulder effectively conveys how the power of imagination and a sudden wind (coincidental or otherwise) contrive to give the obi a life of its

Naked Evil (Olaf Pooley)

own. As the victim backs away, he crashes into a window with such force that he actually seems to be sucked through it, and he falls to his death on the street below.

Although the Goulder/White script struggles to maintain that dynamism throughout the full 85 minutes, there are other truly scary moments. The exorcism scene, when Father Goodman is persuaded down to the dark basement to perform a blessing on the body of Amazan, shows what an inventive director Goulder could be: the witch doctor's corpse is hidden out of sight under a sheet and, as the priest starts the rite and that sudden wind reappears, doors slam and thunder crashes; in a flash, the sheet spins from sight and the table is bare. Throughout the tightly-edited sequence, Goulder juxtaposes Amazan's prostrate body with that of the comatose Alderman. The scene closes with the ghostly silhouette of Amazan framed in the

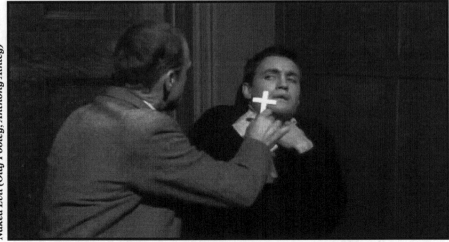

Naked Evil (Olaf Pooley, Anthony Ainley)

4: Excruciating Bad Taste

doorway for a moment and then vanishing. The old man is last glimpsed walking along the rain swept road.

If the exorcism had been at the very end, then *Naked Evil* would have finished on a tense and disconcerting note; unfortunately the running time is instead fleshed out with a dull flashback, dragged out in slow motion, followed by the obligatory uplifting conclusion. 'The evil in this house has left with it,' Goodman says when he realises Amazan's reanimated corpse has fled the scene. 'That evil will surely drag it down to Hell... Those that do the Devil's work forfeit their souls to the Devil—and his torments.'

This tendency towards padding runs through the film and undermines what could have been a taut and nicely balanced script. The open warfare between West Indian gangs, for example, may have held some resonance with the street riots of the 1950s but Goulder's budget means a pitched battle is staged off-camera, while the scenes in the gang-leaders' respective nightclubs look to have been filmed in an otherwise redundant corner of the soundstage and only emphasise how threadbare the production was without adding anything of substance to the story. Even a frantic chase through dimly-lit alleyways merely distracts from the central plot.

The romance between Danny, the promising pupil, and Beverley, the nightclub hostess, is similarly superfluous to the main story and although it arguably serves to humanise the characters, it quickly becomes tedious. A much more interesting relationship is built around the triangle of Danny, Benson and Amazan as they battle for Danny's soul. The witch doctor uses a mix of intimidation and blackmail to enlist the student to his wicked schemes—despite the best efforts of the rational Benson. 'You have the makings of a fine scientist,' the principal barks at him, 'and you are behaving like a superstitious savage.' Dignam's performance turns Benson from the clichéd much-loved teacher into a more complex and ultimately self-destructive character. It was Benson's decision to transplant the ancient and emaciated Amazan from the Caribbean to England, and subsequently it is Benson's threats to sack the 'filthy old wretch' that trigger the voodoo attacks. Benson's mental and physical demise are perfectly realised, and the only weakness is the casual way in which his background is explained. 'When you have lived in the tropics as long as I have,' he says with suitable gravitas, 'you come to know the feel of sheer, outright evil. It's tangible; you can taste it; you can smell it.' No further elaboration is sought or given. Nor does the script dwell too much on why rational science and engineering students drawn from all around the globe should be so in thrall to voodoo superstition in the first place. It seems enough to suggest that because they are not Christian, they are more susceptible to such things.

Dignam aside, the acting is best described as adequate; the student body, prone to burst spontaneously into the singing of calypsos, remain a lightly-sketched group, while Antony Ainley makes a rather dull leading man. The actor, who would become best known for his recreation of *Dr Who* villain 'The Master' after the death of Roger Delgado, conveys a sinister screen presence, excellent for scoundrels but completely at odds with his heroic character. Janet Turrell's Suzanne is so peripheral that she barely registers as a character and other than a spot of bopping at the local 'hop', she is more or less left to fret in the corner. The film's two main protagonists do stand out; in particular the shuffling, cackling Amazan, played by Jazz musician Brylo Forde, who creates a thoroughly repellent heavy—despite looking so physically and mentally frail. By contrast, Olaf Pooley, later a writer and director in his own right, plays the more robust and dynamic Father Goodman as an appropriately sympathetic and sombre creation. The deliberately slow buildup to the final confrontation in the cellar, escalating from whispered speculation in the dining hall to the discovery of decapitated cockerels in the woods and ultimately to the exorcism itself, gives the film its core and more than makes up for its weaker elements.

Despite the obvious merits of the production, Richard Gordon was disappointed with the decision to regard the film as just another B picture. 'That's all that it was intended as,' he concluded, 'and that's all it became. If it had turned out to be the picture I hoped it would be, it might have gone out on a double bill with another X-rated picture and enjoyed far more recognition than it received.'

The film's British distributor, Columbia, took a similar view and, having served its purpose as a supporting feature, *Naked Evil* duly vanished from sight. In the US, where Protelco owned the rights, *Naked Evil* enjoyed a far more colourful (literally) history. Finding itself unable to package the film with one of its own productions, a deal was arranged through Alex Gordon for Robert Saxton to pick up *Naked Evil* for his California-based Hampton International outfit. Saxton looked to widen the film's appeal by adding a colour tint using a process dubbed 'Evil Color', which emphasised the primary colours without much attention being paid to little things like contrast. The gimmick was not enough to guarantee an audience and *Naked Evil* managed only a handful of play-dates paired with near-forgotten Euro-import, *Gorilla Gang* (1968). Then, a decade after it was produced, the film was hauled out of the vault by Sam Sherman of Independent-International, who saw the opportunity of a quick sale to television. The enterprising Sherman concocted a framing sequence featuring Hollywood veteran Lawrence Tierney as a psychiatrist whose patient tells the whole story of the film as a flashback. The colourised sequences were explained as part of a unique laser treatment, blue representing memories of events occurring at night, red being events that frightened the patient, and so on. The new scenes were shot in a single day for a pittance and guaranteed *Naked Evil*, or *Exorcism at Midnight* as it was now titled, a whole new audience on late-night television.

The disappointing theatrical career of *Naked Evil* did nothing to slow down Richard Gordon and Gerry Fernback, however, who chose the Cannes Film Festival to announce an ambitious slate of productions under the Protelco banner, including *The Brainsnatchers*, *Creatures from Under the Sea* and another Allan Ramsen script entitled *Invasion of the Black Death*—all of which would be co-productions with Planet. More acquisitions followed: *The Crooked Cross* (a black magic story for Bryant Haliday) a new John Croydon script called *The Innocence and the Evil* and—Gordon's personal favourite—an adaptation by Val Guest of the Algis Budrys novel, *Who*?

The intention was to get one of the three Planet films into production first, but Blakeley and Chalmers were already developing their own project and were keen to add that to the growing roster of Protelco co-productions. The success of *Island of Terror* in the US convinced Planet of the wisdom of recreating the same elements and the company issued a press release announcing that its next picture would be adapted from the John Lymington novel, *Night of the Big Heat*, about a remote community under attack from alien creatures. The novel had already been adapted for television, and Planet felt that the script required minimal changes for the big screen. With Cushing and Fisher once again ready to sign on, Blakeley and Chalmers confidently sent their script off to the NFFC and Protelco.

NIGHT OF THE BIG HEAT
'A blistering tale of incineration and death!'

A severe heatwave has gripped the tiny island of Fara and tensions are running high among the locals, yet there seems to be no obvious scientific

4: Excruciating Bad Taste

explanation—or sign of a resolution. A somewhat haughty scientist named Hanson, who is staying at the local inn, knows more that he cares to share about the situation but continues to rebuff all approaches for information. Stress levels go higher when landlord Jeff and wife Frankie are confronted with Angela, a former lover of Jeff's, who arrives on the island determined to rekindle their affair. As the temperature soars, the electrical equipment starts to fail and communications with the mainland are cut off. Soon, the locals are squabbling among themselves, with only Hanson rising above the petty dramas; he has realised that the island is not experiencing a natural phenomenon—rather, it is the first battleground in an invasion by unseen aliens. Believing the invaders can be killed if exposed to low temperatures, Hanson resolves to track them to their lair.

Planet's aspirations for the film were almost undone before a scene had been shot, thanks to the precarious state of Britain's balance of payments at the time and the disdain felt in certain quarters for low-budget films in general. Caught in the grip of government cost-cutting, the NFFC had been forced to review its spending and announced that in the future, it would be concentrating on 'more profitable, bigger budget type of productions'—in other words, the sort of films that probably did not need subsidising in the first place. The Corporation promptly deemed *Night of the Big Heat* outside the revised policy and declined to participate. To make matters worse for Blakeley and Chalmers, Richard Gordon disliked the script, thinking it 'too talky and frankly had too many special effects for the budget they (Planet) were proposing.' Protelco followed the example of the NFFC and turned down the offer. Tom Blakeley's response showed typical British stoicism in the face of obstacles: he pressed on regardless, rewriting the script himself with the support of Ronald Liles, his production manager.

Confident that they now had a satisfactory script, Planet signed contracts with Cushing and Fisher and began the construction of sets at Pinewood, but the revised

Night of the Big Heat (Percy Herbert)

Night of the Big Heat (Christopher Lee, Patrick Allen)

script attracted no more interest from investors or distributors than had the earlier version. With the start-date looming, Blakeley hired Pip and Jane Baker for a last rewrite. While the Bakers, who had worked for Blakeley before on films like *Murder Can Be Deadly* (1962), toiled to salvage what they could from the earlier versions and concoct new scenes, Planet continued on with pre-production.

The television version, which had been broadcast on ITV in 1960, centred on an invasion of extraterrestrial, heat-generating spiders and starred Lee Montague and Melissa Stribling. The Planet adaptation pulled off something of a coup when Bob Chalmers announced the casting of Christopher Lee, reuniting him onscreen with his regular Hammer co-star Peter Cushing. For once, Lee was not the heavy but he was nevertheless cast to type as taciturn scientist Godfrey Hanson, who for reasons never satisfactorily explained, sets up a mini-laboratory at 'The Swan' with what appears to be—even by 1960s standards—very primitive looking equipment. Lee had long since cornered the market in low-budget horrors, adding the likes of Rasputin, Fu Manchu and other assorted fiends to his role-call of villainy, but the actor's reputation had suffered by his continued willingness to lend his name to inadequate vehicles, and *Night of the Big Heat* proved to be just that. For most of his screen-time, Hanson scowls and snaps trite observations like 'This heat's bound to lead to irrational behaviour' before disappearing into his room to pore over his findings. Lee's contract guaranteed him top-billing, but the real stars were Patrick Allen and Sarah Lawson, married off-screen as well as on, who played the landlords of the hostelry which seems to have become the focus for all the alien activity, or at least the protracted discussion of it by the locals.

It was not just the invaders that were raising the temperature. The village also welcomed Jane Merrow as Angela Roberts, a bikini-clad sexpot who rubs ice cubes languorously across her cleavage and uses her overt sexuality to taunt the frumpy Lawson. Predictably, red-blooded Patrick Allen cannot resist the fatal attractions of Ms Merrow and succumbs to a quick fumble in the spare room, only to later refer to her in some distinctly ungentlemanly terms. ('She was a slut,' he recriminates,

4: Excruciating Bad Taste

Night of the Big Heat (Jane Merrow, Kenneth Cope)

'and I wanted her!') With nothing much happening in respect of the main narrative, this soap opera sub-plot provides an entertaining distraction, at least for a while. Less agreeable is the attempted rape of Ms Merrow by sweaty local Tinker Mason (Kenneth Cope), a tasteless and unnecessary slice of crude exploitation, which also has nothing to do with the plot.

The term superfluous could also be applied to the character supplied by Peter Cushing. With Lee providing the science and Allen the heroics, Cushing is left to look on as others lose their cool and/or start to strip off—with typical British *sang froid,* he never removes his jacket, no matter how hot it supposedly gets! Apart from gracing the film with his presence and upping the box-office appeal with his name, he justifies his 'guest star' billing by propping up the bar and dispensing sedatives whenever appropriate. The actor was at least given a heroic death, as was Lee, which made for a rare cinematic achievement for the two traditional opponents, both being on the same side *and* both dying well.

With the cast in place, there seems to have been little money to spend on what Gordon felt was the main selling point, the aliens. Making extraterrestrial spiders look convincing would have defeated a budget many times greater than the one on offer from Planet, so the writers transformed the menace into creatures resembling large fried eggs, sliding gracelessly through a chill-looking Black Park. John St John Earl, fresh from *Island of Terror*, did his best, but the effect is laughable and Fisher was wise to keep his monsters out of sight for as long as possible.

Fisher's wife Morag told biographer Wheeler Winston Dixon that her husband 'didn't like science fiction'. 'He felt there wasn't enough human conflict,' she said. 'It was just another monster from outer space. It wasn't human.' With such ineffective special effects, Fisher's preference for the more mundane aspects of inter-planetary conflict is understandable, but *Night of the Big Heat*'s script is not strong enough to sustain this approach for such a long period and by the time the film meanders to its climax, the viewer has lost all interest in the love triangle.

None of these difficulties with the script were apparent when *Kinematograph*

X-Cert

Weekly's roving reporter visited the Pinewood set and found everyone concerned in good spirits including the producers, who were eager to promote their triumph. 'In getting this off the ground, they have beaten the credit squeeze, largely, I gathered, by digging deeply into their own resources,' the magazine recorded. 'But Tom and Bill have stuck to their policy of not seeking financial participation. They prefer to start selling when the production is completed.' That decision not to pre-sell the film, whether a conscious strategy or forced on them by circumstance, would soon come back to haunt Planet. In the meantime, the producers had the challenge of creating a heat wave in the middle of an English winter, which created some discomfort for the cast who needed to look suitably sweltering. All credit to Jane Merrow for enduring a long beach scene in a bikini while the men at least had shirts on; even so, everyone had to be sprayed with glycerine to simulate sweat and suck on ice cubes to hide the vapour trails from their breath.

Despite the low temperatures offscreen, it was the physical interaction between the actors that made the BBFC sit up and take notice and the film's X certificate was a reflection of its desire to protect the under-16s from the steamy sex, rather than the horror. The trade paper *Kinematograph Weekly* picked up on this point observing 'a good bit of hokum...Pity it's an X: the kids would love it.' The mainstream critics were split on the picture's other qualities. The *Los Angeles Times* thought it a 'taut British sci-fi'; *Films and Filming*, on the other hand, noted, 'It's almost a shame that the script got into the hands of a director as modestly efficient as Terence Fisher for his leisurely, atmospheric style does for this awful story-idea all that mortal man can reasonably be expected to do.'

Planet handled the film itself in the UK, opening on a bill with *The Tenth Victim* (1965), an Italian made science-fiction yarn staring Ursula Andress, but neither film encouraged much of a reaction among cinemagoers. Without that crucial pre-sold deal in the US, Planet struggled to interest any distributor and even an intervention by the well-connected Richard Gordon could not find any takers. *Night of the Big Heat* sat on the shelf until the early 1970s, when it was finally picked up by Maron Films, retitled *Island of the Burning Damned*, and paired with the Toho *kaiju* of *Godzilla's Revenge* (1969). Planet's failure to secure an adequate distribution deal pushed the company into bankruptcy soon after, and effectively sounded the death knell for their Protelco co-productions.

Gordon and Fernback did not fare any better than their erstwhile partners and Protelco, too, was wound up. 'Protelco Films was a very ambitious venture,' Gordon summarises, 'which Gerry and I got off the ground with financing from a European syndicate based in Switzerland. But unfortunately they lost interest after the films we made together and took their money elsewhere.' That impressive raft of films just faded away (though the rights to *Who?* were sold to Allied Artists, which jettisoned the Guest screenplay and turned the concept into a political drama starring Elliot Gould). Richard Gordon's contribution to British films of the 1960s was not entirely over; in 1969, he teamed with experimental filmmaker Anthony Balch to produce *Bizarre* (aka *Secrets of Sex*), a series of vignettes exploring the more unusual aspects of sexual gratification. This came as close as the producer ever got to either art or pornography, depending on one's taste in such things, but it certainly was not horror, despite the anachronistic presence of a bandage-swathed mummy voiced by the indomitable Valentine Dyall.

The failure of Planet and Protelco and the credit squeeze in the UK did nothing to dampen the enthusiasm of producers, however, but while the likes of Blakeley and Gordon were happy to be associated with the genre, there were other filmmakers on both sides of the Atlantic who looked to avoid any stigma that might come their way

4: Excruciating Bad Taste

from an affiliation with horror. When Samuel Gallu, an ex-pat American operating in the UK, mounted *Theatre of Death*, he went out of his way to insist that he was making a thriller rather than a horror film—despite the picture in question featuring Christopher Lee in a tale of vampirism in the backstreets of Paris.

THEATRE OF DEATH
'Where acting can be murder.'

> Having inherited the Theatre de la Mort from his father, Philippe Darvas is determined to continue with its lurid repertoire of murder, mayhem and mystery—all in the name of entertainment. Darvas writes and directs tales of violence and bloodletting while running his troupe of actors with a rod of iron. Physical intimidation is nothing new for Darvas, but he goes further with a young starlet, Nicole, whom he hypnotises in order to enhance her performance. He later orders her to move in with him but soon afterwards, Darvas disappears and the police speculate that he might be the latest victim of a vampire killer stalking Paris. The police surgeon, Charles Marquis, who is seeing Dani, one of Darvas's actresses, believes the director is still alive and could be the killer; a psychiatrist substantiates the theory by confirming his belief that Nicole is still under Darvas's control. Convinced that Nicole will be the next victim of the killer, Charles sets out to solve the mystery himself and track down Darvas but in doing so, he inadvertently puts both himself and Dani in mortal danger.

Christopher Lee's unmistakable tones introduce the film and establish the setting as a Parisian theatre company, clearly modelled on the legendary *Théâtre du Grand-Guignol*, which was founded in 1894 and for over sixty years, measured the success of its horror shows by the number of audience-members who fainted. The fictionalised version, *Theatre de Mort*, is also dedicated to offering 'horror, together with avarice, murder and mayhem'—a concise shopping-list of the principle selling points in the screenplay of Ellis Kadison, an American television writer. Kadison's script had been picked up by another graduate from the small screen, Sam Gallu, a producer/director with over 450 television shows under his belt, including the long-running *Navy Log* in the 1950s. Joining the American migration to London, Gallu secured the interest of Michael Smedley-Aston, a former British Lion executive now forging a career as an independent producer. Smedley-Aston's reign at British Lion had included some of the studio's biggest mainstream successes, including *Private's Progress* (1956) and the *St Trinians* series, but there was nothing in his or Gallu's CVs that remotely resembled a horror film and from their subsequent comments to the press, neither man was much interested in making one now.

Interviewed on set by *Kinematograph Weekly*, Gallu said, 'We play the *Grand Guignol* for all the blood and horror that's associated with it'—and then immediately insisted that despite appearances, he was not making a horror film but a murder mystery! To ensure that the project achieved this delicate balancing act of making a film about horror without making a horror film, the producers hired experienced writer Roger Marshall, one of Anglo-Amalgamated's Merton Park regulars, to give the piece a final polish. The production, under the auspices of Pennea Productions, then moved onto its Elstree base for the duration of the shooting.

The film's opening scenes were not shot on soundstages but at the Lyric Theatre in Hammersmith, however, where Gallu directed the 'play within a film'. It is these sequences of beheading, branding, burning and assorted torture that lend the film the look and feel of a horror movie, as well as introducing theatre director Darvas,

X-Cert

whose sadistic treatment of his cast would be a key ingredient in establishing the mystery element. During rehearsals for *The Witches of Salem*, the director sets a hypnotised Nicole loose on the cast with a branding iron. 'Lesson number one,' he smugly lectures horrified onlookers: 'Always catch your audience's involvement; the number one priority in all good theatre.'

But that early promise of blood and horror is left behind on the stage when Gallu launches the action into the night-time streets and rat-infested sewers where the bit players wait to be carved up. The body count rises with vigour but the killings are discreetly arranged so that scarcely a drop of blood is spilled, despite the film's horrific central premise. It seems that a family fleeing the Nazis were trapped by an avalanche and were then forced to kill their eldest child and feed him to his sister to keep her alive; the girl has grown to adulthood with an insatiable craving for blood. As the police surgeon helpfully explains, she has become 'a haemotagiac- someone who needs human blood badly; in your language, it's what you call a vampire.' In his determination to make a murder-mystery, Gallu's bloodthirsty vampire transforms into a common or garden psychopath, and the film's stalk-and-slash credentials are actually those of a routine whodunnit.

Despite his disdain, Gallu borrows liberally from the genre to enhance his film. The theatre is a desanctified chapel where Darvas skulks around in the cobwebbed catacombs fiddling with his favourite torture instruments and watching slide-shows of old horror films (including, rather cheekily, Hammer's 1958 *Dracula*). The killer, creeping in and out of the banks of fog, is swathed from head to toe in black in true Jack the Ripper style, and of course the mere presence of Christopher Lee was enough to entice fans of the macabre into the cinema. Lee, saddled with yet another humourless egotist, manages to suppress even a flicker of self-awareness when he shares a cab with Charles and is asked directly if he has an interest in vampirism. Having thus positioned himself as the prime suspect, Darvas disappears from the action a mere 45 minutes in, and though he is mentioned constantly throughout the remainder of the film's running time, he never reappears—except as a corpse hauled from the Seine.

Theatre of Death (Christopher Lee)

Theatre of Death: UK, Italian and US advertising material

X-Cert

The film immediately suffers from the loss of its star presence. Lee is the perfect red herring, effortlessly capturing the aloofness and arrogance of Darvas as he sums up his philosophy: 'Think of me as a master builder restoring a cathedral. Before you can build up the new ideas, you've got to tear down the old.' He later watches a frenetic voodoo-dance routine, only to sneer that it was 'as frightening as an old woman spearing a cocktail cherry'. Grabbing a spear, Darvas thrusts it towards his leading lady, snarling, 'I suppose you realise I could ram this through your delightful stomach.' Physical threat turns to mental cruelty when he launches a tirade against the psychologically-insecure Dani, forcing her to stand in front of the mirror while he rants, 'Look at that make-up! That eye shadow is grotesque... You are a misfit; you're only happy in the presence of deformity. You are a failure!' Unpleasant he may be, but neither Gallu nor Lee seem interested in making the character a sexual predator, despite Darvas's predilection for hypnotising pretty starlets and making them obey his every command. When Lee caresses Nicole's shoulders and whispers in her ear, it is to do with her acting and not the casting couch.

Even without the sexual *frisson*, Darvas is such a colourful character that the rest of the cast pale in comparison, though Lelia Goldoni, as the tormented Dani, brings vulnerability to an underwritten role. Jenny Till's Nicole is particularly bland although one could argue that the character is kept deliberately one-dimensional so as to avoid giving the game away. But it means that the key figure in the drama is also the least engaging. The men do not fare much better, and the only noteworthy thing about Julian Glover's dull hero is how acceptable British stereotypes had now become in horror films—so much so that none of the actors attempt French accents or mannerisms and could easily have been drafted in from any British film.

Picking up on this theme, Gallu makes only a token effort to evoke a Parisian air with his backdrop; the streets could easily have been London or Hammer's *mittel-*Europe, but the influence seems to be less gothic and more Italian 'giallo' cinema—particularly in Gil Taylor's lurid colour palette and hand-held camerabatics. Taylor was Roman Polanski's cameraman of choice, shooting *Repulsion* and later *Dance of the Vampires*, and his stylish lighting gives Gallu's film a depth that it otherwise lacks. It is a telling point that when the publicity materials were being prepared, the distributor opted to depict the fictional mayhem rather than the actual murders. Gallu's film is so anodyne that the censor was unconcerned by anything untoward in the 'murder and mayhem' and gave the film its X certificate on the strength of the near-nude dance routine.

The critics were generally kind. *Kinematograph Weekly* thought it 'an excellent thriller in its class. Biggest and most convincing red herring of all is Christopher Lee; there is no one who can do this kind of thing better', while the *Daily Cinema* noted, 'Stylishly staged and convincingly plotted...good posh-shocker for popular halls'. Hard-nosed distributors were less impressed by what they saw and despite it being completed at the end of 1965, *Theatre of Death* was held back until 1967 before London Independent Productions gave it a spotty release. In the US, Hemisphere Pictures felt it needed a more provocative title and dreamed up *Blood Fiend*, but the company that had unleashed Al Adamson's *Psycho a Go-Go* (1965) and Philippine-made imports like *The Raiders of Leyte Gulf* (1963) on the world made little ground with the Gallu.

If the makers of *Theatre of Death* had been slightly embarrassed to be making a horror film, producers Harry Field and Lionel Hoare unashamedly set their sights on the horror market with a curious tale which mixed the notion of contemporary vampires first explored in *Devils of Darkness* with some of the most exotic locations yet featured in a British genre film.

4: Excruciating Bad Taste

THE HAND OF NIGHT
'Even now, you're what you wanted to be—one of the dead!'

> American Paul Carver is awakened from a nightmare on board a plane bound for North Africa by a fellow passenger, Gunther, who invites him to visit his home. Carver is guilt-ridden following the accidental death of his wife and children and welcomes the distraction of Gunther, a renowned archaeologist, and his assistant Leclerc, who are celebrating the discovery of a new tomb. The American is introduced to the entrancing Marisa, a 'servant of the night', who tries to seduce Carver into joining her sect. He escapes and is later found unconscious by Gunther and his adopted daughter, Chantal. Leclerc tells them Marisa is a legendary and long-dead princess, a vampire, who has selected Carver to join her in the afterlife. When Chantal is captured by Omar, Marisa's sinister acolyte, the only way that Carver can free her is to confront his inner demons and overcome the supernatural forces which are ranging against him.

One of the more unusual horror films to emerge from a British film studio, *The Hand of Night* was a low-budget effort from Associated British Pathé, a subsidiary of Associated British Pictures Corporation (ABPC), the conglomerate that along with Rank dominated the industry at that time. That ABPC was more often associated with films like *The Dam Busters* (1954) and *Ice Cold in Alex* (1958) made *The Hand of Night* all the more unusual, as were the backgrounds of the men behind the film. Producer Lionel Hoare was a stalwart of Associated British Pathé and in particular its Children's Film Foundation films, and he quickly engaged the involvement of his long-term collaborator, Harry Field. His work with Hoare included the musical *Go Go Mania* (1965), the matinee adventure *Davy Jones' Locker* (1966) and a mystery, *Love is a Woman* (1966). All three of these films were directed by Frederic Goode, who had joined ABPC in the 1950s and whose own CV also included features for the Children's Film Foundation.

Hoare recruited a number of past collaborators behind the camera, including cinematographer William Jordan, art director Peter Moll, editor Frederick Ives and composer Joan Shakespeare. The exception to this cosy group was the writer Bruce Stewart, who had dreamed up the original concept and turned it into a shooting script. A former actor, the New Zealander had been living in England since the mid-1950s and had built a solid reputation as a versatile and inventive scribe; he would eventually script over 200 radio and television plays and win a Silver Dagger award from the Mystery Writers of America for his play, *Shadow of a Pale Horse*. *The Hand of Night* was to represent his sole outing on the big screen and, as he told *The Guardian* newspaper, his stated intention was to write 'a vampire film without blood'. Unlike Gallu, who inserted rational explanations for supernatural happenings, Stewart displayed no reluctance to dip into the bizarre, mixing horror conventions with Egyptian mythology, and he also added more than a timely dash of existentialism and hippy drug-culture.

If the crew were new to this sort of material, at least the leading players were familiar to any regular filmgoer with a penchant for horror. William Sylvester, who had recently bested the Undead in *Devils of Darkness,* played Paul Carver, with *Witchcraft*'s leading lady, Diane Clare cast as Chantal. To play the exotic Marissa, mistress of the dark, Field engaged Alizia Gur, a former Miss Israel, who had made her big screen debut in a cat-fight with Martine Beswick in *From Russia with Love* (1963). The British character actors making up the remainder of the cast including Edward Underdown as Gunther and Terence de Marney, who had appeared in 1965

The Hand of Night

with Boris Karloff in *Monster of Terror*, as the gnarled Omar. De Marney had the rare distinction for an British-based actor of also having appeared with Bela Lugosi in the 1935 film, *The Mystery of the Mary Celeste*.

None of their previous films would have prepared the cast for what lay in store with *The Hand of Night*; the poorly-animated bats may have evoked memories of Hammer but the Moorish castles, desolate landscapes and shadowy crypts create a physical look that could not be more removed from the Bray backlot. The opening credits set the tone for the film and present a mosaic of surreal images, including a hand turning to bones, a skull with a plume of velvety smoke pouring from an eye socket, and a vampire bat twitching in its death-throes. The evocative score by Joan Shakespeare underpins the sense that the psychedelic sixties had now arrived in British horror, and the nightmarish flashback that follows continues in exactly the same vein. In a slow-motion montage, we are taken in to Paul Carver's dream, where he is forced to watch the funeral cortege of his family and then stand helplessly by as his wife, in full bridal gown, turns into a skeleton before his eyes. The scene also includes a brief and slightly-nonsensical shot of the car crash that killed the family, with Carver thrown clear just before impact. Hardly surprising that our hero wakes up screaming to find himself on board a jet bound for North Africa, where the rest of the film is set; curiously, the Moroccan location is never mentioned in the film, although it is clear from the landscape and architecture.

But in aiming to create something unique, Stewart ends up with a storyline that simply meanders through some interesting locations, a situation not helped by the director thinking that the visuals and the performances that he was getting were more interesting than they actually are. The fact that the film's hero is an introverted manic-depressive merely compounds the problem. William Sylvester, a solid but conventional leading man, simply lacks the conviction to pull off lines like 'I don't want to be saved from the consequences of my galloping death wish'. When Chantal

4: Excruciating Bad Taste

The Hand of Night (Aliza Gur, William Sylvester)

loses her temper with Carver's maudlin self-pity, she gives voice to the frustrations of the viewer also. This vacuousness at the centre of the film should have created an opportunity for the supporting cast to step into the breach. Unfortunately, neither Gur nor Clare are up to the task. The dark-haired, olive-skinned beauty queen looks suitably mysterious and enticing, but she acts with the charisma of a wooden stake. 'The darkness isn't strange to those who dwell in it,' she says, to tempt Carver while the audience doze. Blonde, perky Diane Clare is no more accomplished here than she is in her earlier horror films and it is left to Terence de Marney, as the toothless Omar, to inject life into the increasingly moribund proceedings, happily cackling through rubbish like 'Between light and darkness each must choose his side.' Omar's demise, a prolonged entrapment in sunlight, is a rare highlight.

The climax, when it finally arrives, consists of Carver staking Marissa as she sleeps in her coffin and is conducted with the same lethargy as the rest of the film. The downbeat tone continues as Carver, knowing he will become a vampire, wanders off alone into the desert while Gunther pronounces his epitaph, 'He used to say always that he had cheated death. I think after all it is death that has cheated him.' If anyone felt cheated, it would have been the few people who paid to see the film. The *Monthly Film Bulletin* agreed and dismissed it as 'lily-livered vampirism that would make Dracula turn in his shallow grave'. *Films and Filming* was similarly unimpressed: 'A rather ordinary little film...fails dismally on all counts.'

Held back in the UK until 1968, *The Hand of Night* surfaced briefly with another X-certificate film, *Girl on a Motorcycle*, before disappearing. In the US, independent outfit Schoenfield Distributors tried to court an audience by changing the title to the more gruesome-sounding *Beast of Morocco* but were no more successful.

The early summer of 1966 saw the return to the UK, and the genre, of American writer Herbert J Leder, whose early directorial ambitions had been frustrated when Richard Gordon declined his offer to helm *Fiend without a Face*. Leder had gone on to direct two features based on his own screenplays, *Pretty Boy Floyd* (1960) and *Nine Miles to Noon* (1963), neither of which had major studio backing or a circuit release. Nevertheless, the New York-born Leder had managed to convince Warner Bros to back a brace of films aimed well and truly at cashing in on the current boom for British horror.

The Hollywood giant was no stranger to horror films. Warners already had an arrangement in place with Hammer through 7-Arts, which saw the likes of 1965's *Dracula-Prince of Darkness* and *The Plague of the Zombies* carrying the company brand—at least in the UK (they were distributed by Fox in the US). However, the deal with Leder had secured the rights to both sides of the Atlantic and meant a rare excursion for the American major into independent British filmmaking.

The first of Leder's films resurrected one of the screen's earliest monsters, the Golem, originally seen protecting the Jews of 16th-century Prague in the 1915 classic *Der Golem* and now brought back to life in a quiet London suburb for someone with far less altruistic motives in mind.

IT!
'Bullets can't kill it! Fire can't burn it! Water can't drown it! How can we destroy it before it destroys us?'

> *An accidental fire destroys a warehouse with the loss of many priceless artefacts belonging to the local museum—only a statue is unscathed despite being at the centre of the blaze. The statue is moved to the main display hall where the assistant curator, Pimm, is convinced it is somehow implicated in a series of 'accidental' deaths. Pimm believes he can use the statue's secret to secure promotion to curator and win the affection of Ellen, a co-worker at the museum. In the meantime, he freely indulges in his habit of 'borrowing' jewels from the collections and presenting them to his dead mother. By the time Pimm realises the statue is a Golem, a new curator has been appointed who is keen to rush through the sale of the statue to Jim Perkins, representative of an American museum. To make matters worse for Pimm, Perkins falls in love with Ellen and announces that she will accompany him—and the Golem—to the States. Frustrated both professionally and personally, Pimm resolves to unleash the full power of the Golem on those who have offended him.*

Tales and myths about a Golem had circulated throughout Europe for centuries, the most famous of which was the legend of Loew ben Bezalel, the chief rabbi of 16th-century Prague, who sought to protect his people from the anti-Jewish pogroms by fashioning an indestructible man of clay. The stories contain minor variations but all agree on the basic facts: that the creature was uncommonly strong, well-nigh indestructible, and that eventually the power it wields is turned against its creator. Leder took these fundamentals as his starting point and then more or less jettisoned the folklore and ploughed into a story very much of his own creation.

With an unfeeling, unthinking 'clay' juggernaut as the titular character, Leder seems to have pulled out all the stops to make its human master as colourful as possible. The petulant, repressed Pimm is a car-crash of psychoses and insecurities; not only is he greedy, selfish and murderously deranged, the assistant curator is also a sexual fantasist and a megalomaniac. If that were not enough for the audience to cope with, Leder constructed a second-rate Hitchcock sub-plot that turned Pimm into a poor man's Norman Bates, who keeps the dessicated skeleton of his mother in a rocking chair at home, decorated with stolen jewellery. 'Mother, it's silly of you sitting alone in the dark like that,' he chides the corpse. 'It is absolutely ridiculous.'

It! (Alan Sellers)

X-Cert

It! (Roddy McDowall)

To rise to the challenge of bringing this unique personality to the screen, Leder used Warners' dollars to entice Roddy McDowall back to his British homeland and top-billing in the film. A former juvenile lead at Fox during the 1940s, McDowall's career had petered out in the 1950s without him achieving the exalted status of a bankable star. However, regular appearances on the chat show/game show circuit, and close companionships with A-listers of the calibre of Elizabeth Taylor and Judy Garland, had ensured that one of Hollywood's most famous 'confirmed bachelors' remained a celebrity and certainly a big enough name to carry It!

Where Norman Bates had Marion Crane, Arthur Pimm had Ellen Grove, played by Jill Haworth, the fragile 21-year-old beauty who had been discovered by director Otto Preminger for his 1960 adaptation of the Leon Uris best-seller *Exodus*. Winning an exclusive contract, Haworth was plunged into roles in Preminger's subsequent movies, *The Cardinal* (1963) and *In Harm's Way* (1965), neither of which achieved the expected critical and box-office success. Hitting the top rung at the start of her career meant some slippage was inevitable as the actress indicated in an interview with Tom Lisanti. 'I only did this film because I needed the money,' she conceded. 'I hated everything...particularly what they did to my hair!' Haworth's career received a temporary fillip as filming *It!* came to an end, when she was cast as Sally Bowles in the original production of *Cabaret*, but that was only a brief respite and she would spend the next few years mired in British horror films.

By the time the US-based contingent arrived at Merton Park to start shooting what was at that time entitled *Curse of the Golem*, a largely British supporting cast had been booked to provide local colour. This group was augmented by Canadian Paul Maxwell as Perkins—a character who is basically everything that Pimm isn't: good looking, charismatic and enough of an antiquarian to recognise a Golem when

176

4: Excruciating Bad Taste

he sees one. It is Perkins who reveals how the creature can be activated after Pimm dismisses it as 'just a lump of stone'. 'Legend has it that it ran amok one day and is said to have disappeared,' the American remarks. 'My heavens,' Pimm replies, 'You are well informed.'

Leder's script continues at this level of simplicity throughout. When Pimm finds a scroll at the base of the statue, he trots off to the local expert on Hebrew history to be told that it translates as 'He who will find the secret of life at my feet, him I will serve until beyond time'. When Pimm is informed that the Golem is 'probably the most powerful force on Earth today,' his eyes positively glow but the best that he can come up with to test the thesis is to have it smash a glass cabinet that he happens to be standing next to. A later challenge of destroying Hammersmith Bridge is more in keeping with the Golem's power, even if the motivation is somewhat spurious—Pimm is showing off to Ellen. Unfortunately for the film, the more we see of the Golem in action, the less convincing it looks, and the comically-slow movement and obvious rubber suit severely undermine the impact. Leder's direction does not help; his uninspired approach negates some splendid photography by Davis Boulton and sees to it that *It!*, like the Golem, never gets out of second gear.

The human participants perform no better. There is no chemistry at all between Haworth and Maxwell so the audience is as surprised as Pimm when they announce they are off to the US together. McDowall, perhaps sensing that nothing else on the film was going to plan, chews the scenery with a vengeance. Things first start going awry when Pimm uses an umbrella to work out if the Golem is alive and McDowall's hamming creates a scene that is cartoonish in its absurdity. The actor continues on this trajectory later in the film, when he dowses the creature in petrol while snarling and gnashing his teeth like a silent movie villain. In a film mired in such mediocrity, McDowall at least is entertaining, even if for large parts of the action he appears to think he is in a romantic comedy. Having announced to Ellen that he is the happiest he has ever been, he then whispers, 'Would you believe me if I tell you I felt I could do almost anything... I tell you I can do incredible things. See that bridge over there? I can knock that bridge over just like that.'

In the last third of *It!*, McDowall throws out any attempt at credibility. He pouts and preens like a jilted teenage girl and sets an aged librarian on fire just for the hell of it. It comes as something of a relief when the British army decide to drop a tactical nuclear weapon on Pimm's hideaway and put him out of his misery. The Golem, of course, survives unscathed and is last seen disappearing into the sea, presumably for a sequel that mercifully never came.

The cast were under no illusion about the quality of the work. Haworth recalled that McDowall visited her Broadway dressing room and gave her the poster for *It!* which he signed and put a 'Sh...' before the *It!* 'This film really was a piece of shit,' she said. But the critics were not quite so dismissive: the *Hollywood Reporter* felt that the film was a 'trifle long on talk but invested with able production, picturesque Eastmancolor photography and moments of genuine shock'.

Though anyone who has seen *It!* might think it unlikely, Herbert Leder managed to concoct an even more bizarre premise for his second outing for Warners, entitled *The Frozen Dead*. Many of the crew that worked on *It!* including art director Scott MacGregor—who would soon move to Hammer for the likes of *The Vampire Lovers* (1970) and *The Horror of Frankenstein* (1970)—as well as Davis Boulton, make up man Eric Carter and editor Tom Simpson, reunited for Leder's follow-up feature. Robert Goldstein also returned, overseeing the production on behalf of Warners, and once again one is left to wonder if the Hollywood company had actually read the script before parting with its dollars.

X-Cert

THE FROZEN DEAD
'Frozen alive for twenty years! Now they return from their icy graves to seek vengeance!'

Dr Norberg, a brilliant scientist and leading figure in the Nazi regime, has set up a laboratory deep in the English countryside where, with the help of his assistant Karl, he conducts experiments to revive 1,500 soldiers of the Third Reich cryogenically frozen at the end of the war. Despite a number of failures that have left their victims shambling wrecks, General Lubeck and Captain Tirpitz, both fanatical Nazis, insist that they continue. When Norberg's niece Jean and her friend, Elsa, visit from the US, the Nazis realise that they have the opportunity to experiment on living organs and Elsa is decapitated and her head kept alive in a cabinet in the laboratory. Jean refuses to accept the story that Elsa has left for London despite an American scientist, Ted Roberts, insisting that he saw her board the morning train. It seems the girls have a unique telepathic link and Jean starts to sense thoughts and images transferred from her friend. The Nazis realise that Jean has become a risk to their plans and plot to dispose of her while Norberg starts his experiments on brain control using Elsa's living head.

The Frozen Dead starts off promisingly enough: a moonlit night, blood-curdling screams, and the sight of a thug with a whip leading a party of stumbling wretches, chained together, towards an imposing mansion—the home of crackpot scientist Dr Norberg. But from that modest high, the film quickly careers downwards and goes from quirky to the utterly absurd.

At least the requirement of a recognisable name above the title was achieved in impressive style when Dana Andrews arrived at Heathrow airport to board the first taxi to Merton Park. As well as the British-made *Night of the Demon* (1958), Andrews's

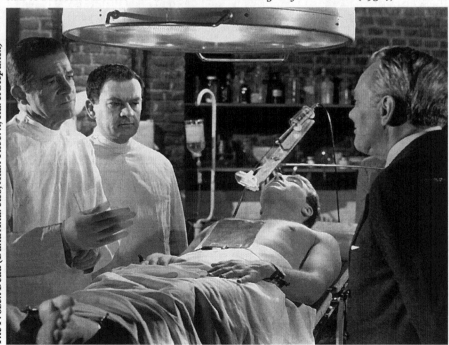

The Frozen Dead (Dana Andrews, Alan Tilvern, Karel Stepanek)

4: Excruciating Bad Taste

CV boasted genuine classics such as *Laura* (1944) and *The Ox-bow Incident* (1943), as well as work with such respected figures as Otto Preminger, Jean Renoir, Eli Kazan and Fritz Lang. Away from the screen, he was president of the Screen Actors Guild from 1963 to 1965 and was outspoken in condemning the increasing demands for female nudity in films. But a very public battle with alcoholism—Andrews became a member of the National Council on Alcoholism—put off a lot of potential employers and his film output slowed considerably. Soon after *The Frozen Dead*, he retired completely from films, bitterly claiming that he had made more money from real estate than he ever had from the movies.

With Andrews in place to attract the American market, British-born Anna Palk was the next in the order of billing. The actress's only previous role of note was in playing the pregnant girlfriend in *The Earth Dies Screaming*, which gave her some preparation for facing silliness with a straight face. Unfortunately, in playing Jean Norberg, the American off-shoot of the family, the 26-year-old is little more than a plot device to add some romance to the story and allow the otherwise obsessive Dr Norberg to show a more caring side. Providing Palk's love interest, Dr Ted Roberts was played by Canadian ex-pat Phillip Gilbert, who had worked in Britain for over a decade without making any noticeable impact. In a film crammed full of stereotypes, Gilbert's nominal hero does stand out as a curiously paradoxical character who has few qualms about Norberg's more nefarious activities. His reaction when he learns that a decapitated head is being kept alive is 'That's what I call a real achievement!' and he later goes on to lie to both the police and his new girlfriend while somehow still managing to retain his hero status.

Surprisingly perhaps, the most challenging role in the film was the unfortunate Elsa Tenney, who ends up making the ultimate organ donation and living—after a fashion—to tell the tale. Kathleen Breck had the dubious honour of fashioning some

The Frozen Dead (Kathleen Breck, Basil Henson, Karel Stepanek)

credibility out of a part that would have posed a severe test to a practised actress, let alone someone whose primary experience was bit-parts on television. Despite the obvious limitations of playing a head in a box, Breck manages to bring a great deal of sympathy to the role, simply by using her eyes and facial expressions—while Boulton defuses the inherent foolishness of the concept by bathing the scene in an eerie blue glow. The closing moments with Elsa's frantic pleading— 'Bury me, bury me'—over and over again are genuinely haunting.

At the opposite end of the spectrum in terms of experience were Basil Henson and Karel Stepanek, who shared 115 years between them—considerably more than necessary for the hackneyed Nazi villains they are required to play. Stepanek, though Czechoslovakian by birth, had propped up many a British war film representing the Third Reich and had also played a small role in Richard Gordon's *Devil Doll*. Making up the trio of evil-doers was Alan Tilvern as Karl; Tilvern had made a career out of playing all-purpose heavies in television series and here essays the kind of thuggish assistant that graced many a B horror film a decade earlier. Karl, it seems, has been killing people for years and passing off the limbs he harvests as spare parts from the morgue. Predictably, it is this doltish assistant who takes it upon himself to behead the most inappropriate person he can find, leaving the basically decent if deluded Norberg to tidy up the abundance of loose ends.

The film also provided employment to the gaggle of bit-part actors who either furnished the amputated limbs—kept alive for reasons never fully explained—or represent the remnants of the Wehrmacht, kept in cold storage or hidden away in the cells. Among this last group, and no doubt still wishing that he could expunge the film from his CV, was Edward Fox; the future star of *The Day of the Jackal* (1973) played prisoner #3, later identified as Norberg's brother.

While none of the performers had much chance with the cardboard characters they were given, the film might have survived had Leder concocted a script that held the viewer's interest without swamping it with trite or ill thought-through ideas. One cannot blame the writer for keeping the scientific logic (or illogic) to a minimum but any credulity to the story is undone by the glaring inconsistencies, the most obvious of which is the rationale for a clearly mad, if rather jaded Nazi setting up a laboratory in the English countryside rather than in some obscure Bavarian Alp or South American republic. A shortlist of unanswered questions would also have to include what the top brass thought they could achieve with 1,500 storm troopers in the days of nuclear proliferation?

Leder's lack of imagination in plotting extends to the direction, which like that of its sister picture, is flat and uninteresting. The opening scene and the arresting sight of Elsa's head in a box aside, there is simply nothing visually engaging going on and when Leder does manage to construct a promising set-up, he overloads the exposition and allows the moment to slip away. *It!* at least had McDowall to distract from the tedium; Dana Andrews struggles manfully to retain his dignity when high-camp might have been more advisable. One can imagine what Vincent Price might have made of the role. The po-faced approach, bar the faux-German accent, creates some sympathy for the character but little in the way of interest.

Critical reaction to *The Frozen Dead* was no better than for *It! Motion Picture Examiner* opined, 'Some moments of horror and some intrigue but the thin and far-fetched plot is drawn out to a length that makes it unwieldy.' The *New York Times* summed up the *It!/Frozen Dead* double-helping with, 'As horror exercises they are horrible bores.' The public shared the critics' indifference and the subsequent failure of the double-bill more or less spelled the end of Leder's directorial ambitions, at least as far as the major studios were concerned. He went to Mexico in 1969 to make

4: Excruciating Bad Taste

The Candy Man, a routine thriller starring George Sanders, but that brought him no more success than his British films and he drifted out of production and into the teaching of film studies. At the time of his death, he was a professor at Jersey City State College, enlightening students on the craft of cinematography.

One American who wrung considerably more success out of the horror genre than Herbert J Leder was Herman Cohen, the architect of many an early AIP/Anglo-Amalgamated co-production, including *The Horrors of the Black Museum* (1959), the film that caused such consternation at the BBFC. Cohen's films had a trademark garishness and outrageousness to them, and when he returned to the UK in 1967, he brought with him a new project very much in the same vein. This time, however, he had a bona fide Hollywood legend in tow—Joan Crawford.

BERSERK!
'Your front row seat to murder!'

> Monica Rivers, the owner and ringmaster of the Rivers Circus, bathes in the box-office glow that accompanies a series of 'accidents' at her circus: a trapeze artist is strangled by his own high-wire, a business manager is impaled on a tent peg, a magician's assistant is sawn in half. The other artists are not so sanguine about the deaths; they think that Rivers has too much to gain and that they are all at risk. The police are convinced that the perpetrator is hiding in the circus and Scotland Yard sends a detective named Brook to flush out the killer. Rivers has other problems to occupy her mind; her daughter Angela has been expelled from school and insists on appearing in a knife-throwing act. At the same time, Rivers' new lover, Frank, is pressuring her for a share of the business. As the circus arrives in London, it seems that it might have beaten the jinx but on the opening night, disaster strikes.

Herman Cohen claimed that he was so determined to cast Joan Crawford that he persuaded Leo Jaffe, the head of Columbia Pictures, to engineer a meeting where he could 'charm' her into accepting the role. The veteran actress, who won an Oscar for *Mildred Pierce* in 1954, had long since abandoned the exalted heights of major studio pictures and was now keeping her career alive by appearing in William Castle slasher movies like *Straitjacket* (1964) and *I Saw What You Did* (1965). Cohen's project, titled *Circus of Blood,* was written by his regular collaborator Aben Kandel and fitted perfectly into this downward trajectory.

Kandel's starting premise could easily have been lifted from *Circus of Horrors*: a series of gruesome 'accidents' plague a 'jinxed' circus as it makes its way to London while the box-office takings soar; Scotland Yard, sensing something amiss, despatch their best man to investigate the circus's owner, Monica Rivers. Crawford seems perfect casting as Rivers, whose matriarchal dominance of the troupe sets off alarms bells both with the performers and the authorities, but the script had to be reworked to accommodate the star. Kandel borrowed an idea or two from *Straitjacket*, where a mother is reunited with her estranged daughter only to find the reunion spoiled by a baffling series of murders. Naturally the mother is the prime suspect and equally predictably, the beatific daughter is revealed in the last act to be the real perpetrator. Tellingly, Kandel's rewrite eased the film away from *Circus of Horrors* and closer in tone to the psychopathic killer-on-the-loose films that flooded into western cinemas in the wake of *Psycho*. To appease Crawford (who was by all accounts unhappy with the original title) Cohen rechristened the film as *Berserk!*, designed to evoke memories of the Hitchcock.

Crucial to Kandel's scenario was the casting of the offspring and Cohen sought

Berserk! (Judy Geeson, Ty Hardin, Joan Crawford, Diana Dors)

to pull off a coup by signing Christina Crawford, Joan's adopted daughter, as errant daughter Angela Rivers. This was a case of her surname getting her the role rather than her CV, which consisted of minor theatre and television credits. Crawford was too shrewd to be upstaged by her own daughter, however, and vetoed the suggestion by insisting that she was too inexperienced. The troubled relationship between the two would later be cruelly exposed by Christina's tawdry autobiography, *Mommie Dearest*, in 1978.

The role of Angela went instead to waif-like Judy Geeson, a British poppet who had just played a schoolgirl in *To Sir with Love* (1967). The appropriately-named Angela arrives after having been expelled from a very proper English school but to ensure that her character was as 'angelic' as possible, the script explains away her misdemeanours as nothing more than 'upsetting the morale of the other students' by hiding in a closet and giggling! Geeson, who bore not even a passing resemblance to her screen mother in either looks or demeanour, would depart the *Berserk!* set and go straight into *Here We Go Round the Mulberry Bush* (1968), a coming-of-age comedy that made her a fantasy figure for a generation of spotty youths and helped to launch her into much higher-profile work.

Cohen was too much of a showman to give up all of his gimmicks and having secured an actress on the cusp of stardom, he signed a star very much on the decline: Diana Dors. Once hailed as Britain's answer to Marilyn Munroe, Dors had entered her 37th year on the back of a decade of poor film choices and salacious headlines. Whatever glamour had been associated with her name had long since evaporated and she was reduced to performing a nightclub act in working men's clubs and taking whatever film work she could get. On the verge of bankruptcy, she reportedly spent her time offset dodging the bailiffs who stalked her to and from the studio. Dors was cast as the boozy, brassy Matilda, described by Rivers as 'attractive in a cheap sort of way', who sobers up just long enough to pour her ample charms into a tight-fitting outfit and flop over the handsome young acrobat.

4: Excruciating Bad Taste

Berserk! (Diana Dors, Philip Madoc)

Michael Gough, who had already starred in three films for Cohen, took a back seat on this one and accepted the small role of Albert Durando, River's inconvenient business manager and former lover who gets the tent peg rammed through his skull relatively early in the proceedings, clearing the way for his muscle-bound successor, Frank Hawkins, played by Ty Hardin. Raised in Texas, Hardin's 'all-American boy' good looks and statuesque 6' 2" physique had won him a Hollywood contract that cast him as TV's *Bronco* and eventually led to appearances in films like *The Battle of the Bulge* (1967) and *Custer of the West* (1967), but his career as a leading man was short-lived, a situation probably not helped by the sight of his smoothly-oiled chest cuddling up to the elderly Crawford. Rivers succumbs to his fiscal and physical demands simultaneously: 'You'll have twenty-five per cent of the circus,' coos the love-smitten pensioner, 'and a hundred per cent of me'.

The most accomplished actor on the film is Robert Hardy, who plays Brooks, the dogged policeman, as a bit of a dandy in Savile Row suit and hand-made Italian shoes, who is never seen without his button-hole. It is not explained how he affords all this on a copper's salary, something that would require too much in the way of character exposition for an Aben Kandel script, and it is left to a single reference from the grumpy chief inspector (Geoffrey Keen), who says, 'Dressing smartly is a fetish of yours'. The screenplay takes one of its frequent lurches into the surreal by having Brooks move into Durando's vacant caravan to allow him, so we are told, '..to hunt a wild animal in its native habitat.'

For all the talent of the supporting players, it was Crawford's film and the star made sure that everyone knew it. She breezed into London in the spring of 1967 and caused an immediate stir among the assembled press corps who dubbed her 'Her Serene Crawfordness'—a title she took as a sign of affection. During the remainder of her stay, she happily entertained reporters to champagne breakfasts in her hotel suite or patiently indulged star-struck chat-show hosts on national television. In terms of publicity alone, Crawford more than earned her salary.

X-Cert

Berserk! (Joan Crawford, Ty Hardin, Michael Gough)

On the set, things were slightly different. Crawford was drinking to excess and needed a considerable volume of alcohol to get her through the working day. But Herman Cohen told Tom Weaver, 'In spite of her sipping hundred-proof vodka, she was very professional with me, and she would never take a drink unless I okayed it. She always knew her lines and she was always on time.' The actress seems to have taken Cohen's strictures in her stride and if anything was more concerned by the way she looked. Crawford admitted at the time to being 59 years old (although

4: Excruciating Bad Taste

her birth certificate said 62) but she insisted that M-G-M's Oscar-winning costume designer Edith Head design a leotard to show off her legs to full advantage—a sight that had many an aged film correspondent drooling. The critic for *Hollywood Screen Parade* spoke for many of his colleagues when he gushed, 'Her legs rival Dietrich's and her tigress personality puts to shame most of the newest kittens who call themselves 1968-style actresses.'

According to her biographer Bob Thomas, the actress was equally proud of her other physical assets and treated Cohen to flashes of her breasts. 'What about these?' she demanded brazenly, 'No operations on 'em either.' Mercifully, Cohen was not tempted to include any such displays on screen. For all her exhibitionism, Crawford was only too aware of her physical decline and she had hairstylist Ramon Guy devise invisible lifts—six tapes connected behind the head with rubber bands that stretched the skin and reduced wrinkles, although it left the actress with a fixed expression on her face throughout. That stiffness extended to Crawford's performance; in fact the only time she really looks comfortable is when she is in the circus ring. Elsewhere, her gestures are simply too theatrical and her delivery deadpan. 'I know how terribly shocked we all are,' she says, having witnessed Michael Gough get spiked, 'but there is no point is staying up any longer. Please go back to sleep.'

Crawford had played dominating women before, but Monica Rivers sets a new standard. Farming her only child out to boarding school without so much as the promise of a visit, she runs the circus as a private stud farm, picking up and casually discarding muscled young lovers, one after the other. This sexually-voracious harridan brushes off the deaths as a bit of bad luck but essentially good for business. 'How can you sit there so calmly and check box-office receipts? It's a good thing you are inhuman,' observes Michael Gough. 'We're running a circus, not a charm school,' shrugs Joan, her eyes fixed on the piles of money. 'People must be entertained.'

Simpler entertainment was provided by the real-life performers in Billy Smart's Circus, and director Jim O'Connolly seems intent on documenting the acts almost as a slice of nostalgia. When he isn't filling the screen with La Crawford's machinations, he is treating the viewer to the 'World's greatest elephant act' or 'Phyllis Allan and her intelligent poodles'. The over-use of genuine circus acts only impedes the narrative and O'Connolly takes a further detour with a song-and-dance scene by the circus's human skeleton, the bearded lady, a midget and the strong man, which is actually not quite as grotesque as it sounds but does not bring us any closer to identifying the killer. The big reveal, when it finally comes, is something of a let-down: Geeson seems intimidated by the screen presence of her co-star; she giggles and pouts like a child and is simply not forceful enough to carry off psychopathy convincingly. The dénouement sees her stamping her foot and squealing, 'I had to kill them. I had to kill them all...Kill, kill, kill!'. Her death scene is also curiously underwhelming: she runs into the stormy night dressed only in her basque and fishnets and is summarily electrocuted on a loose cable.

This lack of drama onscreen was also of concern to the critics. The *Daily Cinema's* reviewer quipped, 'The film has built-in embarrassments. To tell you the truth I liked the performing poodles best.' The *New York Times* was more forgiving, considering Joan to be 'certainly the shapeliest ringmaster ever to handle a microphone' while also warning its readers, 'Remember George Baxt's excellent *Circus of Horrors* six years ago, also from England? *Berserk!* can't hold a candle to it.'

Herman Cohen later insisted that *Berserk!* was his most successful film, but a healthy box-office return did not prevent him from abandoning the fantasy genre— at least temporarily—to make the crime-caper *Crooks and Coronets* in 1969. Jim O'Connolly directed a cast headed by Telly Savalas and Warren Oates and featuring a clutch of British performers, all of whom failed to impress—which sent Cohen scurrying back to his comfort-zone for his next venture. Warner Bros, which got its fingers burned over *Crooks and Coronets,* was forgiving enough to sponsor what would prove to be one of the most maligned genre films made in Britain.

TROG

'You'll laugh at yourself for being so scared...but don't laugh at Trog!'

> Students exploring a cave are attacked by an ape-like creature. One is killed when his skull is crushed and although his companion, Cliff, manages to escape, he is in a state of extreme shock. A third student, Malcolm, who did not witness the attack, is persuaded by Dr Brockton to lead an expedition back into the cavern to capture the creature. Brockton believes the animal is a troglodyte or a primitive cave dweller that has somehow managed to survive since the Ice Age. The village is soon in uproar about the 'monster'; television crews arrive and local resident Sam Murdock is outspoken in his opposition. The creature is lured out of the cave, captured and entrusted to the care of Brockton, who now believes that she has found the missing link. Brockton begins a process of educating the creature she dubs 'Trog' but its primitive instincts are never far from the surface and when Murdock breaks into the lab, it escapes and embarks upon a rampage through the town.

Trog started his trek to the screen under the guidance of Tony Tenser at Tigon, who announced the project in 1967 as *Trog, One Million Year Old Man*. 'I had the idea of making a film set in prehistoric times but without the dinosaurs,' the producer said. 'We had troglodytes or cave dwellers, who were almost human but covered in hair. I wanted to use troglodytes the same way that they used monkeys in *Planet of the Apes* and I wanted to make it a love story.' Tigon tried unsuccessfully to mount the project several times but it wasn't until Herman Cohen emerged with a co-production deal that Tenser was able to get Peter Bryan to write a script that was acceptable to potential distributors. By then, Tigon's *Witchfinder General* (1968) had opened and Tenser was forging ahead with a slate of horror films financed by AIP; *Trog* was deemed surplus to requirements and the rights were sold to Herman Cohen Productions Ltd for a nominal sum.

Cohen brought in John Gilling to rework the Bryan screenplay and it was Gilling who wrote in the film's main protagonist, Dr Brockton, a hard-nosed but humane scientist, very much in the Quatermass mould, who battles to stop the creature from being destroyed or kept in a zoo. Cohen remained unconvinced by the script and Gilling left the project in a state of suspended animation and, if the director had his way, that's how it would have remained. 'I heard they had about five writers working on it after I left,' Gilling told Gilbert Verschooten in *Little Shoppe of Horrors,* 'and it annoyed me intensely that my name should appear on the credit card, associating me with the abortion that finally emerged.'

The rewriting that so incensed Gilling was more than just a cosmetic exercise to interest a distributor; it was driven by Cohen's decision to offer the leading role to Joan Crawford. Since appearing in *Berserk!* the actress had limited her appearances to chat-shows and day-time soaps, while rumours about her uncontrolled drinking rendered her practically unemployable in Hollywood. Cohen, who had previously coaxed something approaching restraint out of her, was one of the few producers still prepared to take a chance and he instructed Aben Kandel to alter the sex of

Trog (Joe Cornelius, Chloe Franks)

Brockton and soften the characterisation. Crawford's name on the package was enough for Cohen to secure financial backing from Warner Bros and after more than two years on the shelf, *Trog* was suddenly a 'go' project.

Her career may have been in irreversible decline but 'Her Serene Crawfordness' proved that she was still a commanding figure—at least to the British press, which gleefully reported her arrival at Heathrow airport with no less than forty items of luggage. Crawford was soon warbling happily to reporters, telling *Today's Cinema*, '*Planet of the Apes* is one of the greatest films I have ever seen. I'd never done any science fiction before, I'd never played a lady scientist, and I'd never played a doctor before. I am going to play everything!' Cohen, his arms linked with those of his star, took the opportunity to manage expectations about content by insisting he made family films and 'good clean horror is escapism: it is no more harmful than Disney's witches and goblins.'

Accommodating Crawford, whose salary reportedly accounted for 25% of the film's budget, limited Cohen's options for the scope of the film. At the press launch, he had boasted that the film would have 'extensive special effects'—by the time Joan Crawford and her mountain of suitcases arrived in London, these had been reduced to some (Ray Harryhausen) animation footage lifted from a Warner Bros' release of 1956, *The Animal World*.

The man charged with bringing all the elements together was Freddie Francis,

X-Cert

Trog / INSET: Joan Crawford

the Oscar-winning cinematographer who had helmed such stylish horrors as *The Skull* (1965) and *Dracula Has Risen from the Grave* (1968). 'As soon as they said the words "Joan Crawford" I signed on,' Francis confessed. 'I would have done anything just to work with her. I thought she would add a touch of real class.' The mystique associated with that name also worked its magic on the supporting players, who included such reliable performers as Thorley Walters, Bernard Kay, Robert Hutton and Michael Gough. Gough was cast as Sam Murdock, a one-man village mob who campaigns vociferously to have Trog put down and in the end frees the creature just to prove that it is indeed a menace. Later additions to the cast brought in David Warbeck, who became something of a cult figure in Italian horror films, and Chloe Frank, the child actress who appeared for Milton Subotsky in a number of Amicus pictures.

Almost from the moment principle photography started, it was obvious that Crawford was going to be trouble. 'Her drinking was worse than it was when we were doing *Berserk!*,' Cohen told *The Dark Side* magazine, 'I had to reprimand her a few times for drinking without asking. She had a frosted glass that said Pepsi-Cola—but inside it was hundred-proof vodka!' It was not just the drinking that was causing problems. 'It was a bit sad by then,' Francis laments. 'She was getting on and losing

4: Excruciating Bad Taste

it a bit. She couldn't remember her lines and we had to use idiot boards a lot of the time and I had to try and shoot round her.' Francis was reduced to filming scenes as early as possible in the day and shooting as few takes as possible, which limited the coverage the editor had available. Veteran Oswald Hafenrichter had to assemble the first cut with whatever shots he had to hand and even in the final film, there are shots where Crawford is seen fumbling with props or struggling to focus.

Despite the difficulties, Francis remained respectful of his star. 'Whatever else is said about her,' he insists, 'she was 100% committed to what she did'—a view shared by actor David Warbeck, who remembers the actress telling him, 'What we're paid for is to turn shit into gold.' Making that transformation was proving a challenge, and Bernard Kay believed that Cohen was placing too much faith in his director. 'The budget was disgustingly low,' he insists, 'but that was how they operated. They thought that Freddie had the knack of making rubbish look good; he could take a cheap cardboard set and because he was such a wonderful cameraman, he made it look wonderful.'

In the end, the cast were all defeated by the script. Even Joan Crawford at the top of her game would have struggled to keep a straight face and mouth lines like, 'How large was it compared to a human? Did it walk upright? Did it crawl? Did it make sounds? If so, were they sounds like the human voice?' Cohen's earlier Disney reference springs to mind in the scene where Dr Brockton tries to domesticate the creature, telling it to fetch a ball and then teaching it the fundamentals of English: 'This is blue, Trog. Bluuuuuuue.'

Faced with a poor script, Francis tries unsuccessfully to steer a path between the more infantile touches and the potential for pure sensationalism. When perennial bit-parter Bartlett Mullins's luckless butcher is hung from his own meat-hook, the director missed the chance for a graphic and shocking scene and instead opted for an anaemic bit of horseplay. The censor, perhaps recalling Cohen's pronouncements about family entertainment, offered the producer an A certificate in exchange for the briefest of cuts. BBFC files record with some disappointment that Cohen 'seems determined to sell this film as a horror movie and...refuses to make the cuts.' The resulting compromise, an AA certificate, allowed Cohen to promise audiences 'One missing link—and all the terror that goes with it'. But the tagline hardly held out the sort of illicit promise inherent in the X.

Critics barely noticed the certificate anyway and buried *Trog* with damning reviews. 'It's probably the worst film ever made,' crowed *The Sun*, while *The Times* was no kinder, noting that 'the script is idiotic beyond belief.' The *Morning Star*'s correspondent was incredulous: 'Did I really see this gormless horror weepie or was it just a bad dream? Can anyone make a film as bad as this?' The public were equally unforgiving. *Trog* opened in the 570-seat Rialto in London to a spectacularly-bad gross of £1,358. To put that into perspective: at the same time over at the 290-seat Windmill, *Alyse and Chloe* (1970) completed its 19th week with over £1,900. Even Crawford herself seemed immune to *Trog*'s charms; asked by an American reporter why she did it, the veteran star replied, 'For the money! I'm an actress and it doesn't matter these days what the hell I do as long as the role has guts.' She went a little further in conversation with writer Roy Newquist and declared, 'If I weren't a Christian Scientist, and I saw *Trog* advertised on a marquee across the street I'd think I'd contemplate suicide.' Sadly, it proved to be the last chapter in the actress's glittering career. She continued with her television appearances but she never made another feature.

Trog! did not quite put an end to Herman Cohen's filmmaking ambitions, but it did put them on hold. It was 1973 before he returned to Britain to pick up more

X-Cert

Trog: Director Freddie Francis, Joan Crawford, producer Herman Cohen

or less where he left off. In the meantime, one had to seriously wonder if *The Sun* film critic who thought that *Trog!* was the worst film ever made had seen some of the others that were pouring out of British studios, in particular a little gem from veteran British writer/director Lawrence Huntington called *The Vulture*.

THE VULTURE
'Half-man, half birdbeast...swooping on his human prey...drinking blood...mutilating them!'

> Ellen West is the only witness to the vandalism of the grave of Francis Real, a long-dead seaman thought to have been in league with the Devil. Ellen, who was walking through the graveyard, insists that she saw a creature with the head of a man and the body of a large bird, the sight of which was enough to turn her hair white with terror. A 200-year-old parchment predicts that Real will avenge himself on the Stroud family and Superintendent Wendell calls on the family home to speak to Trudy and her husband Eric, a nuclear scientist. When the Strouds start to fall victim to mysterious attacks, Eric reveals that he believes Ellen's story and is sure that the creature is the result of a failed nuclear experiment. Convinced that the attacks will continue and that Ellen is in danger, he sets out on an investigation of his own, starting with a visit to an old friend of the family: Professor Koniglich, a seemingly harmless collector of antiques...

It often happens in the world of horror films that one man alone is associated with the success or failure of a particular picture and in the case of *The Vulture*, that honour goes to Lawrence Huntington, who conceived the original story and wrote the script, as well as producing and directing. Huntington was a colourful character; a former dance-hall musician who turned his hand to film-making and had been

4: Excruciating Bad Taste

crafting passable B pictures since the 1930s, with only an occasional step-up to co-feature status. *The Vulture* was something of a departure from his usual thrillers and was inspired, according to the press release, by an unpleasant deity found on Easter Island—a giant hybrid of man and bird called *Manutara*, that thrived on human sacrifice. It is a fanciful tale with only a passing connection to the truth; the natives did have an obscure cult connected to the migratory patterns of the *Manutara,* also known as a Sooty Tern, but it was a seabird considerably smaller than a vulture!

Nevertheless the 'legend', as outlined in Huntington's script, originally called *Manutara,* was enough to hook Hollywood producer Jack O Lamont, who in turn persuaded Paramount to sink its money into the project, subject to the signing of American stars in the lead roles. Lamont, who accepted 'executive producer' credit although he was present throughout shooting, had known Robert Hutton since the actor was at Warner Bros, and he had no difficulty in persuading him to play the dim-witted atomic scientist whose knowledge of animal research seems acutely developed for a physicist. Since his encounter with *The Man without a Body*, Hutton had turned director with *The Slime People* (1963) and relocated to the UK, where the 'high point' of his sojourn to date had been an encounter with Cliff Richard in *Finders Keepers* (1966).

Homeric Films was established to produce the film and it raised the required £50,000 budget from the Canadian Ihod Productions and the NFFC, a combination which enabled Lamont to strengthen the Hollywood connection with two acting heavyweights in supporting roles. Russian-born Akim Tamiroff played the kindly but eccentric Professor Hans Koniglich, who provides the piece with its only real suspect. Tamiroff was a double Oscar nominee who had enjoyed a long association with 'art-house' directors like Orson Welles and Jean-Luc Goddard in films such as *Touch of Evil* (1958) and *Alphaville* (1965). Since the early sixties, he had been active in European films playing a range of bizarre and often menacing characters, but nothing quite like Koniglich, who hides his darker side quite literally under a shabby raincoat. Third-billed Broderick Crawford had gone a step further than Tamiroff and actually picked up a Best Actor Oscar for *All the Kings Men* (1949). Invariably cast as a fast-talking tough guy, he was now best-known as Chief Dan Mathews in television's *Highway Patrol*, and he famously summed up his screen persona to a Hollywood journalist thus: 'My trademarks are a hoarse, grating voice and the face of a retired pugilist: small narrowed eyes set in puffy features which look as though they might, years ago, have lost on points.' Crawford, who had shared an agent with Robert Hutton in the 1950s, played Brian Stroud, the overbearing patriarch of the Stroud family.

Actors of this calibre, even those on their uppers, come at a price, and Lamont and Huntington were left with a depleted budget to flesh out the supporting cast; the only familiar name was Diane Clare playing Trudy, essentially the same endangered heroine role that she had essayed with little distinction in *Witchcraft*. She simply swapped Lon Chaney for Broderick Crawford and carried on as before. Clare, who enjoyed more regular and varied work on the small screen, was particularly unlucky in her choice of films and *The Vulture* was easily the least inspiring. She would soon marry noted author and playwright Barry England and retire completely from the profession thereafter.

To create an environment for these characters to inhabit, Huntington looked no further than another of those fictitious Cornish villages so beloved of horror filmmakers. Tolferro, as it was known, was created during five weeks of location shooting in Devon and Cornwall with interiors filmed at Pinewood. Stephen Dade, who had proved his mettle with the Cornish coastline in *Doctor Blood's Coffin* and *City in the Sea* (1965), handled the cinematography. Dade's contribution was essential to the film's opening scene, a well-staged and beautifully photographed sequence where Ellen West (Annette Carell) walks across a rainy graveyard at night, after scoffing at the bus driver who warns, 'You wouldn't get me in there after dark. Don't you know the place is haunted?' The audience are treated to a flurry of beating wings and manic cackling, and the poor woman is so traumatised that her hair turns white and she is reduced to a trembling wreck.

From this nicely-realised opening, the film rapidly descends into a typical 1950s monster flick with an irradiated creature loose in the countryside and stalking its enemies one by one. Denied a budget for even the most rudimentary special effects, Huntington relies on sound and reactions for impact in the early scenes but quickly resorts to the laughable sight of a pair of giant talons descending from the heavens to pluck victims aloft. Robert Hutton summed up the situation when he told Tom Weaver, 'I think this was one film where they needed more horror...it called for less talk and more horror.'

If the killings were tame, the script commits the cardinal sin of setting up some interesting ideas and just discarding them in favour another attack from above. The prospect of stolen treasure, for example, occupies everyone's thoughts but plays no part at all in the drama. Instead, Huntington throws logic to the wind and heaps coincidence on top of cliché on top of coincidence. An American atomic researcher holidaying in Cornwall at exactly the same time as his wife's family are being picked off by a centuries-old curse and a bird-brained (literally) homicidal lunatic. As all the victims require to be in the open, the situations become increasingly contrived, particularly the final attack on Trudy, who has been warned not to wander off but decides that a bit of fresh air cannot hurt.

Hutton recalls questioning his director about the rationale for a particular action, only to be told, 'Bobby, please just do it. I don't care if it doesn't make sense, just do it.' The actor was left to conclude, 'They just wanted to get the thing on film and forget it.' Despite the ludicrous script, both Hutton and Crawford take the film seriously but neither can rise above a mechanical performance. Akim Tamiroff, on the other hand, pulls out all the stops and attacks his role with all the zeal of a pantomime dame, his scenery-chewing only helping to reinforce the total absurdity of the rest of the film.

The *Daily Cinema* was one of the few reviews to have anything good to say about the film: 'Fair to middling creepy...painless panic for the timorous.' *Kinematograph Weekly* was more scathing: 'Its thrills will chill only the simple-minded.' A decade earlier, *The Vulture* might have been picked up by AIP in the US as perfect drive-in fodder and Paramount pitched the film at the same audience if not the same venue. Doubling it up with the lame Amicus effort, *The Deadly Bees*, it promised patrons 'Talons of Terror!—Hives of Horror!' The press campaign went on to suggest that theatre managers should 'dress an usher in a half-man/half-bird outfit. Have him walk the streets of your community with a sandwich board prominently featuring your theatre and play-date.'

The public largely ignored Huntington's picture but it did spark some interest at AIP, which engaged the Englishman to write and direct its latest Poe opus, *The Oblong Box*, the first to be mounted through its newly-opened London office. But the director fell ill shortly after starting pre-production and was replaced by Michael Reeves, who was himself then replaced by Gordon Hessler. The subsequent film from Huntington's script (revised by Christopher Wicking) was successful enough to reinvigorate the series and win Hessler a three-film contract. Huntington did not live to see what would probably be considered his biggest success as a writer; he died in

4: Excruciating Bad Taste

The Vulture: US advertising materials / INSET: Akim Tamiroff

November 1968.

While Lawrence Huntington's career was drawing to a close, another British filmmaker, Robert Hartford-Davis, was planning a return to the horror genre. Hartford-Davis had made his name with exploitation films like *The Yellow Teddy-Bears* (aka *Gutter Girl*; 1963) for Compton before graduating to *The Black Torment* (1964), a Gainsborough-style gothic horror film, jam-packed with heaving bosoms, stormy nights and mad aristocrats. Tiring of corporate interference, Hartford-Davis and his regular cinematographer Peter Newbrook struck out on their own with Titan Films, later Titan International, to make two typical Sixties oddities: *Gonks Go Beat* (1965) and *The Sandwich Man* (1966). Tony Tenser, Hartford-Davis's employer at Compton, described the director as 'an exploitation man first and foremost' and in 1967, Titan announced a film that seemed determined to push the boundaries of exploitation as far as they could possibly go.

CORRUPTION
'Corruption is not a woman's picture.'

> Sir John Rowan is racked with guilt after an accident leaves his model girlfriend, Lynn, permanently disfigured and seriously depressed. Finding a way of restoring her beauty and her confidence becomes an obsession and he spends long hours researching a cure and conducting experiments on animals before eventually proving that he can restore damaged tissue. Stealing the pituitary gland of a road-accident victim, he successfully operates with Lynn's sister Val assisting. Dr Harris, a colleague and Val's boyfriend, warns that the effects may be short-lived but Rowan and Lynn ignore him and announce that they will marry. As Harris predicted, the astonishing results do not last and Rowan needs to kill a prostitute to obtain the necessary gland—but again the effects are temporary. Rowan and Val are forced into increasingly desperate measures to get the glands and their gruesome activities eventually attract the attention of a gang of transient hippies determined to turn the situation to their advantage.

The script for *Corruption* came from Derek and Donald Ford, who had worked with Hartford-Davis at Compton and had also scripted its efficient Sherlock Holmes versus Jack the Ripper film, *A Study in Terror* (1965). Claiming inspiration from an article in the *New Scientist*, the Fords also seem to have been influenced by *Les Yeux Sans Visage, (Eyes without a Face)*, the 1960 Georges Franju thriller about a brilliant surgeon whose daughter is disfigured in a car crash and forced to wear a mask to hide her face. The doctor becomes fascinated with the idea of restoring

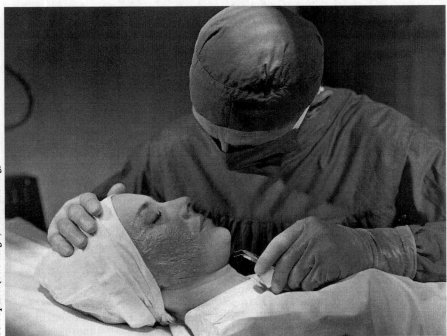

Corruption (Sue Lloyd, Peter Cushing)

4: Excruciating Bad Taste

her beauty, kidnapping and operating on a series of women while searching for the elusive cure. In *Corruption*, Franju's basic plot, with its themes of vanity and guilt, is updated to include a David Bailey-style photographer, the latest laser technology and a gang of drugged-out hippies who seem already to have completely forgotten about the summer of love. The lyrical and disturbing imagery of *Les Yeux Sans Visage* is left behind in favour of a more vulgar and gratuitous approach, perfectly in line with the director's exploitation background. To play the architect of all this bedlam, Hartford-Davis chose to cast the grand old man of British horror films, Peter Cushing.

Aside from Baron Frankenstein, Cushing's screen activities had seldom strayed to the dark side and not since *The Flesh and the Fiends* had the actor being cast in such a despicable role. At least that film's period setting removed it somewhat, but *Corruption* was part of a growing trend for urban horrors, a trail blazed by Michael Reeves's *The Sorcerers* (1967), which would reach a peak with Pete Walker's horrors in the 1970s. This was all new territory for Cushing and the experience was not a particularly happy one for the actor. 'I did not like the film at all,' he told biographer Gary Parfitt. 'With any film you participate in, when you're finished your role, the company, if they so wish, can destroy your original interpretation.'

One can sympathise with Cushing's disapproval of the film's murder sequences, which Hartford-Davis sets out make as uncomfortable as possible for the viewer. The scene in which Rowan attacks a girl (Valerie Van Ost) in a train carriage is the perfect example of the approach adopted by the director; rapid-fire edits, a tangle of flailing limbs and extreme close-ups of Cushing's face, sweat dripping from his brow, hair dishevelled and eyes bulging maniacally. The actor was a long way from the more considered mayhem of Hammer and Terence Fisher. He could not have been any more pleased by the 'continental' version of the film, and the scene where a nervous-looking Rowan visits the prostitute is particularly grotesque. The British version is almost demure, with the girl (Jan Waters, outfitted in a fetching dressing gown) dispatched with relative speed and discretion. The alternative version, never intended for screening in the UK, allows Hartford-Davis to give free rein to his baser instincts. Rowan and the now-topless girl wrestle violently across the room, kicking and scratching each other in another frenzy of hand-held camera shots and close-ups. Cushing, always an energetic actor, launches himself into the physical action with gusto, throwing the tart to the floor and straddling her naked torso as he repeatedly plunges his knife into her stomach. Panting for breath, he then wipes his bloody hands on her breasts. The sequence is shocking enough, but all the more so because of the utter conviction of Cushing's acting and the remorseless intrusion of Hartford-Davis's camera. Incidentally, the doll motif that appeared prominently in the film's advertising features here, with children's toys dotted casually around the flat, presumably to say something about lost innocence.

Cushing is equally powerful during the film's quieter sequences and he effectively captures Rowan's discomfort at the swinging party (which presumably reflected the actor's own unease at being surrounded by all these pretty young things). Later when Lynn's sister, Val (Kate O'Mara), gently rebukes him for working too hard, the actor's expression captures all the frustration and guilt that the character is feeling. 'You are becoming obsessed,' she says, 'shut in here with all these old books. You've got to face facts and get back to your own work.' Rowan's composure snaps: 'Please leave me alone,' he shouts, slamming a book down onto the desk. In a split-second, he is contrite at the outburst and begging forgiveness—a throwaway scene but indicative of how consummate a screen actor Cushing actually was.

The credibility of the story, such as it is, rests on convincing the viewer that

X-Cert

Corruption (Peter Cushing, Valerie Van Ost)

Rowan and Lynn, two people from different generations, backgrounds and interests, had the sort of relationship that would motivate the extreme behaviour depicted. That Lynn needed to be spectacularly beautiful goes without saying; she also needed to be vain, precocious but fascinating enough to enthral an intelligent older man. The producers were fortunate in the casting of Sue Lloyd, a former model and showgirl, who had featured in *The Ipcress File* (1965) but was best known for a recurring role on the popular television series *The Baron*. Despite her relative inexperience with screen acting and the age difference with her romantic interest (Cushing was 26 years her senior), the pairing works well. Lloyd is at her best as Lynn's dementia starts to grow. When Rowan produces a guinea pig he has been using in his experiments, she is appalled, 'You deliberately burned the creature?' she asks. 'Oh, John, how can you be so cruel?' Before long, she is extolling her husband to kill everything in sight in order to acquire the glands.

Hartford-Davis's supporting cast were professional if not especially well known. Kate O'Mara would go on to star in a brace of Hammer horrors while her screen beau, Noel Trevarthen, already had his genre baptism in *It!* and now switched profession from police to medicine to play Dr Harris. The 'normal' relationship between Val and Harris is supposed to counterpoint the destructive fixations of the leads but in fact, insufficient screen time is allowed to them to build that sort of subtext.

The best-known faces amongst the coterie of hippies were Billy Murray, who would carve out a lucrative niche playing East End gangsters and corrupt policemen in British films, and David Lodge, a supporting player in films since the early 1950s, usually as rock-hard soldiers or officious policemen. Lodge was something of a talisman for Hartford-Davis; the two men had first worked together on *Saturday Night Out* (1962) and whenever possible the director would cast him in his latest work. In the case of *Corruption,* the 46-year old was clearly not suitable for a hippy so the writers specifically rewrote the character to make him mentally retarded.

4: Excruciating Bad Taste

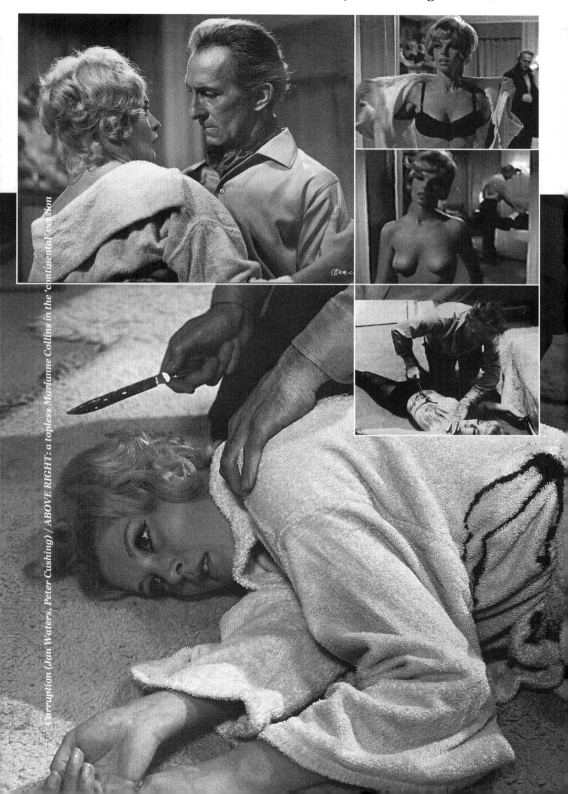

Corruption (Ian Waters, Peter Cushing) / ABOVE RIGHT: a topless Marianne Collins in the 'continental' version

X-Cert

During the early summer of 1967, Hartford-Davies and his crew were decamped to the beachfront at Seaford in East Sussex and on the railway line between Lewes and Brighton, shooting graphic murder sequences. The honour of hosting the most bizarre sequence belongs to Isleworth Studios, however, where the director staged one of the most breath-taking climaxes yet seen in a British horror film. The set up is simple enough: Rowan and Lynn are cornered in their cottage by the hippy gang, who are anxious to know what happened to their missing friend. 'Teri was casing the pad for us,' Rowan is told, as the creeping horror of the situation begins to play over his features. 'We were going to turn you over'. What the hippies do not know is that Teri has been murdered and that the upstanding gent they have at their mercy has a decaptated head in his fridge. The stress of it becomes too much for Lynn's sanity; she activates the powerful laser that has been installed for use in her latest operation but immediately loses control of it and the machine goes haywire. While Cushing wrestles with one of the thugs, the laser slices through everything and everyone in the room, including Val and Dr Harris, who inexplicably reappear at the critical moment. The whole thing is filmed with the same frantic, unstructured approach as the murder scenes and played out against a fractious jazz score. The closing shot features the bodies of all the principle players lying cut and slashed in heaps on the floor, only for Hartford-Davis to reveal that the preceding was a dream/premonition of Rowan's, who is actually still at the earlier party!

The cheat-ending was presumably a ploy to justify the various excesses but the distributors felt no compunction to disguise the filmmaker's true intent. Columbia, which took the worldwide rights, mounted a campaign that played up to the most sensational elements of the film. British patrons were warned that 'Corruption is a super shock film! Therefore no woman will be admitted to see it alone!' The message to Americans was even blunter: 'Corruption is not a woman's picture!' The US press book also contained the helpful suggestion that cinema managers might like to hang the severed heads of female mannequins from the ceiling of the foyer.

Such moves, to say nothing of the film's style and content, were a red rag to the critics, including the *Western Daily Press* which condemned what it saw as 'an ill-directed, ill photographed piece of work in excruciating bad taste. It is, moreover, artistically and morally indefensible, and it is a sad thought that such a film can be made, let alone attract an audience to see it.' The more mainstream reviews were milder; the *Hollywood Reporter* liked the production values but thought the result 'offensive to sense and sensibility', while *Variety* saw 'some genuine suspense, but the pacing and the performances are generally limp.'

If Peter Cushing is to be believed, audiences voted with their wallets and made *Corruption* a resounding commercial success. 'A fortune was made on that picture,' the actor told Gary Parfitt. 'I've heard that Bob was practically able to retire on his share of the proceeds.' Cushing may well have been right on the box-office receipts but Hartford-Davis gave no indication of wishing to retire and instead poured Titan's ill-gotten gains into *The Smashing Bird I Used to Know* (1969), a trashy schoolgirl sex film with the same 'Torn from today's headlines!' theme as his earlier Compton efforts. The director misjudged his market, however, and despite a good cast and some effective moments, *The Smashing Bird I Used to Know* flopped, leaving Titan desperate for a quick win to restore its ailing coffers.

Predictably Hartford-Davis and Newbrook went scurrying down the path they had traversed so successfully with *Corruption* and constructed a modern horror film with seasoned professionals and recognisable genre situations. Then, as with *Corruption*, they packed in as much gratuitous sex and violence as the censorship regime would let them get away with.

4: Excruciating Bad Taste

INCENSE FOR THE DAMNED
'A distorted world comes to life—forbidden secrets sensationally revealed! It's way out!'

> While holidaying in Greece, Richard Fountain, an Oxford don, falls under the spell of a beautiful Greek girl, Chriseis, and her coven of perverted socialites. The group practice the black arts, including orgiastic rituals, human sacrifices and vampirism. Given Richard's family connections, the British and Greek governments are keen to avoid a scandal and Richard's friends Tony and Bob Kirby, his fiancé Penelope, and Derek Longbow, an embassy official, are despatched to the island of Hydra to bring him home. The group arrive in time to prevent the worst excesses but in a subsequent struggle, Chriseis falls to her death and her hold over Richard seems to have been broken. Richard is rescued and returned to Oxford where his future father-in-law, Goodrich, welcomes him as his anointed successor. But Richard is listless and prone to erotic fantasies and nightmares. It becomes apparent that although Chriseis has been defeated, she has not yet been banished and is still exerting a powerful influence over her protege.

Incense for the Damned, or *Bloodsuckers* as it was later retitled, was derived from *Doctors Wear Scarlet*, a rather ponderous and pretentious novel written in 1960 by Simon Raven, a renowned author who was probably better known for his personal life. The *Daily Telegraph* once wrote of him in terms of Lord Byron, highlighting 'the same energy, contempt for cant, unshocked 18th-century acceptance of human folly, urge towards sexual experiment and—underlying the hedonistic philosophy—the same desire to court retribution.' It was a description that Raven did his best to live up to; so much so that when he died at the age of 73 in 2001, *The Guardian's* obituary writer suggested, 'He ought, by rights, to have died of shame at thirty, or of drink at fifty.'

Terence Fisher had reportedly tried to interest Hammer in the novel in the early 1960s, but the studio was more attached to its traditional horrors and the rights were never taken up. Despite the presence of vampires and a complex love triangle, *Doctors Wear Scarlet* could hardly have been called a typical Fisher project. The novel

Incense for the Damned (Patrick Mower, Peter Cushing)

X-Cert

Incense for the Damned: additional footage (Francoise Pascal, Imogen Hassall)

is essentially an acerbic attack on the Establishment and particularly the vice-like hold that the social order's oligarchs exert over the young and impressionable. The author used academia, specifically the Oxbridge universities and their out-moded traditions, to mock society as a whole, and he linked the lax morals and recreational drug-use of the youth of the day to destructive cults and sexual decadence. This was hardly the run-of-the-mill morality tale churned out by Hammer; not only was the story from an infamous profligate but it was being made at a time when anxiety about the so-called counterculture movement was coming to its peak and the drugs, psychedelic music and anti-Vietnam War protests were taking a darker and more sinister turn. In August 1969, the Tate-La Bianca murders on the orders of Charles Manson would forever associate the word 'cult' with random and brutal violence.

It is against this background that writer Julian More constructed his screenplay. More, who had written the lyrics for two huge West End shows, *Expresso Bongo* and *Irma la Douce,* stayed closely to the core of Raven's tale while dispensing with much of the Oxford back story and moving the action onto the Hellenic debauchery as quickly as possible. This approach offered plenty of opportunities for Hartford-Davis to indulge his artistic inclinations as actor Patrick Mower observed while filming a particularly nasty scene where Fountain attacks his girlfriend and rips her throat out with his teeth. Mower, who played Fountain, recorded in his autobiography, 'To Bob's salivating satisfaction, the scene was shot seven times until the blood slowly and sensuously made its way over the impressive contours. He, of course, insisted on personally wiping the poor girl's breasts clean between every take.'

Lucinda Films, which had also backed *The Smashing Bird I Used to Know,* trusted

4: Excruciating Bad Taste

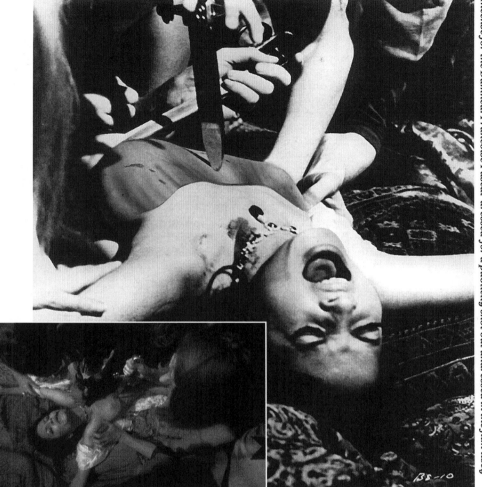

Incense for the Damned: Francoise Pascal 'dressed' for a publicity shot but undressed in the film itself

the director's instincts for this sort of fare and together with Titan pooled enough money to allow not only location filming in Greece and Cyprus—the director's first experience of shooting abroad—but what seems, at first glance, to be an impressive cast list. The aforementioned Patrick Mower, who played the impressionable young intellectual seduced to the dark side, had worked for Hartford-Davis before but he was probably best known for Hammer's *The Devil Rides Out* (1968), in which he played…an impressionable young intellectual seduced to the dark side! Striding to Mower's assistance in that film was Christopher Lee and while Titan's budget could not stretch that far, it did manage to entice Patrick MacNee, erstwhile star of the recently-cancelled *The Avengers*. MacNee took top-billing for the supporting role of Longbow, the urbane consular official who guides the intrepid party through the shadier regions of the Mediterranean. It is MacNee who lightens the sombre tone with some nicely-observed humour; when he is told that 'Richard came to Greece in search of some sort of freedom—to seek his manhood!' Longbow quips, 'Oh? Well, they say this climate works wonders for that sort of thing.' However, his credibility is completely undermined during the hot pursuit of the gang up a mountain path when he leads the charge sitting astride a donkey!

Hartford-Davis also signed another big name from the small screen, Edward Woodward, aka 'Callan' from the television show of the same name. Woodward, whose horror genre credentials would be enshrined by 1972's *The Wicker Man,* had to content himself with a single scene, playing an 'occult expert' whose contribution is limited to espousing vampirism as a sexual perversion. The hat-trick of cameos was completed by Peter Cushing, who had evidently forgiven the director for the aberration of *Corruption* and who took the equally unpleasant but far less psychotic character of Walter Goodrich, a passive-aggressive bully of the first order who is the latent object of Fountain's hatred and fear. Cushing makes the most of his limited screen-time to establish an imposing and powerful figure, arrogantly controlling the destiny of others without even being aware of it. The actor's best scene is at the end of the film after he has seen the death of both his daughter and his prodigy and he lets his mask of stoicism slip for the first time.

In contrast to the starring roles, the trio of would-be rescuers from Oxford are given much more screen time but achieve far less with it. Alex Davion, Senegalese actor Johnny Sekka and Madeline Hinde, who had been the 'smashing bird' in the director's previous outing, all had better and more interesting things on their CVs and none of them would count their flimsy characterisations here among their best work. Imogen Hassall, better known to the tabloids as the 'Countess of Cleavage' than as an actress, plays the dark-skinned Chriseis, but she too is given little opportunity to establish her character as anything other than a voluptuous *houri*. Of course the film also contained an obligatory appearance by David Lodge, complete with a fake moustache and comedy accent, as a Greek policeman.

One would have expected the cast, the locations and the cinematic possibilities of a tale about psychological domination and sexual obsessions to coalesce rather better than it did, but *Incense for the Damned* is a film that failed on almost every level—to the extent that even the director disowned it. It is no longer possible to say how much blame for the inept and barely watchable mess that emerged can be laid at the feet of Hartford-Davis and how much was the result of post-production interference. The production was in trouble long before it reached the editing suite after the money ran out during shooting in the Mediterranean. Cast and crew were recalled while the producers (who in Hartford-Davis's version of events are always unnamed) opened discussions with the completion guarantors to decide whether to write the investment off or to struggle on.

This was in the spring of 1969 and the decision reached was to seek alternative finance and resume filming at a later stage, which is more or less what happened. New scenes were written, new actors engaged (including Mauritian beauty Francoise Pascal) and, according to Hartford-Davis, a new director was hired. The new footage, an explicit orgy, had no bearing on the original script and existed purely to pad out the running time and boost the film's already significant exploitable elements. The old and new scenes were then cobbled together into something loosely approaching a coherent storyline, with the gaps in the narrative bridged by an unconvincing voice-over. As lawsuits started to fly between the various parties involved, the director was so appalled by the new cut that he insisted his name was removed and the direction credited to the fictitious 'Michael Burrowes'.

In the messy aftermath of the shambles, Titan Productions was dissolved and the professional partnership between Robert Hartford-Davis and Peter Newbrook was ended. Both men continued to work in the horror genre but their long-standing collaboration was over. The 'new' bastardised version of the film was submitted to

4: Excruciating Bad Taste

the BBFC, which raised some concerns over the 'girl on girl' coupling glimpsed in the inserts but otherwise was content to pass the film with an X certificate.

Despite all the difficulties with *Incense for the Damned*, the critics seemed quite satisfied with Hartford-Davis's efforts. *Time Out* even suggested it 'was the first time in screen history that a director has disowned the only remotely good thing he has done.' The *Daily Cinema* considered that the 'visual excitement' was 'more effective than the dialogue which strains at the colloquial but remains obstinately literary.' The public were given little opportunity to agree or disagree; the film had a trade screening in 1972 but its release was barely worthy of the term and it was consigned to brief appearances over the next few years, propping up obscure double-bills.

In March 1969, a young film producer started to work on her debut film, a low budget horror which, like *Corruption*, was influenced less by contemporary British studios and more by the subtle but chillingly-effective style of French cinema. In the case of *The Corpse*, Gabrielle Beaumont and husband Olaf Pooley looked to Henri-Georges Clouzot and his 1955 suspense masterpiece, *Les Diaboliques*.

THE CORPSE
'Terror ends with murder...but nightmares begin with the corpse!'

> *Edith is trapped in a desperately unhappy marriage with the tyrannical Eastwood, a pompous and overbearing patriarch who dominates his two children, Rupert and Jane, particularly the latter, a 16-year-old who is kept away from all contact with the opposite sex. Eastwood seems to delight in mentally and physically torturing Jane, but he goes too far when he whips her for stealing some money from the local golf club. Edith and Jane conspire together to murder him by staging a drug overdose and leaving the body to be discovered at their weekend cottage. But the expected call from the authorities telling them of Eastwood's accidental death never comes, and mother and daughter become convinced that someone witnessed the crime and is now stalking them at the family home. Strange noises are heard in the attic, a window is smashed, and the two women are forced to barricade themselves in, not knowing if their tormentor is in or outside of the house.*

Clouzot's black-and-white *Les Diaboliques* (*The Fiends*) is set in a boy's school and tells of a conspiracy between two abused women to rid themselves of the headmaster who has made their life so miserable and who happens to be the husband of one and the lover of the other. The two conspirators murder the headmaster in the bathtub and then throw the body into the school's outdoor swimming pool, hoping he will be found and diagnosed as a suicide. Things start to go wrong when the pool is drained and turns out to be empty, after which a series of strange incidents suggest that the headmaster is actually still alive and tormenting his would-be murderers.

Olaf Pooley, who starred in *Naked Evil*, wrote a script under the title of *Velvet House* which was effectively an updating of Clouzot's story, but rather than set his protagonists loose through the shadowy corridors of an empty boy's school, Pooley's location was a far more cost-effective London suburb. In transferring his action to a leafy stockbroker belt, Pooley ensures that its more limited scope does not impact on the virulence of his terrors and he adds layers of complexity not found in Clouzot. More as a result of financial constraint than design, Pooley's screenplay becomes an exploration of modern society's soft underbelly and he provides a unsettling peek at the behaviours that can be hidden behind chintz curtains.

Husband and wife team Pooley and Gabrielle Beaumont set up the project at Abacus Films with financing, to the princely sum of £55,000, coming from London-

The Corpse (Yvonne Mitchell, Sharon Gurney)

Cannon Film Distributors, the British subsidiary of Cannon Films. At this stage in its history, Cannon was associated with low-budget films like the Oscar nominated *Joe* (1969) and the cult sex film *Maid in Sweden* (1969). Founders Dennis Friedland and Christopher C Dewey, both in their twenties, would lose control of their company in 1979 when it was taken over by Menahem Golem and Yoram Globus, whose business strategy yielded the likes of *Lifeforce* (1985) and *Masters of the Universe* (1987). Cannon Film Distributors also took the US rights while UK distribution was picked up the tiny Grand National Pictures, the company that coincidentally had fared so badly with Hratford-Davis's *The Smashing Bird I Used to Know*.

Pooley and Beaumont would later both try their hands at directing—the latter with considerable success on American television—but for their debut as producers, it was decided that more experienced hands were required at the tiller. Latvian-born Viktors Ritelis, who had practiced his craft at the BBC for a number of years, with work including Peter Cushing's BBC-TV *Sherlock Holmes* series, was selected. *The Corpse* would represent Ritelis's one and only venture into feature films but he did enjoy a long and fruitful career as a television director, working extensively for the BBC and independent companies until his retirement in 1998.

Joining Ritelis behind the camera was cinematographer John Mackey, who was best known for his effects photography on *The Deadly Bees*, as well as some of the model work on *2001: A Space Odyssey* (1968). Also on the crew was Christopher Toyne, Gabrielle Beaumont's younger brother, who helped out as a camera assistant and would eventually graduate to producer status in Hollywood.

To play the leading (titular!) role, Beaumont signed Herman Cohen's favourite heavy, Michael Gough, a man whose reputation as a stage actor was being eroded by poor screen choices—not that Gough seemed unduly concerned. 'I am what they call a "jobbing actor",' he told David Del Valle in *Little Shoppe of Horrors*. 'I basically do whatever is asked of me within my ability. I am not a starry kind of actor nor am I expensive to hire. That is to say I can always afford to do this as I have had too many wives and too many children, so I rarely can turn things down—hence all the horror films.' By 1969, Gough had perfected the imperious and disdainful screen persona

4: Excruciating Bad Taste

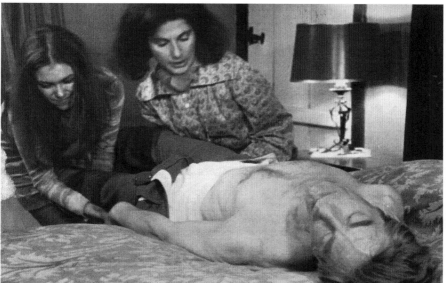

The Corpse (Yvonne Mitchell, Sharon Gurney)

that made him ideal casting as Walter Eastwood, a man with few discernable good qualities. Despite playing a passive role for much of the film, the actor made the most of his opportunities to create a thoroughly odious character; not only does he delight in physical abuse, taking a cane to the 16-year-old Jane, but he goes out of his way to humiliate her by reading her private letters aloud at the breakfast table. With so much of the success of the film resting on the audience feeling that mother and daughter have natural justice on their side, Gough does more than enough to alienate his character in the name of art, although Pooley's script does stop short of tackling one of the screen's last taboos. There is enough in the flashback sequence to suggest that incest can be added to the catalogue of Eastwood's crimes, and in case anyone does not pick up on the inference, the viewer is treated to the bizarre sight of Eastwood caressing his daughter's still warm bicycle seat.

If Michael Gough's philosophy was indeed to feed his wives and children first and foremost, then he must have been pleased by the decision to cast his son Simon as the supercilious Rupert, a self-satisfied chip off the old block who has followed his father into the family business. Rupert turns his music up full volume to drown out the sounds of Jane's screams but can't restrain himself from smugly asking, 'What's sis done now?' as Gough emerges. The family connection was extended when the producers came to cast Jane and hired Sharon Gurney, Simon Gough's fiancée, who was to become Michael Gough's daughter-in-law in 1970. The 20-year-old Gurney looks much older than her character's scripted age but imbues the part with a knowing sexuality and worldliness that moves the schoolgirl away from being merely victim and suggests a predatory quality about her also. This is most obvious in her dealings with the middle-aged Gregson, Eastwood's friend from the golf club, who calls round to reveal that Jane has been stealing from him; Ritelis leaves the audience in no doubt that the two are engaged in a sexual relationship.

Edith, the final member of the family quartet, and arguably the most complex role in the film, was played by the formidable stage actress Yvonne Mitchell, who was perhaps best known on screen for those other much-put-upon wives, Amy Preston in *Woman in a Dressing Gown* (1957) and Constance Wilde in *The Trials of Oscar*

X-Cert

Wilde (1960). Edith Eastwood is spared any direct physical abuse but it is clear from Walter's attitude that he believes her to be mentally unstable (in the later flashback scenes, we learn just how unstable she actually is). Walter's domination of Edith reduces the woman to a dependency on prescription medicine and forces her to hide away in the next room while Walter administers his punishment. Nevertheless, it is Edith rather than Jane who dares to whisper the words, 'Let's kill him'.

Surprisingly, perhaps, the only scene of actual violence in the film is not the murder where Gough is force-fed a cocktail of booze and drugs, but Jane's flogging which borders on the tasteless. Clever editing ensures that the scene stays well within the constraints of the X certificate, however. Ritelis maintains the same approach throughout the film and avoids the temptation to lurch into anything too explicit, preferring to exploit a careful build-up and convincing performances to create the impact. It is testament to his restrained approach that the BBFC snipped around the edges of the whipping scene but with the exception of the use of the word 'fucking'—which was replaced by 'bloody'—the censors left the film largely as presented.

With an efficient but not entirely original script and a miniscule budget, Ritelis deserves much of the credit for such a finely-crafted thriller, combining well-staged action sequences and convincing performances from the leads. Fundamental to the director's success was the use of the well-lit modern house to underpin the action and he manages to emphasis the claustrophobia and strangeness of such a familiar setting by careful use of close-ups and startling angles. (The interiors were all shot in an actual house, which cut down considerably on costs but in a nod to nostalgia, some of the pick-ups were filmed in the now-empty Merton Park Studios.)

Only the disappointing ending lets *The Corpse* down, a flaw which may explain

4: Excruciating Bad Taste

the lack of enthusiasm of distributors when it came to releasing the film. It was not picked up for British release until 1971, when Grand National Pictures distributed it on a bill with *Psycho Killer* (1970). For its US release, Cannon changed the title to *Crucible of Horror*, presumably to make it seem like a better running-mate for its co-feature, Boris Karloff's *Cauldron of Blood* (1969). At least the critics were impressed: *The New York Times* observed, 'It probes a seething family quartet with spider cunning, often brilliance. Superbly directed by Viktors Ritelis and beautifully played.. For tight, merciless tension and venom, the movie is uncommonly effective and engrossing. Add the twist of a civilised, very British fadeout that is the most horrifying thing of all. Quite a picture.'

Pooley and Beaumont stayed together as a team—he, writing and directing the children's film *The Johnstown Monster* in 1971; she, directing the horror film *The Godsend* from Pooley's script in 1980. In 1982, they transferred their base of operations to Los Angeles, where they found a new outlet for their undoubted talents on the small screen.

Although it was shot in March 1969, *The Corpse* was not submitted to the BBFC until late 1971—by which time the much coveted X certificate had received its first significant overhaul since its introduction nearly two decades earlier. John Trevelyan had long felt that the classification regime was struggling to cope with Hollywood films which had become increasingly adult in content (*Bonnie and Clyde* and *The Wild Bunch,* for example, in 1967 and 1969 respectively). European filmmakers in particular were also exploiting the freedom on the continent to make increasingly explicit sex films, which added to the impression that the UK, not for the first time, was out of step in terms of screen censorship.

The BBFC's solution was to raise the threshold of the X category from 16 to 18 years of age, and to introduce a new AA rating designed to accommodate films which were currently designated X due to their subject matter but which with minor cuts could reasonably be seen by 14-year-olds. The new X certificate came into effect in July 1970 and in the opinion of Board Secretary John Trevelyan, it heralded a new age 'where censorship of films for this category was virtually unnecessary'. It was a bold statement from a man who had been a massive influence on British filmmaking in the 1950s and '60s, and one might have expected that someone with his insight and extensive experience really should have known better.

Trevelyan's 'new age' of liberal censorship gave the movie executives in Wardour Street something to smile about at a time when things were looking particularly grim for the British industry as a whole. The Americans, who had arrived in such numbers only a few years earlier, had started to abandon London as their production base of choice. The economic situation in the US had deteriorated to the extent that President Johnson was forced to announce restrictions on American investment in Europe to help address the massive balance of payments deficit which had been caused, in part, by the escalating costs of the continuing Vietnam War. At the same time, Hollywood moguls had formed the view that Britain was no longer 'swinging' and big-budget films made at Pinewood and Shepperton were not enticing American cinemagoers as they once had; indigenous product, like *The Graduate* (1967) and *Rosemary's Baby* (1968), were now what was scaling the box-office heights. M-G-M announced that it was closing its British studios and cutting back on its overseas investments; the other Hollywood majors would very soon join it in the stampede back to California.

Paradoxically, the horror genre was at its most buoyant. Trevelyan's prediction was to prove the truth of the old adage: that the only two types of films that always

X-Cert

find an audience are sex and horror. The departure of the Americans left a vacuum in the UK industry that local filmmakers rushed headlong to fill, and the more relaxed censorship model allowed British producers the freedom to indulge excessively in both. The big players in this market—Hammer, Amicus, Tigon and AIP—all reached production peaks over the next few years and their perceived success encouraged a veritable explosion of horror product.

The previous decade had seen a flowering of some of the best and most creative talent to work in a genre that was still considered the bastard child of mainstream cinema. Now, with all the recent upheavals, it was practically the only game in town and in terms of quantity at least, the 1970s were to represent a golden age for the independent British horror film.

To be continued...

Afterword

Remembering Richard Gordon

Few admirers of indpendent British horror movies could have failed to notice that Richard Gordon, the London-born film producer, died in New York on November 1, 2011, following several months of illness. He was 85. Gordon's passing was noted by many of the mainstream newspapers including *The Guardian* in the UK, which hailed a 'canny film producer known for his horror and sci-fi classics'.

Canny though he undoubtedly was, Richard Gordon was so much more than just another low budget filmmaker. I first met Dick (he insisted on everyone calling him Dick) in 1997 when he was attending the Festival of Fantastic Films in Manchester and he agreed to spare me a quarter of an hour to talk about his 1966 science fiction film, *The Projected Man*. Meeting him in the hotel bar with my trusty tape recorder in hand, we quickly moved on from that rather minor effort to his wider

Richard Gordon and X-Cert author John Hamilton, circa 2005

career and a whole range of peripheral subjects. In fact, we were having so much fun that the brief interview ending up running to several hours. Not only was Dick more than accommodating when it came to meeting with a complete stranger, but he demonstrated an encyclopaedic knowledge of his own films and was a fount of facts, witticisms and tid-bits about cinema in general. We subsequently stayed in touch, writing to each other constantly to share news and meeting up once a year for what became a very welcome ritual of a meal and a good chat, usually in Manchester but on one memorable occasion in New York.

Although his first love was film, and in particular the Hollywood films that he had watched as a youth, our conversations over the years ranged from travel in the Far East, history and Dick's service in the navy, through to the theatre and just general gossip. Again his factual knowledge was staggering and his enthusiasm for detail was undimmed by the passing of time; when he found out my wife was born in Orpington, Kent, he was desperately keen to know what had happened to a cinema that he had visited there as a child, and most disappointed to find out it was now a McDonalds restaurant!

Although I was familiar with Dick's filmography, it was not until I sat down to write about a history of Independent British Horrors from 1953 onwards, that I realised just what a significant figure he had been. If you remove Hammer/Amicus/Tigon from the mix, Dick Gordon, through a number of companies, emerges as the most consistent producer of the 1950s, '60s and '70s. Gordon was immensely proud to have worked with two of his idols, Bela Lugosi and Boris Karloff, whom he met in the early 1950s while writing articles for film magazines. He briefly acted as Lugosi's agent, getting him some desperately needed cash from an ill-fated *Dracula* tour of the British provinces. He later went on to produce two of Karloff's last decent films, *Grip of the Stranger* and *Corridors of Blood*. By the late 1950s, Gordon was hitting

Richard Gordon, Pat O'Brien and producer Charles F Vetter

Afterword: Remembering Richard Gordon

Dennis Price, Richard Gordon and Lisa Daniely

his stride, producing a raft of creditable *noir* thrillers including Terence Fisher's *Kill Me Tomorrow*, starring former Hollywood 'heavy' Pat O'Brien, as well as the minor science fiction classics *Fiend without a Face* and the Quatermass-esque *First Man into Space*, both starring Marshall Thompson. In the 1960s, Gordon befriended Bryant Haliday and starred him in three pictures: *Devil Doll*, *Curse of the Voodoo* and the aforementioned *The Projected Man*. He recruited Peter Cushing and Terence Fisher for *Island of Terror* and made that rarest of beasts—a decent British voodoo picture, *Naked Evil*. Gordon's heart may have been in the Hollywood classics, but he proved that he could move with the times in 1970 when he produced Antony Balch's sex comedy *Bizarre*, before moving into the slasher genre with *Tower of Evil* in 1972. Perhaps Gordon's most memorable film was the hugely entertaining mad scientist parody *Horror Hospital* in 1973. He was also behind a 1978 remake of *The Cat and the Canary* and (his last film) the *Alien* exploitation classic, *Inseminoid*, directed by Norman J Warren.

All of Gordon's films were made in Britain though his office was in New York, the city where he first established Gordon Films Inc in 1949, having arrived on a one-way ticket from London with his brother Alex. While Dick made his home in New York, Alex—who shared his love of the cinema—moved to the West Coast and became a notable B-movie maker in his own right. Dick preferred to take advantage of the tax subsidies in England and commute between film productions in Britain and film distribution in the US, where he also acted as an agent and distributor of selected imported films, a role he maintained for over 60 years. In 2010, Gordon Films Inc acquired the rights to Hammer's *The Abominable Snowman* for home entertainment. Later the same year, Dick snapped up the overseas rights to a library of Kit Parker movies and in April 2012, he sold the television and home video rights to *The Romantic Englishwomen* and *Priest of Love*. Although he made no more films after *Inseminiod*, he never totally gave up and for many years talked about a CGI remake of *Fiend without a Face*. He had several scripts written but was unable to find the finance.

X-Cert

Impressive though his CV was, Dick is probably most fondly remembered for his appearances at numerous fantasy conventions and festivals where he was happy to introduce films dredged up from the vaults, discuss his own movies or simply hang out with fellow fans. Dick's films of choice may have been in the fantasy genre but he was anything but parochial in his tastes; he loved Chaplin's silent comedies, for example, and he owned them all on DVD. He had a voracious appetite for films on DVD, watching everything from *The Mad Doctor* with Basil Rathbone to *Doctor in the House* with Dirk Bogarde. He remained, to the end, a keen cinemagoer and regular visitor to the Film Forum in New York, as well as the local multiplex where his choices were just as varied; he liked *Orson Welles and Me* so much that he went to see it twice but hated *Black Swan*. He rated Colin Firth as one of the best actors of his generation and thought *A Single Man* and *The King's Speech* were excellent. Woody Allen was less to his taste and *You Will Meet a Tall Dark Stranger* was dismissed as 'awful'. Dick stayed in touch with the genre, devouring film magazines like *Little Shoppe of Horrors* and *Midnight Marquee* and, having seen *The Woman in Black* on stage both in London and on Broadway, was looking forward to seeing what sort of a job Hammer and Daniel Radcliffe would make of it.

Dick's last public appearance was in June at the Monster Mash in Pittsburgh, one of his favourite festivals, where he launched his 'biography', an in-depth interview covering the whole of his career and assembled by his close friend, Tom Weaver. Soon afterwards, he suffered a fall walking to his office and was admitted to hospital with related complications. My wife and I visited Dick there in July, knowing from Tom that he was refusing to see anyone until such time as he was in a position to entertain them properly. The hospital was about as nice as these things can be and the staff were very helpful and friendly but we did not find Dick in the best of moods. He was angry, I think at his illness, and annoyed that it was keeping him from the office where he felt the work was piling up. After he apologised for what he called his 'reduced circumstances' for the umpteenth time, I said, 'Honestly, Dick, it's fine.' 'No, it isn't,' he said, looking around the somewhat spartan room, 'I feel I am in a Monogram film!' We all laughed and it broke the ice; we spent the next 20 minutes or so chatting and left with Dick promising that he would be back at Manchester in October, come what may. It was a trip that he never made.

Many horror film magazines and fan sites carried glowing tributes in the months following the news, and Dick deserves all the plaudits he received. Some described him as a last link to a golden era. The tragedy, though, is not the passing of Richard Gordon the film producer, but of Richard Gordon the man.

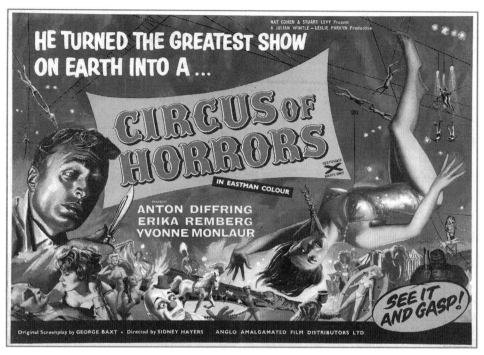

Mother Riley Meets the Vampire

(AKA My Son, the Vampire)

Cast
Arthur Lucan..Mrs Riley
Bela Lugosi...Von Housen
Dora Bryan..Tilly
Philip Leaver.............................Anton Daschomb
Richard Wattis................Police Constable Freddie
Graham Moffat...Yokel
María Mercedes................................Julia Loretti
Roderick Lovell...Douglas
David Hurst..Mugsy
Judith Furse..Freda
Ian Wilson...Hitchcock
Hattie Jacques....................................Mrs Jenks
Dandy Nichols...........................Humphrey's wife
George Benson....................................Humphrey
Bill Shine..................................Mugsy's assistant
David Hannaford............. Man washing windows
Charles Lloyd-Pack...................................Mr Pain
Cyril Smith/Peter Bathurst/Arthur Brander ......
....Police brass
Tom Macaulay...............................Delivery driver
Alexander Gauge........................Police Constable
Laurence Naismith..................Policeman at desk
With John Le Mesurier

Selected Credits
Directed by *John Gilling*
Screenplay by *Val Valentine*
Produced by *John Gilling*
Original Music by *Lindo Southworth*
Sound Recordist *W H Lindop*
Cinematographer *Stan Pavey*
Camera Operator *Dudley Lovell*
Editor *Len Trumm*

X-Cert

Art Director Bernard Robinson
Makeup Eric Carter
Hairdresser Betty Lee
Assistant Director Denis O'Dell

74 minutes
Released July, 1952
Renown Pictures Corp/Blue Chip Productions Inc (US)

Robert Moore............................Police Inspector
Ewen Solon............................Plain clothes man
Jock Finlay......................................Policeman
Madoline Thomas............................Mrs Morgan
Graham Stuart/Gordon Bell....................Guests
Patricia Owens...Joyce
Melissa Stribling..Vera

Selected Credits
Directed by Vernon Sewell
Screenplay by Vernon Sewell
Produced by Nat Cohen/Stuart Levy/Vernon Sewell
Associate Producer Henry Geddes
Original Music by Eric Spear
Director of Photography Stanley Grant
Editor Francis Bieber
Art Director George Haslam
Sound Recordist R G W Smith

74 minutes
Released October, 1952
Anglo-Amalgamated Film Distributors/Lippert Pictures (US)

Three Cases of Murder

Cast
Orson Welles............................Lord Mountdrago
John Gregson................................Edgar Curtain
Elizabeth Sellars....................................Elizabeth
Emrys Jones..................................George Wheeler
Alan Badel...............................Owen/Mr X/Harry
André Morell..Dr Audlin
Hugh Pryse..Jarvis
Leueen MacGrath................Woman in the house
Eddie Byrne..Snyder
Helen Cherry..................................Lady Mountdrago
Eamonn Andrews........................Introductions
Peter Burton .. Under secretary for foreign affairs
Philip Dale..Sgt Mallot
Christina Forrest....................................Susan
Evelyn Hall............................Lady Connemara
Ann Hanslip..The girl
David Horne..................................Sir James
John Humphry..................Private secretary
Maurice Kaufmann..........................Pemberton
Jack Lambert....................Inspector Acheson
Zena Marshall........................Beautiful blonde
John Salew..Rooke
Harry Welchman............................Connoisseur
Colette Wilde..Jane
Arthur Wontner................Leader of the house

Ghost Ship

Cast
Hazel Court............................Margaret Thornton
Dermot Walsh................................Guy Thornton
Hugh Burden..Dr Fawcett
John Robinson.......Professor Mansel Martineau
Joss Ambler.........................Yacht port manager
Joan Carol..Mrs Martineau
Hugh Latimer..Peter
Laidman Browne.......................................Coroner
Mignon O'Doherty............................Mrs Manley
Meadows White....................................Mr Leech
Pat McGrath...Bert
Joss Ackland...Ron
John King-Kelly..Sid
Colin Douglas/Jack Stewart................Engineers
Anthony Marlowe........................Thomas Salter
Geoffrey Dunn........................Strange passenger
Ian Carmichael..Bernard
Anthony Hayes...Pianist
Barry Phelps..Steward

214

Filmography

Patrick Macnee..........................Guard/Subaltern
Marc Sheldon..........................Man in background

Selected Credits
Directed by David Eady/George More O'Ferrall/Wendy Toye
Screenplays by Sidney Carroll/Ian Dalrymple/Donald B Wilson
Stories by Brett Halliday/W Somerset Maugham/Roderick Wilkinson
Produced by Ian Dalrymple/Alexander Paal/Hugh Perceval
Original Music by Doreen Carwithen
Director of Photography Georges Perinal
Camera Operator Denys N Coop
Editor Gerald Turney-Smith
Asst Art Director Maurice Fowler
Sound Recordists Red Law/Bert Ross
Dubbing Editor Lee Doig
Sound Supervisor John Cox
Production Manager RLM Davidson
Makeup George Frost
Wardrobe Supervisor Bridget Sellers
Continuity Olga Brook
Assistant Director John Bremer
Second Asst Director Peter Maxwell

99 minutes

Released May 12, 1955
British Lion Film Corporation/Allied Artists (US)

Grip of the Strangler
(AKA The Haunted Strangler)

Cast

Boris Karloff...............................James Rankin
Jean Kent..Cora Seth
Elizabeth Allan..........................Barbara Rankin
Anthony Dawson..................................Supt Burk
Vera Day..Pearl
Tim Turner...........................Dr Kenneth McColl
Diane Aubrey.....................................Lily Rankin
Max Brimmell................Newgate prison turnkey
Leslie Perrins...............Newgate prison governor
Jessica Cairns....................................Asylum maid
Dorothy Gordon....................................Hannah
Desmond Roberts............................Dr Johnson
Roy Russell.....................Medical superintendent
Derek Birch.........Guyse hospital superintendent
Peggy Ann Clifford..Kate
John Fabian.....................................Young blood
Joan Elvin...Can-Can girl
Michael Atkinson..........................Edward Styles

X-Cert

Yvonne Buckingham..................................Whore
John G Heller......................................Male nurse
George Hirste..........................Lost property man
Arthur Mullard..................................Male nurse
George Spence.......................................Hangman
Jeremy Young..............................Asylum guard
With Robert Day and Marie Devereux

Selected Credits
Directed by Robert Day
Screenplay by John C Cooper/Jan Read
From a Novel by Jan Read
Produced by John Croydon
Original Music Buxton Orr
Director of Photography Lionel Banes
Camera Operator Leo Rogers
Editor Peter Mayhew
Sound HC Pearson
Dubbing Editor Terry Poulton
Production Manager Ronald Kinnock
Makeup Jim Hydes
Hair Stylist Barbara Barnard
Continuity Hazel Swift
Assistant Director Douglas Hickox
Special Effects Les Bowie
Wardrobe Anna Duse

78 minutes

Released July 3, 1958
Eros Film Distributors/M-G-M (US)

Fiend Without a Face

Cast
Marshall Thompson.................Major Cummings
Kynaston Reeves........................Prof R E Walgate
Kim Parker..................................Barbara Griselle
Stanley Maxted....................................Col Butler
Terence Kilburn..........................Capt Al Chester
James Dyrenforth..Mayor
Robert MacKenzie.......................Const Gibbons
Peter Madden......................................Dr Bradley
Gil Winfield...Dr Warren
Michael Balfour..................................Sgt Kasper
Launce Maraschal...................................Melville
R Meadows White.............................Ben Adams
Kerrigan Prescott......................Atomic engineer
Lala Lloyd......................................Amelia Adams
Shane Cordell...Nurse
Sheldon Allan...Sentry
Alexander Archdale..............................Minister
Tom Watson..........................Technical sergeant

Filmography

Selected Credits
Directed by Arthur Crabtree
Screenplay by Herbert J Leder
Produced by John Croydon
Original Music by Buxton Orr
Director of Photography Lionel Barnes
Camera Operator Leo Rogers
Editor R Q McNaughton
Sound Recordist Peter Davies
Dubbing Editor Terry Poulton
Set Designer John Elphick
Makeup Jim Hydes
Hair Stylist Barbara Barnard
Wardrobe Anna Duse
Continuity Hazel Swift
Assistant Director Douglas Hickox
Special Effects Peter Neilson/Ruppel & Nordhoff

74 minutes
Released July 3, 1958
Eros Film Distributors/M-G-M (US)

First Man into Space

Cast
Marshall Thompson ....
....................Commander Charles Ernest Prescott
Marla Landi....................Tia Francesca
Bill Edwards......Lieutenant Dan Milton Prescott
Robert Ayres....................Captain Ben Richards
Bill Nagy..............................Police Chief Wilson
Carl Jaffe.................................Dr Paul von Essen
Roger Delgado ....Ramon de Guerrera
John McLaren ....Harold Atkins
Spencer Teakle/Chuck Keyser/John Fabian ......
..............................Ratings control room
Richard Shaw..Witney
Bill Nick..Clancy
Helen Forrest..................Secretary/Helen Forest
Rowland Brand..............................Truck driver
Barry Shawzin..Sanchez
Mark Sheldon..Doctor
Michael Bell.....................................State trooper
Sheree Winton...Nurse
Franklyn Fox..Larson
Laurence Taylor...Taylor

Selected Credits
Directed by Robert Day
Screenplay by John C Cooper/
Lance Z Hargreaves
Story by Wyott Ordung
Produced by John Croydon/Charles Vetter Jr
Original Music by Buxton Orr

Director of Photography Geoffrey Faithful
Camera Operator Frank Drake
Editor Peter Mayhew
Art Director Denys Pavitt
Sound Recordist Terence Cotter
Sound Editor Peter Musgrave
Production Manager George Mills
Makeup Michael Morris
Hairdressing Eileen Warwick
Wardrobe Charles Guerin
Continuity Kay Rawlings
Assistant Director Stanley Goulder

77 minutes
Released Feburary 27, 1959
M-G-M (UK/US)

Corridors of Blood

Cast
Boris Karloff............................Dr Thomas Bolton
Betta St John..Susan
Christopher Lee........................Resurrection Joe
Finlay Currie...................Supt Charles Matheson
Adrienne Corri..Rachel
Francis De Wolff..................................Black Ben
Francis Matthews.....................Jonathan Bolton
Frank Pettingell..................................Mr Blount
Basil Dignam.........................Hospital chairman
Marian Spencer............................Mrs Matheson
Carl Bernard...Ned
John Gabriel...Baker
Nigel Green.............................Insp Donovan
Yvonne Warren...Rosa
Howard Lang..............................Chief Inspector
Julian D'Albie.................................Bald man
Roddy Hughes...........................Man with watch
Robert Raglan..Wilkes
Charles Lloyd Pack............................Hardcastle
Bernard Archard.........................Hospital official
Frank Sieman..Evans
Josephine Bailey..Child
Gilda Emmanuelli..Annie
Desmond Llewelyn..........Assistant at operations
Marianne Stone........................Woman arrested
Brian Wilde ....
....................Man in operating theatre audience
With Skip Martin, Malcolm Ranson, Mavis Ranson, Charmian Eyre, Anthea Holloway, Kaplan Kaye, Maureen Beck and Anne Castaldini

Selected Credits
Directed by Robert Day

217

Filmography

Screenplay by Jean Scott Rogers
Produced by John Croydon/Charles Vetter Jr
Ass Producer Peter Mayhew
Original Music by Buxton Orr
Director of Photography Geoffrey Faithful
Camera Operator Frank Drake
Editor Peter Mayhew
Art Director Anthony Masters
Sound Recordists Maurice Askew/Cyril Swern
Dubbing Editor Peter Musgrave
Production Manager George Mills
Makeup Walter Schneidermann
Wardrobe Mistress Doris Turner
Continuity Susan Dyson
Assistant Director Peter Bolton

86 minutes
Released September 6, 1962
M-G-M (UK/US)

The Trollenberg Terror

Cast
Forrest Tucker..................Alan Brooks
Laurence Payne..................Philip Truscott
Jennifer Jayne..................Sarah Pilgrim
Janet Munro..................Anne Pilgrim
Warren Mitchell..................Prof Crevett
Frederick Schiller..................Mayor Klein
Andrew Faulds..................Brett
Stuart Saunders..................Dewhurst
Colin Douglas..................Hans
Derek Sydney..................Wilde
Richard Golding..................First villager
George Herbert..................Second villager
Anne Sharp..........German woman with little girl
Leslie Heritage..................Carl
Jeremy Longhurst/Anthony Parker ....
..................Student climbers
Theodore Wilhelm..................Fritz
Garard Green..................Search plane pilot
Caroline Glaser..................Little girl
Jack Taylor..................Jim

Selected Credits
Directed by Quentin Lawrence
Screenplay by Jimmy Sangster
Story by Peter Key
Produced by Robert S Baker
Original Music by Stanley Black
Director of Photography Monty Berman
Camera Operator Desmond Davis
Art Director Duncan Sutherland
Sound Recordist Dick Smith
Production Manager Charles Permane

Makeup Eleanor Jones
Hair Stylist Joy Vigo
Continuity Yvonne Richards
Special Effects Les Bowie
Assistant Director Norman Harrison

84 minutes
Released October 7, 1958
Eros Film Distributors/DCA (US)

Blood of the Vampire

Cast
Donald Wolfit..................Doctor Callistratus
Vincent Ball..................Dr John Pierre
Barbara Shelley..................Madeleine Duval
Victor Maddern..................Carl
William Devlin..................Kurt Urach
Andrew Faulds..................Chief guard Wetzler
John Le Mesurier..................Judge
Bryan Coleman..................Monsieur Auron
Cameron Hall..................Drunken doctor
George Murcell/ Julian Strange/
Bruce Whiteman..................Guards
Barbara Burke..................Housekeeper
Bernard Bresslaw..................Tall sneak thief
Hal Osmond..................Small sneak thief
Henry Vidon..........Professor Bernhardt Meinster
John Stuart..................Uncle Phillippe
Colin Tapley..................Commissioner of prisons
Muriel Ali..................Gypsy dancer
Max Brimmell..................Warder
Dennis Shaw..................Blacksmith
Otto Diamant..................Gravedigger
Milton Read..................Executioner
Richard Golding..................Official
Theodore Wilhelm..................Emaciated prisoner
Yvonne Buckingham..................Serving wench
Sylvia Casimir..........Laughing woman in tavern
Gordon Honeycombe/Carlos Williams ....
..................Stretcher bearers
Patricia Phoenix..................Woman

Selected Credits
Directed by Henry Cass
Screenplay by Jimmy Sangster
Produced by Robert S Baker/Monty Berman
Original Music by Stanley Black
Director of Photography Monty Berman
Camera Operator Geoffrey Seaholme
Production Designer John Elphick
Editor Douglas Myers
Sound Recordist Bill Bulkley
Production Manager Charles Permane
Makeup Jimmy Evans

X-Cert

Hairdressing Joyce James
Wardrobe Muriel Dickson
Assistant Director Luciano Sacripanti

87 minutes
Released August 26, 1958
Eros Film Distributors/Universal Pictures (US)

Jack the Ripper

Cast
Lee Patterson.........................Sam Lowry
Eddie Byrne.......................Inspt O'Neill
Betty McDowall....................Anne Ford
Ewen Solon................Sir David Rogers
John Le Mesurier.................Dr Tranter

George Rose..Clarke
Philip Leaver........................Music hall manager
Barbara Burke................................Kitty Knowles
Anne Sharp...Helen
Denis Shaw...Simes
Jack Allen.................Asst Commissioner Hodges
Jane Taylor..Hazel
Dorinda Stevens....................................Margaret
Hal Osmonde..................Snakey the pickpocket
George Street..........................Station sergeant
Olwen Brooks..............................Lady Almoner
Endre Muller..Louis Benz
Esma Cannon...Nelly
George Woodbridge....................................Blake
Bill Shine................................Lord Tom Sopwith
Marianne Stone........................Drunken woman
Garard Green..................................Dr Urquhart
Charles Lamb..Harry
Jennifer White...Beth
Cameron Hall..............................Hospital porter
Alan Robinson..Coroner
Anthony Sagar...Drunk
John Mott..Singer
Lucy Griffiths..................Salvation Army woman
Ballet Montparnasse........................Themselves
John Barrett........Onlooker at 2nd murder scene
Katy Cashfield............................Blonde girl
Helena Digby..1st victim
Paul Frees...Narrator

Selected Credits
Directed by Robert S Baker/Monty Berman
Screenplay by Jimmy Sangster
Story by Perter Hammond/Colin Craig
Produced by Robert S Baker/Monty Berman
Original Music by Stanley Black/Jimmy McHugh/Pete Rugolo
Art Director William Kellner
Director of Photography Robert S Baker/Monty Berman
Camera Operator Dudley Lovell
Editor Peter Bezencenet
Sound Recordist Buster Ambler
Dubbing Editor Jeanne Henderson
Production Manager Jack Swinburne
Makeup Jimmy Evans
Hairdressing Bill Griffiths
Wardrobe Supervisor Jack Verity
Continuity Yvonne Richards
Assistant Director Peter Manley

84 minutes
Released May 28, 1959
Regal Films International/
Paramount Pictures (US)

Filmography

The Flesh and the Fiends

Cast
Peter Cushing.............................Dr Robert Knox
June Laverick.................................Martha Knox
Donald Pleasence..........................William Hare
George Rose.....................................William Burke
Renee Houston.....................................Helen Burke
Dermot Walsh..................Dr Geoffrey Mitchell
Billie Whitelaw..........................Mary Patterson
John Cairney..................................Chris Jackson
Melvyn Hayes.................................Daft Jamie
June Powell...............................Maggie O'Hara
Andrew Faulds.................Inspector McCulloch
Philip Leaver...................................Dr Elliott
George Woodbridge......................Dr Ferguson
Garard Green...............................Dr Andrews
Esma Cannon..................................Aggie
Geoffrey Tyrrell............................Old Davey
George Bishop...............................Blind man
Becket Bould..................................Old Angus
George Street....................................Publican
Michael Balfour..........................Drunken sailor
Stephen Scott/Raf De La Torre.....Grave robbers
Steven Berkoff.........................Medical student
Golda Casimir..................................Gypsy
Robert Checksfield/Paul Craig/Glyn Dearman/
Anthony Valentine/John Murray Scott ....
....Students
Gilda Emmanuelli...............................Jennie
Moris Farhi/Jack McNaughton........Stallholders
Janice Field/Dorothy Grumbar/Norman Fisher/Ann Lancaster/Vivienne Lacey/Vernon Morris/Don Vernon ....
....Minuet dancers
Ian Fleming..................................Priest
Eric Francis.......................Clerk of the court
Lucy Griffiths..................................Crone
Frank Henderson..........................Artist
Robert Hunter ....Artist's friend
Olive Kirby..Maid
Michael Mulcaster...........................Undertaker
Sylvia Osborne.......................Blowsy woman
Gordon Phillott........................Nightwatchman
John Rae................................Reverend Lincoln
Charles Stanley..............................Town crier
Marita Stanton.................................Barmaid
Peter Stephens....................................McBain
Graham Stuart.................................Smedley
Hazel Sutton.......................................Blonde

Selected Credits
Directed by John Gilling
Screenplay by John Gilling/Leon Griffiths

X-Cert

Produced by Robert S Baker/Monty Berman
Original Music by Stanley Black
Director of Photography Monty Berman
Camera Operator Chic Waterson
Editor Jack Slade
Art Director John Elphick
Sound Recordists Bob Jones/George Stephenson
Dubbing Editor Jeanne Henderson
Production Manager Jack Swinburne
Makeup Jimmy Evans
Hairdressing Betty Sherriff
Wardrobe Laura Nightingale
Continuity Kay Rawlings

97 minutes
Released February 2, 1960
Regal Films International/Valiant Films (US)

The Man Without a Body

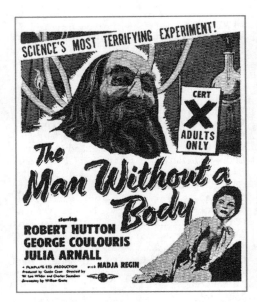

Cast
Robert Hutton	Dr Phil R Merritt
George Coulouris	Karl Brussard
Julia Arnall	Jean Cramer
Nadja Regin	Odette Vernet
Sheldon Lawrence	Dr Lew Waldenhouse
Peter Copley	Leslie
Michael Golden	Michel de Notre Dame
Norman Shelley	Dr Alexander
Stanley van Beers	Madame Tussaud's guide
Tony Quinn	Dr Brandon
Maurice Kaufmann	Chauffer
William Sherwood	Dr Charot
Edwin Ellis	Publican
Donald Morley	Stock broker
Frank Forsyth	Detective
Kim Parker	Suzanne
Ernest Bale	Customs officer

Selected Credits
Directed by Charles Saunders/W Lee Wilder
Screenplay by William Grote
Produced by Guido Coen
Original Music by Albert Elms
Director of Photography Brendan J Stafford
Camera Operator Anthony Heller
Editor Tom Simpson
Production Designer Harry White
Sound Recordist Cyril Collick
Production Manager John 'Pinky' Green
Makeup Jim Hydes
Hairdressing Ivy Emmerton
Continuity Splinters Deason
Assistant Director William Lang

80 minutes
Released May 1957
Budd Rogers Releasing Corp (US)

Woman Eater

Filmography

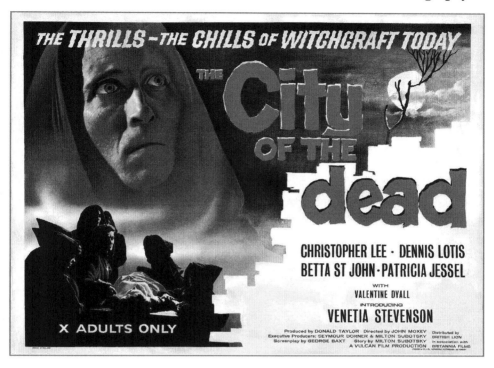

Cast
George Coulouris......................Dr James Moran
Vera Day...Sally Norton
Peter Wayn.....................................Jack Venner
Joyce Gregg.......................Mrs Margaret Santor
Joy Webster..Judy
Jimmy Vaughn..Tanga
Robert MacKenzie.........................Lewis Carling
Norman Claridge......................Doctor Patterson
Marpessa Dawn..................................Native girl
Sara Leighton................................Susan Curtis
Edward Higgins.......................Sergeant Bolton
Harry Ross...Bristow
Alexander Field............................Fair attendant
David Lawton...................Man at club with Judy
John Tinn...Lascar
Maxwell Foster...................Inspector Brownlow
Peter Lewiston........Detective Sergeant Freeman
Roger Avon................................Desk Constable
Shief Ashanti..................................Witch doctor
John Grant...........................Rescue party leader
Susan Neill..................Orange-juice counter girl
Stanley Platts..................Explorers club steward
With Marie Devereux

Selected Credits
Directed by Charles Saunders
Screenplay/Story by Brandon Fleming

Produced by Guido Coen
Original Music by Edwin Astley
Director of Photography Ernest Palmer
Camera Operator Anthony Heller
Editor Seymour Logie
Sound Mickey Jay
Art Director Herbert Smith
Production Manager Frank Bevis
Makeup Terry Terrington
Hairdresser Doris Pollard
Continuity Vera Pavey
Assistant Director Douglas Hermes

70 minutes
Released April, 1958
Eros Films/Columbia Pictures (US)

The City of the Dead

Cast
Dennis Lotis...............................Richard Barlow
Christopher Lee......................Prof Alan Driscoll
Patricia Jessel.....Elizabeth Selwyn/Mrs Newless
Tom Naylor....................................Bill Maitland
Betta St John..............................Patricia Russell
Venetia Stephenson..........................Nan Barlow

X-Cert

Valentine Dyall	Jethrow Keane
Ann Beach	Lottie
Norman Macowan	Reverend Russell
Fred Johnson	The Elder
Jimmy Dyrenforth	Garage attendant
Maxine Holden	Sue
William Abney	Policeman

With Nickolas Grace

Selected Credits
Directed by John Moxey
Screenplay by George Baxt
Story by Milton Subotsky
Produced by Donald Taylor/Max Rosenberg
Original Music by Douglas Gamley
Director of Photography Desmond Dickinson
Camera Operator Jack Atcheler
Editor John Pomeroy
Art Director John Blezard
Sound Mixer Richard Bird
Makeup George Claff
Hairdresser Barbara Bernard
Wardrobe Freda Gibson
Production Manager Ben Arbeid
Special Effects Cliff Richardson
Continuity Splinters Deason
Assistant Director Tom Pevsner

76 minutes
Released September, 1960
Britannia Films/Trans Lux (US)

Peeping Tom

Cast

Carl Boehm	Mark Lewis
Moira Shearer	Vivian
Anna Massey	Helen Stephens
Maxine Audley	Mrs Stephens
Brenda Bruce	Dora
Miles Malleson	Elderly gentleman customer
Esmond Knight	Arthur Baden
Michael Goodliffe	Don Jarvis
Martin Miller	Dr Rosen
Jack Watson	Chief Insp Gregg
Shirley Ann Field	Pauline Shields
Pamela Green	Milly
John Barrard	Small man
Keith Baxter	Det Baxter
John Chappell	Clapper boy
Robert Crewdson	Shop assistant on film set
Roland Curram	Young man in sports car
Nigel Davenport	Det Sgt Miller
John Dunbar	Police doctor
Maurice Durant	Publicity chief
Paddy Edwards	Girl electrician
Cornelia Frances	Girl in sports car
Veronica Hurst	Miss Simpson
M Le Compte/Mme Le Compte	Lovers in garden
Bartlett Mullins	Mr Peters
Pete Murray	Young man embracing girl
Margaret Neale	Mark's stepmother
Columba Powell	Mark as a child
Michael Powell	Mark's father
Guy Kingsley Poynter	P Tate
Frankie Reidy	Mark's mother
Alan Rolfe	Store detective
Frank Singuineau	Electrician
Peggy Thorpe-Bates	Mrs Partridge
Susan Travers	Lorraine
Brian Wallace	Tony
Brian Worth	Assistant director

Selected Credits
Directed by Michael Powell
Screenplay by Leo Marks
Produced by Michael Powell/Albert Fennell
Original Music by Brian Easdale
Director of Photography Otto Heller
Camera Operator Gerry Turpin
Editor Noreen Ackland
Art Director Arthur Lawson
Assistant Art Director Ivor Beddoes
Production Manager Al Marcus
Sound Recordist Gordon McCallum/C C

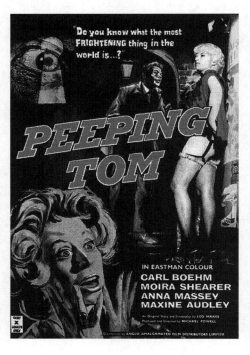

Stevens
Sound Editor Malcolm Cooke
Makeup W J Partleton
Hairdresser Pearl Orton
Costumes Dickie Richardson
Continuity Rita Davison
Assistant Director Ted Sturgis
Second Assistant Directors Denis Johnson/
Denis Johnson Jr

101 minutes
Released April 7, 1960
Anglo-Amalgamated Film Distributors/
Astor Pictures Corp (US)

Circus of Horrors

Cast
Anton Diffring......................................Dr Schuler
Erika Remberg..................................Elissa Caro
Yvonne Monlaur............................Nicole Vanet
Donald Pleasence..Vanet
Jane Hylton...Angela
Kenneth Griffith...Martin
Conrad Phillips........................Insp Arthur Ames
Jack Gwillim...............................Supt Andrews
Vanda Hudson..........................Magda von Meck
Yvonne Romain...Melina
Colette Wilde.................Evelyn Morley Finsbury
William Mervyn............................Doctor Morley
John Merivale............................Edward Finsbury
Peter Swanwick ....
...........................German Police Inspector Knopf
Carla Challoner...........................Nicole as a child
Kenny Baker..Dwarf
Jack Carson.............................Chief Eagle Eye
Chris Christian....................................Ringmaster
Sasha Coco..Luis
Walter Gotell..........................Baron Von Gruber
Fred Haggerty........................Second roustabout
Glyn Houston.............................Carnival barker
Kenneth J Warren......................First roustabout
Malcolm Watson..............Murdered Frenchman

Selected Credits
Directed by Sidney Hayers
Screenplay by George Baxt
Produced by Samuel Z Arkoff/Leslie Parkyn/
Julian Wintle/Norman Priggen
Original Music by Muir Mathieson/Franz
Reizenstein
Sound Recordists Len Page/Ken Cameron
Sound Editor Lionel Selwyn
Director of Photography Douglas Slocombe
Camera Operator Chic Waterson

Filmography

Editors Reginald Mills/Sidney Hayers
Art Director Jack Shampan
Production Manager Charles Permane
Makeup Trevor Crole-Rees
Hairdressing Maud Onslow
Wardrobe Vi Murray
Continuity June Randall

88 minutes
Released April, 1960
Anglo-Amalgamated Film Distributors/
American International Pictures (US)

The Hands of Orlac

Cast
Mel Ferrer.....................................Stephen Orlac
Christopher Lee....................Nero the magician
Dany Carrel................................Régina/Li-Lang
Lucile Saint-Simon..........Louise Cochrane Orlac
Felix Aylmer........................Dr Francis Cochrane
Peter Reynolds.......................................Mr Felix
Basil Sydney.........................Maurice Seidelman
Campbell Singer................Inspector Henderson
Sir Donald Wolfit.....................Professor Volchett
Donald Pleasence.......................Graham Coates
Peter Bennett/George Merritt.............Members
Arnold Diamond......................................Dresser
Janina Faye...Child
Gertan Klauber.................Fairground attendant
Mireille Perrey.........................Madame Aliberti
David Peel..................................Airplane's pilot
Walter Randall..Waiter
Anita Sharp-Bolster.............Volchett's assistant
Manning Wilson......................Inspector Jagger
Yanilou...Emilie
Edouard Hemme...Auge
Jean Fountaine............................French waiter
Pierre Ferrari..............Ambulance attendant
Beulah Hughes....................................Pub whore
Franca Bellj/Anne Clune/Vicki Woolf ....
....Cell whores
Peter R Hunt..Pleasants
Charles Lamb..Guard
Tallulah Miller....................................Pub whore
Philip Ryan..............................Police Constable
Ann Way..Seamstress
Molly Weir...Maid
With Jean Combal Antoine Balpêtré and Andrée Florence

Selected Credits
Directed by Edmond T Greville
Writers John Baines/Edmond T Greville/Max
Montagut/Maurice Renard/Donald Taylor

225

X-Cert

Produced by Steven Pallos/Donald Taylor
Original Music by Claude Bolling
Sound Buster Ambler/Robert Biart/Bob Jones
Directors of Photography Desmond Dickinson/Jacques Lemare
Camera Operator Harry Gillam
Editors Oswald Hafenrichter/Jean Ravel
Production Managers Ben Arbeid/Eugene Nase
Production Designer Eugene Pierac
Makeup Stuart Freeborn
Hairdressing Barbara Bernard
Wardrobe Jackie Breed
Continuity Yvonne Richards
Assistant Director Basil Rabin
Second Assistant Director Timothy Burrill

95 minutes
Released December, 1960
Britannia Films/Continental Distributing (US)

House of Mystery

Cast
Peter Dyneley..............................Mark Lemming
Jane Hylton................................Stella Lemming
Nanette Newman..........................Joan Trevor
Maurice Kaufmann........................Henry Trevor
Colin Gordon...............................Burdon
John Merivale..............................Clive
Ronald Hines..............................Young husband
Colette Wilde..............................Wife
Molly Urquhart............................Mrs Bucknall
George Selway.............................Constable
John Abineri...............................Milkman
With Pearson Dodd, Freda Bamford, Roy Purcell

Selected Credits
Directed by Vernon Sewell
Writers Pierre Mills/Vernon Sewell/C Vylars
Produced by Leslie Parkyn/Julian Wintle
Original Music by Stanley Black
Sound Recordist John W Mitchell/Ken Cameron
Director of Photography Ernest Steward
Camera Operator James Bawden
Editor John Trumper
Production Managers Arthur Alcott/Geoffrey Haine
Art Director Jack Shampan
Makeup Trevor Crole-Rees
Hairdressing Maud Onslow
Wardrobe Vi Murray
Continuity Joy Mercer
Assistant Director Jan Saunders

56 minutes
Released May, 1962
Anglo-Amalgamated Film Distributors/National Broadcasting Company (US)

The Man in the Back Seat

Cast
Derren Nesbitt..............................Tony
Keith Faulkner..............................Frank
Carol White..................................Jean
Harry Locke.................................Joe Carter

Selected Credits
Directed by Vernon Sewell
Writers Malcolm Hulke/Eric Paice/Edgar Wallace
Produced by Leslie Parkyn/Julian Wintle
Original Music by Stanley Black
Sound Recordist John W Mitchell/Ken Cameron
Director of Photography Reg Wyer
Camera Operator Noel Rowland
Editor John Trumper
Production Manager Arthur Alcott
Art Director Harry Pottle
Makeup Trevor Crole-Rees
Hairdressing Maud Onslow
Wardrobe Vi Murray
Continuity Joy Mercer
Assistant Director Jan Saunders

57 minutes
Released June, 1961
Anglo-Amalgamated Film Distributors

Night of the Eagle
(AKA Burn, Witch, Burn)

Cast
Peter Wyngarde............................Norman Taylor
Janet Blair..................................Tansy Taylor
Margaret Johnston........................Flora Carr
Anthony Nicholls.........................Harvey Sawtelle
Colin Gordon...............................Lindsay Carr
Kathleen Byron............................Evelyn Sawtelle
Reginald Beckwith........................Harold Gunnison
Jessica Dunning...........................Hilda Gunnison
Norman Bird...............................Doctor
Judith Stott................................Margaret Abbott
Bill Mitchell.................................Fred Jennings

Filmography

Paul Frees..............................Prologue Narrator
George Roubicek.....................................Cleaner
Frank Singuineau...........................Truck driver
Gary Woolf......................................Relief driver

Selected Credits
Directed by Sidney Hayers
Screenplay by Charles Beaumont/Richard Matheson/George Baxt
Original Story by Fritz Leiber
Produced by Samuel Z Arkoff/Albert Fennell
Original Music by William Alwyn
Sound Recordists Eric Bayman/Len Shilton
Sound Effects Ted Mason/Alastair McIntyre
Director of Photography Reginald Wyer
Camera Operator Gerry Turpin
Editor Ralph Sheldon
Art Director Jack Shampan
Production Managers Arthur Alcott/Geoffrey Haine
Makeup Basil Newall
Hairdressing Iris Tilley
Costume Designer Sophie Devine
Wardrobe Maude Churchill
Continuity Jane Buck
Assistant Director David Bracknell

90 minutes
Released April 25, 1962
Anglo-Amalgamated Film Distributors/ American International Pictures (US)

Unearthly Stranger

Cast
John Neville..........................Dr Mark Davidson
Philip Stone.........................Prof John Lancaster
Gabriella Licudi...........................Julie Davidson
Patrick Newell....................................Maj Clarke
Jean Marsh.......................................Miss Ballard
Warren Mitchell..............Prof Geoffrey D Munro

Selected Credits
Directed by John Kirsh
Screenplay by Rex Carlton
Original Story by Jeffrey Stone
Produced by Albert Fennell
Executive Producers Leslie Parkyn/Julian Wintle
Original Music by Edward Williams
Sound Recordists Simon Kaye/Ken Cameron
Sound Editor Lionel Selwyn
Director of Photography Reg Wyer
Camera Operator Frank Ellis
Editor Tom Priestley
Production Managers Arthur Alcott/Geoffrey Haine
Production Designer Harry Pottle
Makeup Trevor Crole-Rees

X-Cert

Hairdressing Maude Onslow
Continuity Estelle Stewart
Assistant Director Frank Hollands

78 minutes
Released April, 1964
Anglo-Amalgamated Film Distributors/
American International Pictures (US)

Dr Blood's Coffin

Cast
Kieron Moore..............................Dr Peter Blood
Hazel Court..........................Nurse Linda Parker
Ian Hunter...............................Dr Robert Blood
Kenneth J Warren........................Sergeant Cook
Gerald C Lawson..........................Mr G F Morton
Fred Johnson...Tregaye
Paul Hardtmuth...................Professor Luckman
Paul Stockman...............................Steve Parker
Andy Alston......................................George Beale
Ruth Lee..Girl
John Romane..Hanson

Selected Credits
Directed by Sidney J Furie
Screenplay/Story by Jerry Juran
Produced by George Fowler

Original Music by Buxton Orr
Sound Mixer William Galter
Dubbing Mixer Fred Ryan
Director of Photography Stephen Dade
Camera Operator Nicolas Roeg
Editor Antony Gibbs
Special Effects Leslie Bowie/Peter Neilson
Production Manager Buddy Booth
Art Director Scott Macgregor
Makeup Freddie Williamson
Hairdressing Helen Penfold
Wardrobe Dulcie Midwinter
Continuity Gladys Reeve
Assistant Director John Comfort

92 minutes
Released January, 1961
United Artists (UK/US)

The Snake Woman

Cast
Susan Travers...Atheris
John McCarthy.........................Charles Prentice
Geoffrey Denton....................Col Clyde Wynborn
Elsie Wagstaff................................Aggie Harker
Arnold Marlé.......................................Dr Murton
Michael Logan...Barkis

Stevenson Lang........................Shepherd
John Cazabon......................Dr Horace Adderson
Dorothy Frere..........................Martha Adderson
Hugh Moxey...........................Inspector
Frances Bennett............................Polly
Jack Cunningham........................Constable Alfie

Selected Credits
Directed by Sidney J Furie
Writer Orville H Hampton
Produced by George Fowler
Original Music by Buxton Orr
Sound H C Pearson/Bob Winter
Director of Photography Stephen Dade
Camera Operator Harry Gillam
Editor Antony Gibbs
Prodution Manager Buddy Booth
Art Director John Earl
Makeup Freddie Williamson
Hairdressing Helen Penfold
Wardrobe Dulcie Midwinter
Assistant Director Douglas Hickox

68 minutes
Released April 26, 1961
United Artists (UK/US)

The Tell-Tale Heart

Cast
Laurence Payne...............................Edgar Marsh
Adrienne Corri................................Betty Clare
Dermot Walsh...................................Carl Loomis
Selma Vaz Díaz.....................................Mrs Vine
John Scott.................................Police Inspector
John Martin..............................Police Sergeant
Annette Carell............................Betty's landlady
David Lander.................................Jeweller
Rosemary Rotheray...................................Jackie
Suzanne Fuller...Dorothy
Yvonne Buckingham..................................Mina
Richard Bennett..Mike
Joan Peart..................................Street girl
Elizabeth Paget...............................Elsie
Nade Beall....................................Old crone
Pamela Plant.....................................Manageress
Graham Ashley...Neston
Patsy Smart.........................Mrs Marlow
Brian Cobby..........................Young man
Madeline Leon..............................Young woman
Frank Thornton................................Barman
With David Courtney

Selected Credits
Directed by Ernest Morris

Filmography

Writers Brian Clemens/Eldon Howard
Story by Edgar Allan Poe
Produced by Edward J Danziger/Harry Lee Danziger
Original Music by Tony Crombie/Bill LeSage
Sound Recordist George Adams
Sound Editor John Smith
Director of Photography Jimmy Wilson
Camera Operator Paddy Aherne
Editor Derek Parsons
Production Manager John Draper
Art Directors Norman G Arnold/Peter Russell
Makeup Aldo Manganaro
Wardrobe Rene Jerrold Coke
Continuity Phyllis Townshend
Assistant Director Geoffrey Holman

78 minutes
Released December, 1960
Warner-Pathe Distributors/
Brigadier Films (US)

Witchcraft

Cast
Lon Chaney.............................Morgan Whitlock
Jack Hedley...............................Bill Lanier
Jill Dixon..Tracy Lanier
Viola Keats.................................Helen Lanier
Marie Ney....................................Malvina Lanier
David Weston..................................Todd Lanier
Diane Clare..................................Amy Whitlock
Yvette Rees.............................Vanessa Whitlock
Barry Linehan..........................Myles Forrester
Victor Brooks........................Inspector Baldwin
Marianne Stone.................Forrester's Secretary
John Dunbar...Doctor
Hilda Fennemore..Nurse

Selected Credits
Directed by Don Sharp
Screenplay Harry Spalding
Produced by Robert L Lippert/Jack Parsons
Original Music by Carlo Martelli
Sound Recordist Buster Ambler
Sound Editor Spencer Reeve
Director of Photography Arthur Lavis
Camera Operator Len Harris
Editor Robert Winter
Assistant Editor Clive Smith
Production Manager Clifton Brandon
Art Director George Provis
Makeup Harold Fletcher
Hairdressing Joyce James
Wardrobe Jean Fairlie

X-Cert

Continuity Renee Glynne
Assistant Director Frank Nesbitt

79 minutes
Released March, 1964
20th Century Fox (UK/US)

The Earth Dies Screaming

Cast
Willard Parker.....................................Jeff Nolan
Virginia Field...Peggy
Dennis Price..................................Quinn Taggart
Thorley Walters...................................Edgar Otis
Vanda Godsell..........................Violet Courtland
David Spenser..Mel
Anna Palk..Lorna

Selected Credits
Directed by Terence Fisher
Screenplay by Henry Cross
Produced by Robert L Lippert/Jack Parsons
Original Music by Elisabeth Lutyens
Sound Recordist Buster Ambler
Sound Editor Spencer Reeve
Music Director Philip Martell
Director of Photography Arthur Lavis

Camera Operator Len Harris
Editors Clive Smith/Robert Winter
Production Manager Clifton Brandon
Art Director George Provis
Makeup Harold Fletcher
Hairdressing Joyce James
Wardrobe Jean Fairlie
Continuity Renee Glynne
Assistant Director Gordon Gilbert

62 minutes
Released January, 1961
20th Century Fox (UK/US)

Curse of the Fly

Cast
Brian Donlevy...........................Henri Delambre
George Baker...........................Martin Delambre
Carole Gray...............................Patricia Stanley
Yvette Rees...Wan
Burt Kwouk...Tai
Michael Graham.......................Albert Delambre
Jeremy Wilkins..........................Inspector Ronet
Charles Carson.........................Inspector Charas
Mary Manson............................Judith Delambre
Rachel Kempson....................Madame Fournier
Warren Stanhope........................Hotel manager
Mia Anderson..Nurse
Arnold Bell....................................Hotel porter
Stan Simmons.........................Heavyset creature

Selected Credits
Directed by Don Sharp
Screenplay by Harry Spalding/George Langelaan
Produced by Robert L Lippert/Jack Parsons
Original Music by Bert Shefter
Sound Recordist Jock May
Sound Editor Clive Smith
Director of Photography Basil Emmott
Camera Operator Frank Drake
Editors Colin Miller/Robert Winter
Special Effects Harold Fletcher
Production Manager Teresa Bolland
Art Director Harry White
Makeup John O'Gorman
Hairdressing Barbara Barnardie
Continuity Renee Glynne
Assistant Director Gordon Gilbert

86 minutes
Released January, 1966
20th Century Fox (UK/US)

Filmography

X-Cert

Devil Doll

Cast
Bryant Haliday..........................The Great Vorelli
William Sylvester............................Mark English
Yvonne Romain..........................Marianne Horn
Sandra Dorne.............................Magda
Nora Nicholson..........................Aunt Eva
Alan Gifford.......................Bob Garrett
Karel Stepanek........................Dr Heller
Francis De Wolff................Dr Keisling
Anthony Baird..........................Soldier
David Charlesworth.........................Hugo Novik
Lorenza Colville....................Mercedes
Sadie Corre.......................Hugo
Trixie Dallas...................Miss Penton
Guy Deghy.......................Hans
Margaret Durnell..................Countess
Heidi Erich.....................Grace
Ray Landor..........................Expert twist dancer
Pamela Law.........................Woman with Garrett
Jackie Ramsden........................Nurse
Philip Ray......................Uncle Walter
Ella Tracey.................................Louisa

Dennis Price.....................Major Lomas
Lisa Danielly.....................Janet Stacey
Ronald Leigh-Hunt...................Doctor
Mary Kerridge.............................Janet's mother
John Wittey..............................Police Inspector
Jean Lodge.........................Mrs Lomas
Beryl Cunningham..................Nightclub dancer
Danny Daniels.........................Simbaza
Dennis Alaba Peters...................Saidi
Tony Thawnton........................Radlett
Michael Nightingale..............................Hunter
Nigel Feyisetan.....................Simbaza in London
Louis Mahoney...........................African expert
Valli Newby..............................Nightclub pickup
Andy Meyers.................Tommy Stacey
Jimmy Feldgate.....................Barman

Selected Credits
*Directed by Lindsay Shonteff
Screenplay by George Barclay/Lance Z Hargreaves
Story by Frederick E Smith
Produced by Kenneth Rive/Lindsay Shonteff
Sound Recordist Derek McCalm
Dubbing Editor Reginald Court
Director of Photography Gerald Gibbs
Camera Operator Brian Elvin
Editor Ernest Bullingham
Production Manager Fred Slark
Makeup Jack Craig
Hairdressing Ann Fordyce
Wardrobe Mary Gibson
Assistant Director Ernie Lewis
Executive Producers Richard Gordon/Gerald A Fernback*

**81 minutes
Released September, 1964
Associated Film Distribution Corp (US)**

Curse of the Voodoo
(AKA Voodoo Blood Death)

Cast
Bryant Halliday........................Mike Stacey

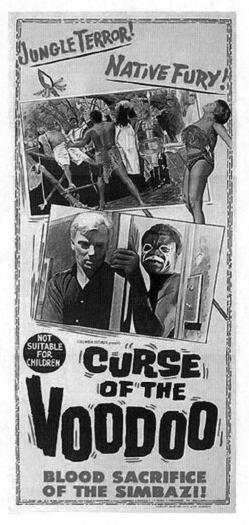

232

Filmography

Selected Credits
Directed by Lindsay Shonteff
Screenplay by Tony O'Grady/Leigh Vance
Produced by Richard Gordon/Kenneth Rive/
Gerald A Fernback
Original Music by Brian Fahey
Sound Recordist Jock May
Director of Photography Gerald Gibbs
Camera Operator Brian Elvin
Editor Barry Vince
Production Manager Fred Slark
Art Director Tony Inglis
Makeup Gerry Fletcher
Assistant Director Bill Snaith

77 minutes
Released August 22, 1965
Gala Film Distributors/Allied Artists (US)

Director of Photography Reg Wyer
Camera Operator Frank Drake
Editor John Trumper
Production Manager John Comfort
Art Director John St John Earl
Makeup George Blackler
Hairdressing Biddy Chrystal
Wardrobe Muriel Dickson
Continuity Muirne Mathieson
Assistant Director Roy Baird
Second Assistant Directors Ian Goddard/
Barry Melrose

88 minutes
Released September, 1965
Planet Film Distributors/20th Century Fox (US)

Devils of Darkness

Cast
William Sylvester................................Paul Baxter
Hubert Noel...................................Count Sinistre
Carole Gray..Tania
Tracy Reed......................................Karen Steele
Diana Decker..........................Madeleine Braun
Rona Anderson..............................Anne Forest
Peter Illing............................Inspector Malin
Gerard Heinz..Bouvier
Brian Oulton..................................The Colonel
Walter Brown...Bruno
Eddie Byrne.........................Dr Robert Kelsey
Victor Brooks..................Inspector Hardwick
Marie Burke.........................Old gypsy woman
Marianne Stone..........................The Duchess
Avril Angers..Midge
John Taylor...Sgt Miller
Frank Forsyth................Antique shop caretaker
Geoffrey Kenion..............................Keith Forest
Rod McLennan..Dave
Murray Kash....................................Gypsy chief
Burnell Tucker..Derek
Margaret Denyer.........................Tania's mother
Olwen Brookes....................................Landlady
Billy Milton...Librarian
Julie Mendez.................................Snake dancer

Selected Credits
Directed by Lance Comfort
Screenplay/Story by Lyn Fairhurst
Produced by Tom Blakeley
Original Music by Bernie Fenton
Sound Recordists Robert T Macphee/Gordon K McCallum/Otto Snel

The Projected Man

Cast
Mary Peach................................Dr Patricia Hill
Bryant Haliday..........................Dr Paul Steiner
Norman Wooland....................Dr LG Blanchard
Ronald Allen...............................Dr Chris Mitchel
Derek Farr...................................Inspector Davis
Tracey Crisp.........................Sheila Anderson
Derrick de Marney....................................Latham
Gerard Heinz..............................Prof Lembach
Sam Kydd..............................Harry Slinger
Terry Scully.................................Steve Lowe
Norma West..............................Gloria King
Frank Gatliff...................................Dr Wilson
John Watson..........................Sergeant Martin
Alfred Joint.................................Security man
Rosemary Donnelly..Girl
David Scheuer..Boy

Selected Credits
Directed by Ian Curteis/John Croydon
Screenplay by John C Cooper/Peter Bryan
Story by Frank Quattrocchi
Produced by John Croydon/Maurice Foster/
Pat Green/Michael Klinger/Tony Tenser/
Richard Gordon
Original Music by Kenneth V Jones
Sound Red Law/S G Rider
Dubbing Editor Brian Blamey
Director of Photography Stanley Pavey
Camera Operator Cece Cooney
Editor Derek Holding
Special Effects Robert Hedges/Mike Hope/Flo Nordhoff
Art Director Peter Mullins
Makeup Eric Carter
Hairdressing Joan Carpenter

233

X-Cert

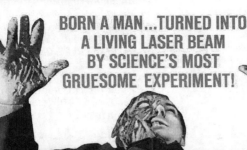

Wardrobe Kathleen Moore
Continuity Olga Brook
Assistant Directors Tom Sachs/Derek Whitehurst

77 minutes
Released February, 1967
Compton-Cameo Films/
Universal Pictures (US)

Island of Terror

Cast
Peter Cushing.............................Dr Brian Stanley
Edward Judd...............................Dr David West
Carole Gray......................................Toni Merrill
Eddie Byrne.......................Dr Reginald Landers
Sam Kydd.....................Constable John Harris
Niall MacGinnis...................Mr Roger Campbell
James Caffrey..................................Peter Argyle
Liam Gaffney....................................Ian Bellows
Roger Heathcote..Dunley
Keith Bell...Halsey
Margaret Lacey...............................Old woman
Shay Gorman..Morton
Peter Forbes Robertson.....Dr Lawrence Phillips
Richard Bidlake...Carson
Joyce Hemson................................Mrs Bellows
Edward Ogden...........................Helicopter pilot

Selected Credits
Directed by Terence Fisher
Screenplay by Edward Andrew Mann/Alan Ramsen
Produced by Tom Blakeley/Gerald A Fernback/Richard Gordon
Original Music by Malcolm Lockyer
Sound Barry Gray/Bob MacPhee/Gordon K McCallum
Director of Photography Reginald H Wyer
Camera Operator Frank Drake
Editor Thelma Connell
Special Effects Michael Albrechtsen/John St John Earl/W T Partleton
Art Directors John St John Earl/Fred Hole
Production Manager Roy Baird
Makeup W T Partleton/Bunty Philips
Hairdressing Stella Rivers
Costume Designer Rosemary Burrows
Continuity Kay Mander
Assistant Director Don Weeks

89 minutes
Released June 20, 1966
Planet Film Distributors/Universal Pictures (US)

Filmography

Naked Evil
(AKA Exorcism at Midnight)

Cast
Basil Dignam....................................Jim Benson
Anthony Ainley.............................Dick Alderson
Suzanne Neve..................................Janet Tuttle
Richard Coleman.......................Inspector Hollis
Olaf Pooley...............................Father Goodman
George A Saunders..................................Danny
Carmen Munroe..................................Beverley
Brylo Forde...Amizan
Dan Jackson...Lloyd
Ronald Bridges...Wilkins
Bob Allen..Doctor
Catharine Erhardt............................Ann Norris
Addison Greene..Blair
Pearl Prescod....................................Landlady
Lawrence Tierney..............................The doctor
With Nuba Stuart John Bates Oscar James and Bari Jonson

Selected Credits
Directed by Stanley Goulder
Screenplay by Stanley Goulder/Jon Manchip White
Produced by Steven Pallos/Gerald A Fernback
Original Music by Bernard Ebbinghouse
Sound Recordist Clive Winter
Director of Photography Geoffrey Faithful
Camera Operator Len Harris
Editor Peter Musgrave
Art Directors Denys Pavitt/George Provis
Makeup Stella Morris
Hairdressing Mervyn Medalie
Continuity Lorna Selwyn
Assistant Director Malcolm M Johnson

80 minutes
Released 1966
Columbia Pictures/ Hampton International (US)

Night of the Big Heat
(AKA Island of the Burning Damned)

Cast
Christopher Lee........................Godfrey Hanson
Patrick Allen......................................Jeff Callum
Peter Cushing..........................Dr Vernon Stone
Jane Merrow...............................Angela Roberts
Sarah Lawson.............................Frankie Callum
William Lucas....................................Ken Stanley

X-Cert

Kenneth Cope	Tinker Mason
Percy Herbert	Gerald Foster
Tom Heathcote	Bob Hayward
Anna Turner	Stella Hayward
Jack Bligh	Ben Siddle
Sidney Bromley	Old tramp
Barry Halliday	Radar operator

Selected Credits
Directed by Terence Fisher
Screenplay by Ronald Liles
Story by John Lymington
Produced by Tom Blakeley/Ronald Liles
Original Music by Malcolm Lockyer
Sound Recordists E Karnon/Dudley Messenger
Dubbing Editor Norman A Cole
Director of Photography Reg Wyer
Camera Operator Frank Drake
Editor Rod Keys
Special Effects Martin Gutteridge/Garth Inns
Art Director Alex Vetchinsky
Makeup Geoffrey Rodway
Hairdressing Stella Rivers
Wardrobe Kathleen Moore
Continuity Joy Mercer
Assistant Director Ray Frift

94 minutes

Released May, 1967
Planet Film Distributors/Maron Films (US)

Theatre of Death
(AKA Blood Fiend)

Cast

Christopher Lee	Philippe Darvas
Julian Glover	Charles Marquis
Lelia Goldoni	Dani Gireaux
Jenny Till	Nicole Chapelle
Evelyn Laye	Madame Angelique
Ivor Dean	Inspector Micheaud
Joseph Furst	Karl Schiller
Betty Woolfe	Colette
Leslie Handford	Joseph
Fraser Kerr	Pierre
Dilys Watling	Heidi
Steve Plytas	Andre
Miki Iveria	Patron's wife
Terence Soall	Ferdi
Esther Anderson	La Poule
Peter Cleoll	Jean
Suzanne Owens	Girl on scooter
Julie Mendez	Belly dancer
Lita Scott/Evrol Puckerin	Voodoo dancers

Filmography

Selected Credits
Directed by Samuel Gallu
Screenplay by Ellis Kadison/Roger Marshall
Produced by William J Gell/E M Smedley-Aston
Original Music by Elisabeth Lutyens
Sound Recordist Peter Davies/Len Shilton
Recording Director A W Lumkin
Dubbing Editor Allan Morrison
Director of Photography Gilbert Taylor
Camera Operator Bob Kindred
Editor Barrie Vince
Production Manager Al Marcus
Art Director Peter Proud
Makeup Jill Carpenter
Hairdressing Elsie Alder
Wardrobe Vi Murray
Continuity Angela Martelli
Assistant Director Eric Rattray

91 minutes
Released November, 1967
London Independent Producers/
Hemisphere Pictures (US)

The Hand of Night
(AKA Beast of Morocco)

Cast
William Sylvester.............................Paul Carver
Diane Clare...Chantal
Aliza Gur..Marisa
Edward Underdown.............................Gunther
Terence de Marney....................................Omar
William Dexter..Leclerc
Sylvia Marriott....................................Mrs Petty
Avril Sadler...Mrs Carver
Angela Lovell....................................Air hostess
Maria Hallowi..Nurse

Selected Credits
Directed by Frederic Goode
Written by Bruce Strewart
Produced by Harry Field/Lionel Hoare
Original Music by Joan Shakespeare
Director of Photography William Jordan
Editor Fredrick Ives
Animation Nancy Hanna/Keith Learner/Vera Linnecar
Art Director Peter Moll
Makeup Cliff Sharpe
Assistant Director Ted Morley

88 minutes
Released August 11, 1968
Schoenfeld Films (US)

237

X-Cert

IT!

Cast

Roddy MacDowall	Arthur Pimm
Jill Haworth	Ellen Grove
Paul Maxwell	Jim Perkins
Aubrey Richards	Prof Weal
Ernest Clark	Harold Grove
Oliver Johnston	Curator Trimingham
Noel Trevarthen	Insp White
Ian McCulloch	Detective Wayne
Richard Goolden	The old rabbi
Dorothy Frere	Miss Swanson
Tom Chatto	Young captain
Steve Kirby	Ellis
Russell Napier	Boss
Frank Sieman	Museum workman
Brian Haines	Joe Hill
Mark Burns/Raymond Adamson	Officers
Lindsay Campbell	Policeman
John Baker	Museum guard
Alan Sellers	The Golem

Selected Credits
Directed by Herbert J Leder
Screenplay/Story by Herbert J Leder
Produced by Herbert J Leder/Tom Sachs/ Robert Goldstein
Original Music by Carlo Martelli
Sound Editor Jim Roddan
Sound Mixer Kevin Sutton
Director of Photography Davis Boulton
Camera Operator Ronnie Maasz
Editor Tom Simpson
Art Director Scott MacGregor
Makeup Eric Carter
Hairdressing Mary Sturgess
Wardrobe Mary Gibson
Continuity Doreen Soan
Assistant Director Bill Snaith

96 minutes
Released November 15, 1967
Warner-Pathe Distributors/
Warner Bros-Seven Arts (US)

The Frozen Dead

Cast

Dana Andrews	Dr Norberg
Anna Palk	Jean Norburg
Philip Gilbert	Dr Ted Roberts
Kathleen Breck	Elsa Tenney
Karel Stepanek	General Lubeck
Basil Henson	Dr Tirpitz
Alan Tilvern	Karl Essen
Anne Tirard	Mrs Schmidt
Edward Fox	Norburg's brother
Oliver MacGreevy	Joseph
Tom Chatto	Inspector Witt
John Moore	Bailey
Charles Wade	Alfie

Selected Credits
Directed by Herbert J Leder
Screenplay by Herbert J Leder
Produced by Robert Goldstein/Herbert J Leder
Original Music by Don Banks
Sound Editor Jim Roddan
Sound Mixer Kevin Sutton
Director of Photography Davis Boulton
Camera Operator Ronnie Maasz
Editor Tom Simpson
Production Manager Tom Sachs
Art Director Scott MacGregor
Makeup Eric Carter
Hairdressing Pearl Tipaldi
Wardrobe Mary Gibson
Continuity Doreen Soan
Assistant Director Douglas Hermes

95 minutes
Released October, 1966
Warner-Pathe Distributors/
Warner Brothers-Seven Arts (US)

Berserk!

Cast

Joan Crawford	Monica Rivers
Ty Hardin	Frank Hawkins
Diana Dors	Matilda
Michael Gough	Albert Dorando

Filmography

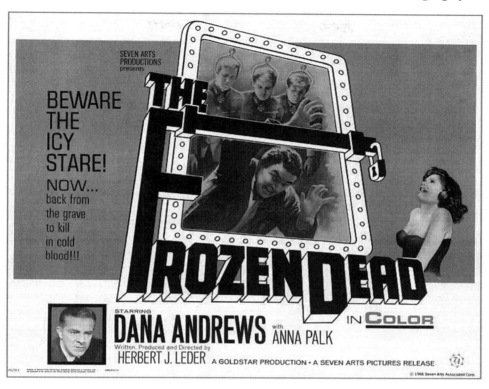

Judy Geeson....................................Angela Rivers
Robert Hardy...................Detective Supt Brooks
Geoffrey Keen.....................Commissioner Dalby
Sydney Tafler.............................Harrison Liston
George Claydon............................Bruno Fontana
Philip Madoc...Lazlo
Ambrosine Phillpotts.....................Miss Burrows
Thomas Cimarro..Gaspar
Peter Burton...Gustavo
Golda Casimir................................Bearded lady
Ted Lune..Skeleton man
Milton Reid..Strong man
Marianne Stone...Wanda
Miki Iveria..Gypsy
Howard Goorney..Emil
Reginald Marsh.............................Sgt Hutchins
Bryan Pringle........................Constable Bradford
Herman Cohen........................Audience member
Robert Rowland.................Big top ticket holder

Selected Credits
Directed by Jim O'Connolly
Screenplay/Story Aben Kandel/Herman Cohen
Produced by Herman Cohen/Robert Sterne
Original Music by Patrick John Scott
Sound John Cox/Mike Le Mare/Bert Ross

Director of Photography Desmond Dickinson
Camera Operator Norman Jones
Editor Raymond Poulton
Production Manager Laurie Greenwood
Art Director Maurice Pelling
Makeup George Partleton
Hairdressing Pearl Tipaldi
Wardrobe Joyce Stoneman
Costume Designer Jay Hutchinson Scott
Continuity Betty Harley
Assistant Director Barry Langley

96 minutes
Released September, 1967
Columbia Pictures (UK/US)

Trog

Cast
Joan Crawford...............................Dr Brockton
Michael Gough.............................Sam Murdock
Bernard Kay.......................Inspector Greenham
Kim Braden................................Anne Brockton
David Griffin............................Malcolm Travers

X-Cert

John Hamill..Cliff
Thorley Walters.....................................Magistrate
Jack May...Dr Selbourne
Geoffrey Case..Bill
Robert Hutton........................Dr Richard Warren
Simon Lack....................................Colonel Vickers
David Warbeck......................................Alan Davis
Chloe Franks..Little girl
Maurice Good/Rona Newton-John.....Reporters
Joe Cornelius..Trog
John Baker...Anaesthetist
Golda Casimir......................................Professor
Herman Cohen.....................................Bartender
John D Collins..................................TV crewman
Shirley Cooklin...............Little girl's mother
Robert Crewdson.........................Dr Pierre Duval
Harry Fielder................................Security guard
Pat Gorman..Army officer
Brian Grellis.....................................John Dennis
Paul Hansard..................................Dr Kurtlimer
Bartlett Mullins...Butcher
Cleo Sylvestre..Nurse

Selected Credits
Directed by Freddie Francis
Screenplay by Aben Kandel
Story by Peter Bryan/John Gilling
Produced by Herman Cohen/Harry Woolveridge
Original Music by John Scott
Sound Maurice Askew/Tony Dawe/
Michael Redbourn
Director of Photography Desmond Dickinson
Camera Operator Norman Jones
Editor Oswald Hafenrichter
Production Manager Eddie Dorian
Art Director Geoffrey Tozer
Makeup Jimmy Evans
Hairdressing Pearl Tipaldi
Wardrobe Ron Beck
Continuity Leonora Hail
Assistant Director Douglas Hermes

93 minutes
Released September, 1970
Warner Bros/Warner Bros Pictures (US)

The Vulture

Cast
Robert Hutton...............................Dr Eric Lutens
Akim Tamiroff....................Prof Hans Koniglich
Broderick Crawford....................Brian F Stroud
Diane Clare.....................................Trudy Lutens
Philip Friend..The vicar
Patrick Holt..Jarvis
Annette Carell......................................Ellen West
Edward Caddick...................................Melcher
Gordon Sterne...........................Edward Stroud
Keith McConnell............................Supt Wendell
Margaret Robertson....................................Nurse
Monte Landis.............................Bus driver
With Arnold Diamond, Peter Elliott, Roy Hanlon, Murray Hayne, Gordon Tanner and George Tovey

Selected Credits
Directed by Lawrence Huntington
Screenplay by Lawrence Huntington
Produced by Lawrence Huntington/
Jack O Lamont
Original Music by Eric Spear
Sound Edgar Vetter
Production Designer Duncan Sutherland
Director of Photography Stephen Dade
Camera Operator Ray Sturgess
Still Photographer John Hardman
Editor John S Smith
Production Manager Philip Shipway
Makeup Geoffrey Rodway
Hairdressing Gordon Bond
Wardrobe Dulcie Midwinter
Continuity Ann Skinner
Assistant Director Bill Snaith
Second Assistant Director Richard Gill

Filmography

Writers Donald Ford/Derek Ford
Produced by Peter Newbrook
Original Music by Bill McGuffie
Sound Mixer Cyril Collick
Dubbing Mixers Peter Gilpin/George Willows
Production Designer Bruce Grimes
Director of Photography Peter Newbrook
Camera Operator Norman Jones
Editor Don Deacon
Assistant Editor Maxine Julius
Special Effects Michael Albrechtsen
Production Manager Robert Sterne
Makeup John O'Gorman
Hairdressing Biddy Chrystall
Costume Designer Hilary Pritchard
Continuity Splinters Deason
Assistant Director Ken Softley

91 minutes
Released December, 1968
Columbia Pictures (UK/US)

91 minutes
Released May 3, 1967
Paramount Pictures (UK/US)

Corruption
(AKA Carnage)

Cast
Peter Cushing...........................Sir John Rowan
Sue Lloyd...Lynn Nolan
Noel Trevarthen............................Steve Harris
Kate O'Mara...Val Nolan
David Lodge...Groper
Wendy Varnals...Terry
Billy Murray...Rik
Vanessa Howard..Kate
Jan Waters.................................Girl in the flat
Phillip Manikum....................................Georgie
Alexandra Dane.....................................Sandy
Valerie Van Ost.......................Girl in the train
Diana Ashley..Claire
Victor Baring.......................Mortuary attendant
Shirley Stelfox...........................Girl at the party
Anthony Booth..................................Mike Orme

Selected Credits
Directed by Robert Hartford-Davis

Incense for the Damned
(AKA Bloodsuckers)

Cast
Patrick Macnee..........................Derek Longbow
Peter Cushing.....................Dr Walter Goodrich
Alex Davion..................................Tony Seymore
Johnny Sekka......................................Bob Kirby
Madeline Hinde....................................Penelope
Edward Woodward.........................Dr Holstrom
William Mervyn.......................Marc Honeydew
Patrick Mower........................Richard Fountain
David Lodge...Colonel
Imogen Hassall.......................................Chriseis
John Barron...Diplomat
Valerie Van Ost...............................Don's wife
Theo Moreos..Mayor
Nick Pandelides.........................Monk superior
Andreas Potamitis.......................Police chief
Theodosia Elefthreadon..................Old woman
Christ Eleftheriades................................Priest
Françoise Pascal.............................Girl at orgy
Marianne Stone................Cheerful lady at party

Selected Credits
Directed by Michael Burrowes
Screenplay by Julian More
Novel by Simon Raven
Produced by Graham Harris/Peter Newbrook
Original Music by Bobby Richards

X-Cert

Sound Recordists Tony Dawe/Dennis Whitlock
Sound Don Deacon/Colin Hobson/Peter Pardo
Production Designer George Provis
Director of Photography Desmond Dickinson
Camera Operator Ronnie Maasz
Editor Peter Thornton
Assistant Editor Maxine Julius
Production Manager Robert Sterne

87 minutes
Released 1972
Titan Film Distribution Ltd/
Chevron Pictures (US)

The Corpse
(AKA Crucible of Horror)

Cast
Michael Gough..........................Walter Eastwood
Yvonne Mitchell..........................Edith Eastwood
Sharon Gurney............................Jane Eastwood
Simon Gough............................Rupert Eastwood
David Butler...Gregson
Olaf Pooley...Reid
Nicholas Jones..................................Benjy Smith
Mary Hignett..Servant
Howard Goorney..............Petrol pump attendant

Selected Credits
Directed by Viktors Ritelis
Screenplay by Olaf Pooley
Produced by Gabrielle Beaumont
Executive Producers Christopher Dewey/
Dennis Friedland
Original Music by John Hotchkis
Sound Mixer Aubrey Lewis
Dubbing Editor Max Bell
Production Designer Peter J Hampton
Director of Photography John Mackey
Second Cinematographer Clive Tickner
Editor Nicholas Pollock
Production Manager Michael Brown
Makeup Fred Williamson
Hairdressing Betty Glasgow
Wardrobe Mary Gibson
Continuity Ann Edwards
Production Assistant Janet Elliott
Assistant Director Richard MacLaine
Second Assistant Director Christopher Toyne

91 minutes
Released November 10, 1971
Grand National Pictures/
Cannon Film Distributors (US)

Bibliography

Magazines and Pictorials

No study of Fifties and Sixties cinema can call itself complete without drawing heavily on the trade papers, Kinematograph Weekly and Daily Cinema, and I am deeply indebted to the reviewers and journalists who contributed to both tomes. I would also like to single out the following magazines:

Films Illustrated, Film Review, Bizarre Magazine, Cinema X, Cinefantastique, The Dark Side, Fangoria, Femme Fatale, Films and Filming, Little Shoppe of Horrors, Photoplay, Scarlet Street, Shivers and *Shock Xpress*.

Books:

Dixon, Wheeler Winston: *The Charm of Evil: the Life and Films of Terence Fisher*; Scarecrow Press Inc, Metuchen NJ 1991
Francis, Anne: *Julian Wintle: A Memoir*; Dukeswood, London 1984
Johnson, Tom and **Miller, Mark A**: *The Christopher Lee Filmography*; McFarland & Company, Jefferson, North Carolina 1994.
Lee, Christopher: *Tall, Dark and Gruesome*; Victor Gollancz, London 1997
Lisanti, Tom: *Fantasy Femmes of Sixties Cinema*; McFarlane & Company, Jefferson, North Carolina, 2001.
McFarlane, Brian: *Autobiography of British Cinema*; Methuen, London 1997
Mower, Patrick: *My Story*; John Blake Publishing Ltd, London 2007
Newquist, Roy: *Conversations with Joan Crawford*; Berkley Pub Group 1981
Parfitt, Gary: *The Films of Peter Cushing*; HFCGB, Bath, Avon, 1977
Pirie, David: *The New Heritage of Horror*; I B Taurus & Co, London 2009
Powell, Michael: *Million Dollar Movie*; Mandarin Paperbacks, London 1992
Sangster, Jimmy: *Do You Want It Good or Tuesday?*; Midnight Marquee, Baltimore, 1997
Smith, Don G.: *Lon Chaney, Jr. Horror Film Star 1906-1973;* McFarland & Co, Jefferson, North Carolina, 1996
Thomas, Bob: *Joan Crawford A Biography*; Weidenfeld and Nicholson, London 1979
Trevelyan, John: *What the Censor Saw;* Michael Joseph Ltd, London 1973
Walker, Alexander: *Hollywood England*; Harrap, London 1986
Weaver, Tom: *Double Feature Creature Attack*: McFarland, Jefferson, N. Carolina, 2003

Additional Sources:
British Board of Film Classification, Soho Square, London
British Film Institute, National Library, Stephen Street, London
Peter Wyngarde fan site

wikipedia.com
imdbpro.com

www.hemlockbooks.co.uk

Hemlock Books is an independent publisher specialising in genre-related film titles, with particular emphasis on horror, mystery and the macabre.